'To Amaze the People with Pleasure and Delight':

The Horsemanship Manuals
Of William Cavendish,
Duke of Newcastle

By Elaine Walker

With a Foreword

By Peter Edwards

 XENOPHON PRESS

Published by Xenophon Press LLC

7518 Bayside Road, Franktown, Virginia 23354-2106, U.S.A.

XenophonPress@gmail.com

www.XenophonPress.com

Cover Image: Copyright Elaine Walker 2015

For Bryan and Christian

Xenophon Press Library

30 Years with Master Nuno Oliveira, Henriquet 2011

A New Method to Dress Horses, Cavendish 2015

A Rider's Survival from Tyranny, de Kunffy 2012

Another Horsemanship, Racinet 1994

Art of the Lusitano, Yglesias de Oliveira 2012

Austrian Art of Riding, Poscharnigg 2015

Breaking and Riding, Fillis 2015

Baucher and His School, Decarpentry 2011

Description of Moderne Manege, D'Eisenberg 2015

Dressage in the French Tradition, Diogo de Bragança 2011

Dressage Principles Illuminated, Expanded Edition, de Kunffy 2015

École de Cavalerie Part II, Expanded Edition, Robichon de la Guérinière 2015

Equine Osteopathy: What the Horses Have Told Me, Ginaux 2014

François Baucher: The Man and His Method, Baucher/Nelson 2013

Great Horsewomen of the 19th Century in the Circus, Nelson 2015

Gymnastic Exercises for Horses Volume II, Russell 2013

H. Dv. 12 Cavalry Manual of Horsemanship, Reinhold 2014

Handbook of Jumping Essentials, Lemaire de Ruffieu 1997

Handbook of Riding Essentials, Lemaire de Ruffieu 2015

Healing Hands, Giniaux, DVM 1998

Horse Training: Outdoors and High School, Beudant 2014

Legacy of Master Nuno Oliveira, Millham 2013

Methodical Dressage of the Riding Horse, Faverot de Kerbrech 2010

Racinet Explains Baucher, Racinet 1997

Science and Art of Riding in Lightness, Stodulka 2015

The Art of Traditional Dressage, Volume I DVD, de Kunffy 2013

The Ethics and Passions of Dressage Expanded Edition, de Kunffy 2013

The Gymnasium of the Horse, Steinbrecht 2011

The Italian Tradition of Equestrian Art, Tomassini 2014

The Maneige Royal, de Pluvinel 2010

The Portuguese School of Equestrian Art, de Oliveira/da Costa 2012

The Spanish Riding School & Piaffe and Passage, Decarpentry 2013

To Amaze the People with Pleasure and Delight, Walker 2015

Total Horsemanship, Racinet 1999

Wisdom of Master Nuno Oliveira, de Coux 2012

Available at **www.XenophonPress.com**

Foreword

Horses were such a ubiquitous presence in the country until comparatively recent times that they often seem to have faded into their surroundings and become invisible. Yet, before the internal combustion engine revolutionised transport, people who did not go on foot travelled by horse, either mounted or in a coach. The centrality of horses in early modern society was such that without them social and economic life could hardly have functioned. Horses also had an iconic as well as a utilitarian value. Indeed, not only did possession of a horse mark an important social divide but among the upper classes the ability to ride well on a powerful, finely proportioned stallion, demonstrated their fitness to rule.

This is what makes this book so important and its subject, William Cavendish, the 1st Duke of Newcastle, such a key figure to study. Because of his unrivalled skill in the manège, the refined set of equine exercises that demanded the highest level of horsemanship, he was widely regarded as the finest horseman in Europe. Dr. Elaine Walker puts his achievement into context and in doing so offers the modern reader insights into the essential nature of early modern society and the attitudes and actions of the ruling elite, who dominated the social, economic, cultural and political life of the time. In this respect, the art of horsemanship and the principles that underpinned Newcastle's training methods served as a metaphor for good government and the right ordering of society.

As Dr. Walker ably argues, Newcastle's method, as set out in his manuals, revolutionised the training of horses. Claiming to be the first person to base his method on a proper understanding of the equine psyche, he sought to work with the grain of these intelligent, sentient creatures rather than against it, and without the use of brute force. Horses should be cherished. But, what gives this book wider appeal is Newcastle's belief that his system had general application and that the correct training of horses was analogous to the way a monarch governed his subjects and how parents brought up their children and teachers taught their pupils. Although authoritarian by nature and a firm supporter of monarchical rule, Newcastle's precepts hint at a more sensitive relationship between ruler and the ruled.

No-one is better qualified than Elaine Walker to write this book. As a leading authority on the life and times of the duke, she has made a detailed study of the manuals in both their English and French forms. Moreover, as she keeps and rides horses, she is well-placed to assess the value of Newcastle's teachings. Her relaxed and uncluttered style makes the importance of this seminal work on horsemanship accessible to a wide readership for the first time.

Peter Edwards
Professor of Early Modern British Social History,
University of Roehampton.

Author's note:

This text began life as a Ph.D. thesis in 2004 and adapted material from it has appeared in many journals and essays. The original research also provided papers for conferences, talks and displays in various locations, including two of Newcastle's own homes, Bolsover Castle and The Harley Gallery at Welbeck Abbey. Development into a book came with publication by the Long Riders Guild Press in 2010. The current edition has been re-edited, revised and updated and has the addition of a foreword but remains essentially the same in argument and overall content.

Contents

Chapter 1

Introduction

> It has been my fortune to spend a great deal of time riding,
> and so I think myself versed in the horseman's art.
> Xenophon, *The Art of Horsemanship*

William Cavendish, first Duke of Newcastle (1593-1676), wrote that, 'there is nothing of more Use than A Horse of Mannage; nor any thing of more State, Manliness, or Pleasure, than Riding; and as it is the Noblest, so it is the Healthfullest Exercise in the World'. Throughout his life, Newcastle put this belief into practice, devoting time, money and faith to his love of horses and the art of the riding house, or manège, through which the soldier's battlefield skills took on new refinement. His many years of experience lead to two horsemanship manuals, published in 1658 and 1667, setting down his life-long pleasure in horses, riding and the symbolism of noble display to establish his ideal pattern for a worthy tradition.[1]

Newcastle's skill with horses helped clarify many of the tensions of his life and the manuals offer insight into a complex man with a strong urge for self-expression. While they are significant in the development of horsemanship literature, they include a biographical subtext found as much in the training method as in the underlying philosophy. A century later, François de la Guérinière, perhaps the most influential of classical horsemanship authors, declared that Newcastle was 'the greatest expert of his age' and that this would be the 'unanimous sentiment of all connoisseurs'.[2] Today connoisseurs of the art are fewer and to fully appreciate the value of Newcastle's manuals involves an understanding that the symbolic importance of horsemanship was rooted in the needs of a practical skill requiring a high level of knowledge. Therefore the method and its execution are bound to the political and philosophical ideas from which they were born and neither can be fully understood without reference to the other.

The importance of this is neatly explained by Ann Hyland:

---

1 *A New Method, and Extraordinary Invention, to Dress Horses* (London: Thomas Milbourn, 1667), pp.13-14; *La Méthode Nouvelle et Invention extraordinaire de dresser les Chevaux* (Antwerp: Jacques van Meurs, 1658). Further references to Newcastle's manuals will be included in the text using the date of publication.

2 François Robichon de la Guérinière, *School of Horsemanship*, trans. by Tracey Boucher (London: J. A. Allen, 1994), p.87. Also available as *Ecole de Cavalerie Part II* (Virginia: Xenophon Press 1992, 2015).

To the historian many references may lack the full meaning that experience of horses can give. To the horseman who lacks an historian's appreciation, many of these same references do not even register as pertaining to the horse except in the broadest sense. Dual appreciation shows a more complete picture of how an equestrian system has come to operate in any age.[3]

Newcastle himself puts the argument more bluntly:

Quant aux hommes de lettres, quoy qu'il é, ils n'étudient pas la Cavalerie, [...] C'est pourqouy on ne doit pas s'étonner, s'ils se trompent un peu en ce dont ils ne sont profession (1658: 'Avant-Propos'). [4]

Like Newcastle, I 'have Practised, and Studyed Horse-manship ever since I was ten years old' (1667: p.41) and my practical knowledge of horses is as much the foundation for this book as my academic background as a scholar of seventeenth-century literature. My lecture-demonstrations in Newcastle's riding house at Bolsover Castle in Derbyshire, with Dr. Geoff Edwards and his classically trained Lusitano horses and Peter Maddison-Greenwell of El Caballo de España, have illustrated that Newcastle's method has practical application. It works on an understanding of the horse which was innovative in his time and, more surprisingly, resonates with approaches to training that are considered new in our own.

The early modern reader or audience would bring understanding gained through an elite education to the riding house so that aspects of the work less widely appreciated today would have been assimilated instinctively. The twenty-first century reader does not need to be a rider to understand these texts, but does need to appreciate that a rider's knowledge uncovers layers of interpretation that may otherwise be overlooked. As Newcastle says, 'Cét art ne consiste pas sulement en l'étude, & contemplation de l'esprit, mais aussy en la pratique du corps'(1658: pp.270-271).[5]

Newcastle's manuals in context.

The large number of horse training manuals published between the mid-sixteenth and late seventeenth centuries testify to the popularity of the art across Europe.[6] The importance of

---

3   *The Medieval War Horse,* (Stroud: Sutton Publishing, 1994), p.xi.
4   'As for men of letters, 'tho they study, they don't study horsemanship [...] wherefore it is not surprising, if they be somewhat mistaken in what is not their profession' (1743: p.13).
5   'This art does not consist only in study and mental contemplation, but in bodily practise likewise' (1743: p.132).
6   R. S. Toole-Stott, *Circus and the Allied Arts: A World Bibliography* (Derby: Harper & Sons, 1960), pp.36-118.

the horsemanship manual to the serious rider is illuminated by Sir Philip Sidney's advice to his younger brother:

> At horsemanship, read Grisone, Claudio, and a book that is called *La Gloria del cavallo* withal, that you may join the thorough contemplation of it with the exercise, and you shal profit more in a month than others in a year.[7]

To the genuine enthusiast, texts analysing the art added an academic and theoretical level to a practical skill, an approach still used today. Difficulties arise in modern study of early manuals owing to the mutability of text at the time, when assimilating another author's work was neither unusual nor especially problematic. Newcastle's use of privileges to protect his work illustrates his awareness of this danger[8] and also of the prestige linked to such action, as explained by Adrian Johns:

> The making of elaborate folio volumes demanded substantial investment, which without protection would only be ventured upon by the extremely foolhardy. But they further averred that gentlemen patentees, soaring above the commercial fray, could produce higher works of greater quality and fidelity than would be possible in an environment of ruthless competition between mercenary Stationers. They explicitly and consistently identified virtuous *people* with veracious *printing*.[9]

A large number of the early manuals are heavily derivative, even though most claim originality. This causes difficulty locating the author's own ideas, especially as there is a strong element of tradition in any learned practical skill. Newcastle's texts are very straightforward in this respect. He deliberately sets out to establish his manuals as unique, through the quality of production, wealth of privileges and, most importantly, strong emphasis on the originality of the content.

The first of Newcastle's horsemanship manuals, setting out his personal method of training, was published in French in 1658, though some early copies lacking the engraved title may have been in circulation in 1657.[10] This is a lavish folio edition with forty-two very fine engraved plates after

---

7   Katherine Duncan-Jones, *Sir Philip Sidney: Courtier Poet* (London: Hamish Hamilton, 1991), p.171.

8   The privileges accorded to the 1658 manual were granted by the Estates General of the United Provinces; Philip IV of Spain 'en son conseil de Brabant', 'en son Conseil Privé'; and Louis XIV of France, followed by 'Transport des Dits Privileges' from Newcastle to the publisher (sig. f-f2ᵛ). A letter dated 1657, in Newcastle's hand to an unnamed recipient, relating to his request for a 'previledge for my booke' from the 'States of Hollande' is transcribed and reproduced in the undated catalogue (late 1990s) of letters and manuscripts offered for sale by Richard Hatchwell, Malmesbury.

9   *The Nature of the Book* (Chicago/London: University of Chicago Press, 1998), p.258.

10   Toole-Stott, p.84.

Abraham van Diepenbeeck. A more modest second manual in English followed in 1667. These texts have a history very similar to Newcastle's own in near misses with the fame and popularity they might have enjoyed.

The first manual was published with borrowed money in a short run, but a fire in the publishing house reduced the available numbers further. The exact number of copies published and the method of distribution is open to conjecture but copies were given as gifts to influential contacts and friends of Newcastle, including John Evelyn.[11]

Within ten years of publication, Newcastle's friend, Jacques de Solleysel, was repeating extracts in his own work, *Le Parfait Mareschal*, because 'his [Newcastle's] book is Rare, and that People can but with difficulty procure it, as well as because of the excessive Rate it is sold at, and because of the small number of Copies which were printed'.[12] This provides useful evidence that the manual was not simply a gift edition but was offered for public sale. However, by 1733, François de la Guérinière was saying it had 'become so rare that one can scarcely find it'.[13]

The second book, published by Thomas Milbourn in 1667, was something of a poor relation to the first as it lacked the plates. Milbourn produced a substandard French translation of the second book in 1671 and 1674, and a translation, corrected by Solleysel but with inferior new plates, was published by Gervaise Clousier in Paris in 1677. It was believed for some time that the original plates had been lost or destroyed but they were in the hands of Newcastle's granddaughter, the Countess of Oxford, by 1737 when John Brindley issued a second edition of the original French text. Brindley went on to publish an English translation in folio in 1743 which included the plates and surpassed the original in quality of production. He also produced a particularly fine Large Paper copy of the 1743 edition ruled throughout with red lines. This translation made Newcastle's original manual widely accessible in his own country for the first time, nearly a hundred years after it first appeared, and it was reprinted in 1748. Further editions in German and Spanish were published before the end of the eighteenth century, alongside a number of adaptations and derivative works, testifying to Newcastle's lasting influence.

The complicated history of the manuals can be confusing, especially as the titles add to the problem. The title of the 1658 French manual is, *La Methode Nouvelle et Invention extraordinaire de dresser les Chevaux les travailler selon la nature, et parfaire la nature par la subtilité de l'art; la quelle n'a jamais été treuvée que Par Le tres-noble, haut tres-puissant Prince Guillaume Marquis et Comte de Newcastle.* The English manual of 1667 is entitled, *A New Method and Extraordinary Invention to Dress Horses, and Work Them according to Nature*: as also, *To Perfect Nature by the Subtilty of Art:*

---

11   Letters thanking Newcastle for gift-copies may be found in *A Collections of Letter & Poems* [...] *to the Late Duke and Duchess of Newcastle* (London: Langley Curtis, 1678); John Evelyn's presentation copy with a personal inscription from Newcastle was Lot no. 1076 in the Evelyn Library Sale at Christie's, London, 15 March, 1978.

12   *Le Parfait Mareschal or Complete Farrier,* trans. by Sir William Hope (Edinburgh: George Mosman, 1696), p.206.

13   La Guérinière, p.78.

Example of new plates produced for translations of Newcastle's 1667 manual

Which was never found out, but by the Thrice Noble, High, and Puissant Prince William Cavendish, Duke, Marquis and Earl of Newcastle. Aside from the alteration of 'La' to 'A' and the addition of Newcastle's new honours in the second manual, the titles are the same. This suggests that the second is a translation of the first. However, the second book is, as Newcastle tells his Reader in a prefatory epistle, 'neither a Translation of the first, nor an absolutely necessary Addition to it' (1667: sig.

b2ᵛ). Therefore, Newcastle wrote two manuals with the same title, one published in French and one in English. They cover the same basic method and techniques and have a considerable amount of material in common, often word-for-word. However, they are not the same. The second manual has a long introduction discussing other horsemanship texts, alongside a retrospective on the importance of Newcastle's riding house in Antwerp, where he lived between 1648 and 1660. Much of the technical material shows progression in his ideas during the intervening years and does not follow the sequential approach to training with the same strict focus as the first. They are two separate, but related, texts. Newcastle himself advises his reader that the second book 'may be of use by it self, without the other, as the other hath been hitherto, and is still, without this; but both together will questionless do best'(1667: sig. b-b2ᵛ).

When John Brindley decided in 1743, 'that I should farther oblige the Lovers of Horsemanship if I procured a Translation of the [1658] Book, and printed it with the same Advantages as the Original', he added 'several ornamental prints' and chose to present the book as the 'First Volume of A Complete System of Horsemanship'. The title page of Volume I calls this anthology of material *A General System of Horsemanship in all its Branches: containing a Faithful Translation Of that most noble and useful work of his Grace, William Cavendish, Duke of Newcastle*. Brindley does not include the title of the 'useful work' on this page, although he does include the original engraved plate with the French title on the page opposite, and refers to it as *The new Method of Dressing Horses* in his dedicatory epistle.[14] Despite this and the change from 'complete' to 'general', Brindley's intention is quite straightforward: Newcastle's work is included as part of this two volume overview of horsemanship. This has, however, led to confusion over the title and provenance of Newcastle's manuals and their relationships with the second volume of Brindley's series, a translation of a French veterinary text, Gaspard de Saunier's, *La parfaite connoissance des Chevaux.*[15]

Brindley's fine translation and largely faithful reproduction of Newcastle's original text has been reissued as a facsimile several times since the 1970s under the title *A General System of Horsemanship*.[16] However, comparing the broad generality suggested by Brindley's title with the emphatic claim for a 'Methode Nouvelle et Invention Extraordinaire', which aims to 'parfaire la nature' and 'n'a jamais été treuvée' by any but Newcastle, it becomes clear that the original title encompasses large elements of self-presentation. The reader has a lively image of the author before the book is opened. This strong sense of character is a feature of Newcastle's work and his reaction to the renaming of his definitive work as *A General System of Horsemanship* is easily imagined.

To add to the confusion, Saunier's text was derived in part from Jacques de Solleysel's first edition of *Le Parfait Marechal* of 1664, which contains considerable reference to Newcastle's work.

---

14   London: John Brindley, 1743, sig. a
15   La Haye: Adrien Moetjens, 1734.
16   First issued by J. A. Allen, 1970.

In *Le Parfait Marechal,* Solleysel indicates when he is quoting Newcastle, but Sir William Hope, translating Solleysel into English in 1696, does not keep this distinction when he adds 'a compendious and excellent Collection of Horsemanship, taken from the best and most modern Writers on that subject such as Mr. De La Brow, Pluvinel and the Great Duke of Newcastle'.[17] Subsequently Newcastle's words appear verbatim under Hope's name, as do those of the other authors he admired, while his plates are a strange merging of features from Newcastle's and Pluvinel's manuals. Only familiarity with the original authors can distinguish their text from his additional material.

Multiple texts, in various translations, with the intervention of scribes, translators and followers are a feature of horsemanship texts and many others during this period. Newcastle's are not unusual in this respect, although the presentation of each manual confounds the matter further in a way that is unique. The French-language manual very carefully and with great detail defines Newcastle, though living in Antwerp in 1658, as an English lord, a 'tres-puissant prince', whose relationship with the rightful British monarch was established in that young man's childhood. The engravings locate him in the impressive estates that establish his lineage while the activity of the riding house provides a cultural point of contact with the Continental elite. The second manual, was published when he, like his monarch, was 'restored' to his demesne. It sets out to record his influence while exiled on the Continent and revive his countrymen's lost enthusiasm for an art rooted in Europe but, in Newcastle's opinion, given an English provenance by his own success there. Each is therefore defined not by the time in which it was written, but by the high points of the previous era in Newcastle's life. Small wonder, that with the detail of essentially the same title in different languages, they become confusing texts for later readers.

However, in an attempt to avoid further confusion, I will rely on the two original manuals of 1658 and 1667. Where the material is common to both, the 1667 text will be used and for further accessibility, all references from the French of 1658 will be footnoted with the corresponding translation from Brindley's 1743 edition.[18] The standard of translation in the Brindley edition is high and the text is easily available via facsimile editions, the most recent being by Xenophon Press in 2015, which is notable for being the first to reclaim Newcastle's original title.[19] The dedications and verses in the 1658 text are not retained by Brindley but are included here in Appendix 1 in full with translations. References to the second manual are to the original 1667 edition and therefore straightforward.

---

17   Paris: Gervais Clousier, 1664*; A Supplement of Horsemanship to* [...] *The Parfait Mareschal,* already cited, title page.

18   Subsequent references to this edition will be made in the text, by the date followed by the page number.

19   William Cavendish, *A New Method to Dress Horses* (Virginia: Xenophon Press, 2015)

The terminology of horsemanship.

Specific terminology is attached to the art of riding and confusion can arise due to changes in this terminology over time and in the nature of the exercises they describe. Horsemanship has always been a developing art with each era using terms in ways that reflect contemporary thinking.

Today the term 'classical dressage' is used to describe the sort of riding Newcastle enjoyed, with 'dressage' used alone referring to the modern derivative. This comes from the original term 'dresser', as used by Newcastle, wherein 'to dress' the horse is to train it. 'High school dressage' is the classical form taken to the most demanding level of achievement in the 'airs above the ground', the highly-skilled leaps wherein all four hooves leave the ground at once. The Spanish Riding School of Vienna, which dates back to the late sixteenth century, and the Cadre Noir at Saumur, are the best known experts in these skills today. Newcastle speaks of all the advanced movements as 'airs', referring to those where four hooves leave the ground as 'leaps' or 'high airs'. However, the term 'haute école' or 'high school' was not used by Newcastle or any of his peers as it dates from the 1850s.

The terms 'ménage' or 'manège' are familiar today and tend to be used interchangeably to refer to the specially designed area in which the horse is ridden. Strictly speaking, one's 'manège', comes within one's 'ménage', as the latter term refers to the overall holding of the owner. Today many amateur riders with modest training ambitions have a manège. This may also be known as the 'school' and the term 'schooling' is as common as 'training', which often, though not always, refers to speed or endurance based sports, such as racing, or long distance riding. When Newcastle speaks of 'mannage', he refers to the art of horsemanship itself, while 'the mannage' refers to the schooling area. He also refers to the art simply as 'horsemanship' and the schooling area as the 'riding house' and I will follow his lead with these terms, though using modern spelling conventions.

The riding house has a long history as the subject of considerable thought in terms of design and construction and remains an ambitious enterprise. Newcastle built riding houses on his estates at Welbeck and Bolsover and converted an existing space for this use during his exile in Antwerp. The enormous symbolic value of these buildings emerges repeatedly. The riding house was almost as much a concept as a place, locating noble display and achievement in a context recognisable to any European of refined discernment.

Within the riding house, while many of the exercises have changed in execution, the terms used to describe them are retained. Also in the development of the art, new airs have been devised which were unknown to early modern riders. The 'levade' for example, a moment of stillness balanced on the hind legs at an angle of 45 degrees, is an air first devised in the nineteenth century. It differs significantly in method, execution and dynamic from the early modern pesade and curvet or courbette from which it evolved, even though they may appear very similar in the context of art. Similarly the courbette has developed into quite a different movement today. [20]

The changes from early modern to current practice illustrates the art as one that has developed and grown over the centuries. However, more importantly in the discussion of early modern texts, precise use of terminology means that both the practice of the exercise and its value to the early modern observer can be understood. Some further discussion of these differences will follow below, but in order to maintain clarity of focus on the early modern context of these exercises, I will employ only the terminology used by Newcastle and his contemporaries.

A final very important term used by Newcastle is 'cavalier'. This obviously has specific links with the English Civil War, in which Newcastle played an active role, but in the context of his manuals, he uses the term to mean a skilled horseman. As a devoted royalist and cavalier himself in every sense of the word, Newcastle's personal definitions of a horseman are linked to his own class. Therefore, while they do not preclude those who turned against the monarch during the Civil War in terms of status, the implicit and explicit hierarchical relationship between monarch and people is paralleled in the rider on horseback. Ideologically, to Newcastle the 'homme de cheval' can only be a royalist.[21]

Horsemanship in Newcastle's life.

Riding as an art formed a touchstone for many aspects of life for Newcastle and his horsemanship manuals were both published during times of great change. The foundation of his interest, however, was laid by his birth, background and upbringing. Newcastle was in many ways the epitome of the Renaissance man. Born in 1593, he was skilled in courtly pursuits, such as fencing, horsemanship and amateur writing, well travelled, able in the administration of his estates, active in the politics of the court, creative yet practical, living his life with self-assurance and theatricality. His fascination with optics, friendships with philosophers such as Thomas Hobbes and René Descartes, and his involvement with circles of literary and scientific acquaintance established him as a forward thinker over a forty year period. Newcastle's eclectic range of interests and enthusiasms led to both fame and ridicule and his life was a combination of intense practicality and self-conscious display.

He was a man of the new era of science and discovery that flourished in the seventeenth century yet remained rooted in ideals of the Elizabethan era. Politically astute, he was inclined also to sweeping romantic gestures. A grandson of the famous Bess of Hardwick, whose four marriages enabled her to amass huge wealth, he inherited her interest in dynastic lineage and the building of great estates through

---

20   I would like to acknowledgment the help of Patrice Franchet d'Espèrey and Brigitte Dupont, Assistante au Centre de Documentation de l'École Nationale d'Equitation, Cadre Noir, Saumur, and Katharina Fuchshuber on behalf of Dr. Georg Kugler, Director of the Spanish Riding School of Vienna in tracing the history of these terms.
21   1658 : 'Aux Cavaliers'; see Appendix I.

his father. Much of his focus was on improving family strength and ambitious building projects.[22]

While undoubtedly a significant figure in both the political and literary history of the seventeenth century, Newcastle's role is hard to define. He held many noble offices, including Governor to the future Charles II and Gentleman of the King's Bedchamber, as a part of the steady upward social mobility that began when he was knighted alongside Prince Henry in 1610. He was elevated to Viscount Mansfield in 1619, made Lord Lieutenant of Nottinghamshire in 1626, Earl of Newcastle in 1628, Marquess in 1643 and finally rose to a dukedom in 1665, before his death at the venerable age of eighty-three in 1676. He lent money to the crown and financed his own troop of cavalry for the Scots War of 1639. When the Civil War began in 1642, his strong reputation as a popular and trusted nobleman brought him the appointment as lord general in supreme command of the Royalist army in the North. His strong personal instinct for civility and generosity lead to fair treatment of his enemies in defeat and he inspired his men on the field with his own courage in battle. His elevation from Earl to Marquess of Newcastle recognised decisive action that secured Yorkshire for the Royalist cause and his army remained strong until outnumbered by 30,000 parliamentarian forces to his own 5,000 men at York in 1644. His famous 'Whitecoats' or 'Newcastle's Lambs', were distinguished at the battle of Marston Moor by fierce courage inspired by devotion to their general and despite the decimation of his army, Newcastle was one of the last to leave the field.

Yet despite these impressive achievements, he is famous in many respects for degrees of failure. His long and expensive years of careful political planning yielded very little and never fulfilled his longing to be Master of the Horse, a role whose honour recognised the vital place of the Royal Stables in the life of the court. His Governorship of the young Prince Charles, a post very dear to his heart, ended abruptly after only three years, a casualty of the so-called 'Army Plot', leaving him with only severe debts from his expenses. While he successfully handled many difficult situations in the North, repeatedly digging deep into his own pocket, his most famous contribution to the Civil War was defeat at the battle of Marston Moor in 1644, even though Prince Rupert's refusal to listen to his advice arguably caused the situation. His debatable decision to leave his own country became famously attributed to his refusal 'to endure the laughter of the court', but was more likely because he was not willing to recruit more men to fight a war he believed was already lost. His importance as a patron of the arts and sciences was undermined by his enthusiasm for publishing his own cheerfully amateur plays and poetry. Even after the Restoration and his return home in 1660, his decision to retire to the country was made only after the rejection of all his offers of his experience to Charles II and in

---

22   See Lucy Worsley, *Cavalier: A Tale of Chivalry, Passion and Great Houses* (London: 2007), Geoffrey Trease, *Portrait of a Cavalier: William Cavendish, First Duke of Newcastle* (London: Macmillan, 1979) and Katie Whitaker, *Mad Madge: Margaret Cavendish, Duchess of Newcastle, Royalist, Writer and Romantic* (London: Chatto & Windus, 2003) for comprehensive recent biographies.

the knowledge that 'many believe I am discontented' (*Life*: pp.68-69). [23]

Contemporary descriptions refer often to his lavish hospitality and huge sphere of influence, balanced by his tendency to risk all in the hope of gaining the monarch's attention. This tension is best illustrated by Lucy Hutchinson, describing the nobility who stood with the King at the outbreak of the Civil War:

> The greatest family was the Earle of Newcastle's, a lord so much once beloved in
> his country that, when the first expedition was against the Scotts, the gentlemen of
> the country sett him forth two troopes, one all of gentlemen, the other of their men,
> who waited on him into the north at their own charge. He had indeed, through his
> greate estate, his liberall hospitality, and constant residence in his country, so endear'd
> them to him, that no man was a greater prince then he in all that northern quarter, till a
> foolish ambition of glorious slavery carried him to court, where he ran himselfe much in
> debt, to purchase neglects of the king and queene, and scornes of the proud courtiers. [24]

The impulse to enjoy 'glorious slavery' and the level of Newcastle's responsibility at Marston Moor, along with his tense relationship with Prince Rupert, damaged his reputation at the time and subsequently, and seemed to outweigh his many achievements. His decision to leave England after the battle sealed his fate and, as Geoffrey Trease says, 'Newcastle is immortalised as the Cavalier who deserted the cause in a huff', though many others took the same course of action. [25] As an ardent Royalist, he devoted much of his life to the service of his king, with few thanks and little recognition. Even his dukedom, while a notable honour held by only six others aside from members of the royal family, involved an financial arrangement whereby he released the king from the considerable debt owed to him by the Crown. However, he is a hugely significant figure in the development of the ongoing relationship between the English and the horse, and an acknowledged master in the eyes of many European horsemen, such as la Guérinière, whose names are better known today.

A gentlemanly education and background informs the philosophy and content of the manuals, but this is grounded in the nature of the author. Newcastle was a man of great enthusiasm, loyalty and willingness to stand by those views, ideas and people he believed in. This may be seen through his patronage of writers and philosophers, his great collections of music and musical instruments and his devotion to his family and his monarch. Evidence of his support of his second wife, Margaret Cavendish, in her writing career is especially notable, being unusual for the time, but great pride in her made his

---

23   Margaret Cavendish, *The Life of William Cavendish, Duke of Newcastle,* ed. by C. H. Firth (London: John C. Nimmo, 1886), subsequently referred to in the text as *Life,* followed by the page number.

24   *Memoirs of Colonel Hutchinson,* ed. by Harold Child (London: Kegan Paul Trench Trübner, 1904), pp.121-122.

25   Already cited, p.141.

admiration unconditional[26] and enthusiastic mutual support was one of the keynotes of their marriage.

While Newcastle may never have had the love he desired from his king, the devotion of his daughters, lifelong closeness with his brother, Charles, and his relationship with Margaret Cavendish suggest a man whose qualities were most clearly recognised by those closest to him. It is not entirely ironic that such recognition seems to have been given readily by his horses, instinctive judges of character. Margaret Cavendish reports that, 'I have observed, and do verily believe, that some of them had a particular love for My Lord; for they seemed to rejoice whensoever he came into the stables, by their trampling action, and the noise they made' (*Life*: p.101).

Newcastle's dedication to his horses, appreciation of their beauty and reluctance to part with them, even when in great financial difficulties, may be seen as a demonstration of his character as important as any of his artistic or philosophical enthusiasms. Cavendish also recalls that during his exile, 'though he was then in distress for money, yet he would sooner have tried all other ways than parted with any of them; for I have heard him say, that good horses are so rare, as not to be valued for money, and that he who would buy him out of his pleasure (meaning his horses), must pay dear for it' (*Life*: pp.72, 71).

Horses played a central role in Newcastle's life from early childhood to old age and his father was pleased when, unlike a friend who had put his money into land, Newcastle bought 'a singing-boy for 50 l, a horse for 50 l, and a dog for 2 l with a boyhood windfall. His father felt that the friend's desire for property before the age of twenty indicated covetousness. This was perhaps a formative opinion, as while Newcastle grew up to have a great love for the fine properties that defined his family, his generosity suggests that he always avoided covetousness (*Life*: p.21).

Edward Hyde, Earl of Clarendon, famously criticised Newcastle as a dilettante by damning him with faint praise:

> He was a very fine Gentleman, active, and full of Courage, and most accomplish'd in
> those Qualities of Horsemanship, Dancing and Fencing, which accompany a good
> breeding; in which his delight was. Besides that he was amorous in Poetry and Musick,
> to which he indulged the greatest part of his time; and nothing could have tempted him
> out of those paths of pleasure, which he enjoy'd […] but Honour and Ambition to
> serve the King […] He liked the Pomp and absolute Authority of a General well,
> and preserv'd the dignity of it to the full […] But the substantial part, and fatigue
> of a General, he did not in any degree understand, (being utterly unacquainted with
> War) nor could submit to; but referr'd all matters of that Nature to the discretion of his
> Lieutenant General King […] In all Actions of the Field he was still present, and
> never absent in any Battle; in all which he gave instances of an invincible courage and

---

26   For example, see Newcastle's introductory verse to *Poems, and Fancies* (London: J. Martin & J. Allestrye, 1653).

fearlessness in danger; in which the exposing of himself notoriously did sometimes change the fortune of the day, when his Troops begun to give ground. Such Articles of Action were no sooner over, than he retired to his delightful Company, Musick, or his softer pleasures, to all which he was so indulgent, and to his ease, that he would not be interrupted upon what occasion soever; insomuch as he sometimes denied Admission to the Chiefest Officers of the Army, even to General King himself, for two days together; from whence many Inconveniencies fell out.[27]

This arch description has done much to damage Newcastle's reputation but balanced against Hutchinson's account highlights both strengths and weaknesses in his character. Both suggest a learned attitude of seeking life's pleasures and refinements, perhaps to balance the tensions of status and martial prowess. An aristocratic engagement with the vital dramas of life but aloofness from mundane necessity indulged through a strictly amateur enjoyment of the arts is promoted in early conduct books. However, this attitude did not extend to Newcastle's horsemanship and he had no patience with those who approached the art in a dilettante style:

> [...] they would be the Finest men in the world, for All things, though they will take Pains for Nothing; and because, forsooth, they cannot Ride by Inspiration, without taking pains, therefore it is worth Nothing [...] The next thing is, That they think it is a disgrace for a Gentleman to any thing Well. What! Be a Rider. Why not? Many Kings and Princes think themselves Graced with being good Horsemen (1667: p.7).

This devotion to the skill of horsemanship goes far beyond aristocratic affectation. Newcastle's personal dedication and expertise surfaces repeatedly in anecdotal and historical evidence, most pointedly in the writing of Margaret Cavendish, and also that of many later and less partial commentators who acknowledge him as a seminal figure in the art.[28] Douglas Grant sums up Newcastle's pattern of behaviour during the years of his exile neatly as, 'the constant search for credit, and, once it was found, the immediate purchase of horses',[29] while Newcastle, in his second horsemanship manual, recalls that during his exile in Antwerp, members of the continental aristocracy having seen him ride 'cried, Miraculo' (1667: sig. c).

Even allowing for self-promotion in this story, his reputation and the detail of his manuals indicates that he achieved a level of skill only attainable over many years. The enjoyment of writing

---

27 *The History of the Rebellion and Civil Wars in England,* ed. by W. D. Macray, 6 Volumes (Oxford: 1888), Vol. II, pp. 392-93.

28 For example, see Jean and Lily Froissard, *The Horseman's International Book of Reference* (London: Stanley Paul, 1980)

29 Douglas Grant, *Margaret the First* (London: Rupert Hart-Davies, 1957), p.60.

and music could be undertaken casually and according to mood, but to ride well, to devise a method and inspire an audience, could not be approached in a dilettante fashion. Regardless of his failings, his love of 'softer pleasures' and his desire for 'glorious slavery', the horsemanship manuals prove that Newcastle was fully capable of long-term rigorous dedicated application.

A boyhood love of horses and fascination with the art of the riding house was not in itself unusual. To ride in a noble style upon a splendid horse was part of the gentlemanly education and aristocratic self-presentation that Newcastle believed maintained the hierarchy vital to social order. As a youth, he trained in horsemanship with Monsieur St. Antoine, a graduate of the Italian academy of Giovanni Battista Pignatelli alongside Antoine de Pluvinel, with whose own riding manuals Newcastle's have much in common. Regardless of his emphatic claims that his method is totally original, he is part of a long lineage. St. Antoine had been sent to England by Henri IV of France to train the golden child, Prince Henry, in whose company Newcastle received his knighthood in 1610, at the age of 16. They shared also a passion for horsemanship and had Prince Henry lived, Newcastle's influence at court and indeed the course of his life could well have been very different, given this common enthusiasm. Sir Balthazar Gerbier claimed that Prince Henry had planned to set up a riding academy in England along French lines, 'that by example of the French [...] our Nobility and Gentry might learn their exercises in England in their youth'. Gerbier did set up an academy that lasted a few years in the middle of the century at his own house in Bethnal Green, but it would seem that without the patronage of the Prince, it failed.[30]

Roy Strong argues that Prince Henry's premature death at the age of eighteen ended a renaissance period for England[31] and a hankering for this style of life, based on noblesse oblige with the tradition and grace this entailed is evident throughout Newcastle's life. The importance of horsemanship as 'fit and proper for a person of quality' to develop a 'noble and heroick nature' was thus established very early in his development (*Life*: pp.80, 34).

With the arrival of St. Antoine, the art of manège aspired to new heights in England and Prince Henry erected the first ever purpose-built riding house between 1607 and 1609. Twelve years later, Newcastle built his own riding house at Welbeck, modelled on the Prince's building.[32] The purchase and breeding of the correct stamp of horse for the riding house was also a particular interest for Prince Henry and horses exceeded all other types of gifts presented to him by foreign royalty and dignitaries. Books dedicated to him included Gervase Markham's *Cavelrice: or the English Horseman* (1607) and Nicholas Morgan's *The Perfection of Horsemanship* (1609). Strong cites the Venetian ambassador as relating Prince Henry's love of Barbary horses so perhaps it is not surprising that Newcastle states,

---

30   Quoted in John Stoye, *English Travellers Abroad 1604-1667* (New Haven/London: Yale University Press, 1989), p.38.

31   *Henry: Prince of Wales and England's Lost Renaissance* (London: Thames & Hudson, 1986), p.3.

32   Mark Girouard, *Robert Smythson and the Elizabethan Country House* (New Haven: Yale University Press, 1983), pp.251-3.

'Quant aux Barbes, il faut que je confesse qu'ils sont mes favouris' (1658: p.16).[33]

Like Prince Henry, Newcastle was interested not only in riding but also in the conformation and the bloodlines of fine horses. Much of his later life was spent in attempting to establish himself on a secure, long-term basis at court, perhaps in the hope of regaining ground that would naturally have become his had Prince Henry lived. While his career included much close contact with both Charles I and Charles II, to have grown to adulthood as a companion to Prince Henry would have established a very different relationship. His belief that he had been repeatedly 'cut down by Lady Fortune' and that 'the wisest way for man was to have as little faith as he could in this world and as much as he could for the next world' was perhaps established when the promise of the young prince was curtailed by his premature death (*Life*: pp.253-254).

Newcastle received an academic education also but he was not an enthusiastic scholar and left St. John's College, Cambridge without graduating, having spent his time 'taking more delight in sports than learning'. However, as Margaret Cavendish is careful to point out, 'although My Lord has not so much scholarship and learning as his brother Charles had, yet he hath an excellent natural wit and judgement' (*Life*: pp.133-134). Of more enjoyment to him doubtless would have been the foreign travel considered an essential experience for the young noblemen and designed to cultivate a refined and cosmopolitan experience of the world. The first Earl of Clare, John Holles, was advised by his father that each of the European nations 'have their virtues, which are with study and due endeavour to be encompassed, and as in times past, eloquence and philosophy were only to be had in Athens […] so in Italy riding, weapons and the mathematics, in France an assured, free and civil conversation [...] qualities at these times most respected in our own court'.[34] This widely-held belief in the value of Continental style and skills forms a significant background to the motivation behind both of Newcastle's manuals.

Newcastle undertook the European tour in 1612, in the company of Sir Henry Wotton, who described him as 'so sweet an ornament of my journey, and a gentleman himself of so excellent nature and disposition'.[35] Horses featured in this tour as gifts for the Duke Charles Emmanuel of Savoy from King James and Newcastle was given a horse as a gift by the Duke himself, who took such a liking to the young man that he wished to keep him in Savoy to give him experience of court life and war. The giving and receiving of horses as gifts reflected their prestige among the nobility and remained a feature of Newcastle's generosity throughout his life. The elegant and skilful handling necessary to enhance their beauty was therefore a highly valued measure of a man's own grace.

As one of the defining pursuits of a gentleman, horsemanship, like swordsmanship, had practical roots in battle, but in the riding house had become entirely a decorative skill. Along with music and

---

33   Already cited, pp.65-66; 'With regard to Barbary horses, I freely confess they are my favourites' (1743: p.21).

34   *Letters of John Holles 1587-1637*, ed. by P. R. Seddon (Nottingham: Thoroton Society Record Series 31, 1975), p.53.

35   *Life and Letters of Sir Henry Wotton*, ed. by L. P. Smith (Oxford: Oxford University Press, 1966), p.23.

dancing, with which horsemanship shared terms such as capriole and *corvetta*, it demonstrated a cultured taste and background. Even without his great love of the art, a man such as Newcastle would consider himself incomplete without some refinement in the skill. It was quite different to racing, a sport growing in popularity throughout Newcastle's life. While he seems to have taken some part, racing is the subject of a bitter little verse, 'Of Runninge horses', written in his latter years, which considers that, 'Theye that keepe horse for race are mutch to blame' for promoting an activity, 'worthless of Honor', most likely at the expense of interest in the riding house.[36] While hunting was highly popular among the nobility, Newcastle was not greatly enthusiastic and Margaret Cavendish does not include hunting or racing among his interests (*Life*: p.208). Although the author of a broadside with details of Newcastle's own race course and the rules thereof, his secretary, John Rolleston, wrote also that 'for other delights, as those of running horses, hawking, hunting, &c, his Grace used them merely for society's sake […] to please others'. He adds though that Newcastle's 'knowledge in them excelled' (*Life*: pp.208; lxvii).[37]

The biblical precedent for man to have dominion over nature gave hunting a spiritual justification which could be transferred to the riding house in the submission of a fiery stallion to the rider's will. The way in which that submission was obtained marks the features of training developments over the passage of time. Unlike the sports of hunting or racing, however, the activities of the riding house were an art, whose ultimate purpose was elevation of the rider through refinement, not bloodshed or competition.

Neither was horsemanship a science in itself. While the term 'science' is used occasionally by Newcastle, the use of 'art' is consistent. The science involved in perfecting the art is the technical precision and analytical understanding of the horse's anatomy that shapes the training. This approach offers an underlying serious intent to counter any accusations of frivolity. Newcastle's stance reflects the definition by Hobbes that 'Science is the knowledge of Consequences, and dependence of one fact upon another […] Because when we see how a thing comes about, upon what causes, and by what manner; when the like causes come into our power, wee see how to make it produce the like effects'.[38]

Suitable skills for a gentleman were earnestly discussed in the writings of the time, including those of Sir Philip Sidney and Sir Thomas Elyot. Sidney's *Defence of Poesy* opens with a description of his own education in horsemanship, during which he was taught that 'no earthly thing bred such wonder to a Prince as to be a good horseman'.[39] A gentleman's education was to be well-rounded, so that academic and practical skills advanced together. In *The Boke Called the Governour,* Sir Thomas Elyot advises that:

---

36 University of Nottingham, Department of Manuscripts and Special Collections, Portland Manuscripts: PwV 25, fol.138.

37 *Being Commanded by* […] *to publish the following articles for his new course* (Oxford: 1662); Epistle to the Duchess of Newcastle, in *Life*: p.lxvii.

38 *Leviathan,* ed. by Kenneth Minogue (London: Everyman, 1994), p.23.

39 *Defence of Poesie, Astrophil and Stella and Other Writings*, ed. by Elizabeth Porges-Watson (London: Everyman, 1997), p.83.

All thoughe I have hitherto aduaunced the commendation of lernyng, specially in gentil men, yet it is to be considered that continuall studie without some maner of exercise, shortly exhausteth the spirites vitall, and hyndereth naturall decoction and digestion, wherby mannes body is the soner corrupted and brought in to diuers sickenessis, and finallye the life is therby made shorter: where contrayrye wise by exercise, whiche is a vehement motion (as Galene prince of phisitions defineth) the helthe of man is preserued, and his strength increased. [40]

This belief in the value of physical exercise as well as 'lernyng' was one Newcastle seems to have embraced. He refers often to the well-being gained from riding and his handwritten manuscript on horsemanship includes a list of the ages of notable horsemen as evidence of its value in maintaining health (PwV 21, fols.83v-84). Elyot's suggestions for exercises improving physical strength and hand to eye co-ordination include skill at arms, as 'Amonge these exercises it shall be conuenient to lerne to handle sondrye waipons, specially the sworde and the batayle axe, whiche be for a noble man moste conuenient'. However, he adds that:

the most honorable exercise, in myne opinion, and that besemeth the astate of euery noble persone, is to ryde suerly and clene on a great horse and a roughe, whiche undoubtedly nat onely importeth a maiestie and drede to inferiour persones, beholding him aboue the common course of other men, dauntyng a fierce and cruell beaste, but also is no litle socour, as well in pursuete of enemies and confoundyng them, as in escapyng imminent daunger, whan wisdome therto exhorteth. [41]

Therefore, as a comprehensive system of personal development, riding could hardly be bettered. As an active, intelligent but not academic man, fully aware of his own role as an aristocrat, Newcastle's personal interest in horses provided the motivation to turn this useful exercise into a source of life-long pleasure.

The importance of self-presentation and noble display had become a key feature in living in the context of the European courts with horsemanship, horses and images of horses forming a central part of this theatricality. An appreciation of fine horses crossed cultural and geographical boundaries to create understanding between men who may not share a common language and display on horseback by or before a prince is a key feature of early horsemanship manuals. The presentation of the horse in art becomes therefore, a double pleasure and a double assertion of the status of the owner who can

40 Thomas Elyot, (London/NewYork: J. M. Dent/E. P. Dutton, n.d.), Book XVI; Elyot's original 1531 text went though seven further editions in the sixteenth century.
41 Elyot, Book XVII.

command and afford such beauty in flesh and on canvas. Newcastle's manuals, as records of art and works of art in themselves, fix the experience and status of ownership and expertise.

Lisa Jardine and Jerry Brotton examine large tapestries as a readily portable 'aspect of the ostentatious occasions on which men and women of distinction visited one another' to be 'unpacked and displayed prominently at crucial moments of diplomatic negotiation and dynastic alliance-formation'.[42] Newcastle had tapestries made of several of the plates from his 1658 manual, including those in which he appears himself, and also had several life-size portraits made of his horses. His awareness of and engagement with European modes of self-expression illustrate the centrality of court culture in his life, as would be expected in a man of his status. The plates of himself on horseback in the 1658 manual relate closely to the images of the time, so that he locates himself in the context of aristocratic display both publicly and privately. Strong similarities may be seen between the portraits of Newcastle in the 1658 plates and those of George Villiers and other key royal and noble figures, all of which illustrate qualities suitable for martial and political prowess.

The horse also appears in emblem books reinforcing the qualities needed in a leader. Andrea Alciati's *Emblemata*, of 1581 includes an emblem 'On one who knows not to flatter', wherein the horse becomes the emblem of the rebellious state that responds only to the dictates of a fierce leader. Geoffrey Whitney's *A Choice of Emblems* of 1586, picks up this same image, dedicating it to Sir Philip Sidney. Whitney alters the emphasis so that the horse is no longer a metaphor for the state, but becomes analogous with it, reminding the rider that a horse will not suffer a fool gladly. As 'His corage fierce, do the crave a better guide', a horse that consents to follow the leadership of his rider testifies to that man's 'judgement grave', as well as 'learning, witte, and ecke of conscience cleare'. This difference between the horse as metaphor and the horse as analogy is an vital consideration in relation to Newcastle's manuals.[43]

The iconography of horsemanship was interwoven both physically and psychologically throughout the culture of the early modern European court. To a man as steeped in the art as Newcastle, this provided a potential occupation for his long years away from home after the collapse of all that he believed in, heralded by personal defeat at Marston Moor. During his exile from England, Newcastle missed his home greatly and suffered both financial insecurity and frustration at being unable to do more to help his king. Cavendish relates that 'his onely and chief intention was to hinder His Majesties enemies' and that he would 'willingly sacrifice himself and all his posterity for the sake of His Majesty'. After Charles I's execution, Newcastle's devotion to his former pupil, Prince Charles, led him to 'wait on His Highness (which he did afterwards at several times, so long as His Highness continued there) expecting some opportunity to serve his king and country' (*Life*: pp.123, 94).

---

42   *Global Interests: Renaissance Art between East and West* (London: Reaktion Books, 2000), pp.132-133.

43   Alciato, Emblem 35; Whitney, p.38, *Alciato Project* <http://www.mun.ca/alciato/desc. html> [accessed 4 May, 2015]; Rosemary Freeman, *English Emblem Books* (New York, Octagon Books, 1978), pp.56-61.

However, he waited in vain as others were closer to the exiled monarch and while he was later appointed to the king's Privy Council, he was too outspoken and when Charles sailed for Scotland, Newcastle was not permitted to accompany him. Feeling, as he often did in his relations with the monarchy, undervalued and overlooked, Newcastle returned to Antwerp where he had found suitable and affordable accommodation for a long exile in the former home of the artist Rubens. Although happy in his second marriage, the burdens of maintaining his household and his inability to help his monarch left him feeling isolated. His sense of abandonment led him to write, to an unnamed recipient, 'My acquaintances hide themselves from me, and my friends and kindred stand afar off'.[44]

He turned to his great love, horsemanship, to occupy and establish himself as an aristocrat holding his head high although 'banished his native country' (*Life*: p.84). This was not, however, evidence of frivolity but a statement of his ability to maintain a recognisably noble lifestyle, particularly important in the context of his exile. His riding house attracted a great many distinguished visitors from the Continental nobility, and while he describes it as 'my own private riding-house' (1667: sig. B[v]), it is likely that by some gentlemanly arrangement his financial situation was eased through the training of horses and riders.

Alongside the displays of his art, he also recorded his expertise in the form of his first published instruction manual. To a man as hungry for public and royal recognition as Newcastle, an individual contribution to history was a necessity. Therefore, in writing his book, he set out to establish a new standard in an art that served as a beautiful parallel to all that noble birth entailed, declaring:

> What can be more Comely or Pleasing, than to see Horses go in all their several
> Ayres? and to see so Excellent a Creature, with so much Spirit and Strength, to be
> Obedient to his Rider, as if having no Will but His, they had but One Body, and One
> Mind, like a Centaur? But above all, What sets Off a King more, than to be on a
> Beautiful Horse at the Head of his Army? (1667: p.13).

The development of horsemanship as an art.

The art so beloved of Newcastle had begun to develop in Renaissance Italy, and in 1550 Frederigo Grisone published *Gli Ordini di cavalcare*, the first important horsemanship manual to be of interest primarily to the elite, rather than the military, horseman, although a great many of his readers would have been both. He also set the precedent for the riding manual itself as a feature of the master's work, and a huge array of manuals followed. Many were derivative, or translations of Grisone's work

---

44   University of Nottingham, Department of Manuscripts and Special Collections, Portland Manuscripts: Pw1, fol. 537, 30 Oct. 1649.

'improved' upon by others and so locating ownership of the material becomes difficult, especially as not all who were influential published their methods. Pignatelli trained under Cesare Fiaschi, then joined Grisone's academy in Naples to become the most celebrated instructor of his time but did not publish his own manual. His influence then, could only be interpreted through oral tradition, constantly filtered through the experience of those who followed him.

This is also true in some respects with regard to the manuals of Antoine de Pluvinel, the next seminal author. Pluvinel's manuals were published posthumously and prepared by a student of his, Rene Menou, partly from rough notes and fragments of writing. Large tracts of the material in Pluvinel's manuals had already appeared in Menou's own text of 1612, so it becomes difficult to separate the student from the master. Therefore, straightforward comparisons between texts based on locating originality are almost impossible. [45]

In this respect Newcastle's manuals are straightforward but his political and personal agenda complicate the motivation behind each manual, adding an additional and complex dimension of subtlety to his work. For Grisone and Pluvinel, to set down their ideas for future riders was a way of recording the ephemeral, one of the functions of the published text. Newcastle's reasons for doing this are not simply to do with being a great horseman but also related to the situation of his life at the time when each manual was written.

One of the primary features of Grisone's work is the acceptance of extreme brutality to counter any resistance from the horse. Developing this with a move away from violence makes the work of Pluvinel the next significant text, taking horse training into a new area of refinement and precision. Pluvinel also works in the context of the riding house exclusively, whereas Grisone uses ploughed fields, ditches and other outdoor locations in the training. Newcastle's method adds further refinement and his claims of innovation are justified, although he also includes developments from earlier practices. This is inevitable as while methods may change and develop, the ways in which the rider influences his mount, namely by his weight and position on the horse's back, are bound by the anatomy of both. The use of these fixed physical features, however, is where the development in both understanding and method is seen.

This sense of progression in the horsemanship text can be traced further by considering the way in which Newcastle influenced later masters, such as la Guérinière. Newcastle stands alone as the first and only British author whose work was not derivative of early Continental texts and became acclaimed as a primary influence by later generations of horsemen. Nevertheless, rather than attempting to see him as he saw himself, in splendid isolation, a more accurate perspective is to see him in the lineage of great horsemen, each with an individual contribution to make.

---

45 *Le Maneige Royal,* trans. by Hilda Nelson (Virginia, Xenophon Press 2010); see pp.v-vi for a consideration of the relationship between Pluvinel's texts and Menou's, *La Pratique du Cavalier* (Paris, 1612). All subsequent references to Pluvinel's work will be to Nelson's translation. Toole-Stott, pp.80-81, 92-95 also considers the highly complicated history of these texts.

The riding house and the battlefield.

The moral purpose of horsemanship was in contention from the Renaissance onwards and Newcastle contributes to the debate in characteristically emphatic style in 1667 with a chapter entitled 'That it is a very Impertinent Error, and of Great prejudice, to think the Mannage Useless' (1667: p.5). This follows his 1658 observation, that those who misunderstand the value of these horses, simply reveal that 'ne sont bons eux mesmes à quoy que ce soit' (1658: 'Avant-Propos').[46] He comments resignedly also that 'There are great Disputes amongst Cavaliers about this Business' when it comes to choosing the best horse 'Either for the War, or for Single-Combat, or for Any Thing Else' (1667: p.77). With his usual wry insight, he comments 'how Difficult a thing it is to have a Good Horse in any Kind, for Any thing' and his conclusion that 'a Knowing Horseman is not so Happy for Horses, as a citizen of London, that knows Nothing' (1667: p.81) illustrates again his ironic acceptance that knowledge is not always a help, because divided opinion then complicates the matter. A tension is apparent as riding moves from the battlefield to the riding house. This seems largely due to attempts, such as those made by Newcastle himself, to retain the links between the two. He does not, however, claim that the exercises were of use on the battlefield, but that the riding house trained a horse to be sufficiently versatile to be of use there.

The movements of the riding house were originally based on the behaviour of stallions in the wild, either displaying to mares or fighting rival stallions. The aggressive kicking or striking nature of many of these movements serves well the male display involved in the art. Newcastle believed strongly that the horseman should 'do nothing against Nature; for Art is but to set Nature in Order' (1667: p.271), giving a masculine imperative of control within the context of shaping nature to man's purpose. However, these natural skills were refined and defined until there was little left to truly resemble wild natural movement. In theory at least, the fighting movements could transfer usefully to the battlefield but there seems to be a gradual move to separate the riding house horse and the war horse which may be traced through the manuals.

In translating Grisone, Sir Thomas Blundeville distinguishes between the war horse and the horse of pleasure so that the latter should learn additional skills more suited for ceremony and display.[47] In *Le Maneige Royale*, Louis XIII's comment to Pluvinel that certain airs 'are not necessarily the best for war', suggests an anticipation that the training could lead to the battlefield. Interestingly Pluvinel seems to avoid being drawn into this discussion, saying, 'I will soon give my opinion to your Majesty' but eventually only adds that some modified exercises may be useful 'when one fights in a duel or in battle'. It may be that this token mention of the matter is a cautious recognition of it as a controversial

---

46 'are good for nothing themselves' (1743: p.14).

47 *A new booke, containing the Arte of Ryding and breaking greate Horses* (London: Willyam Seres, 1560, Preface).

subject. [48] Primary source evidence suggests that the art of the riding house in its advanced form had lost any practical connection with the battlefield by Newcastle's time. No mention at all of any of the school airs appears in *The young Horseman or The honest plain-dealing Cavalier,* written in 1644, by John Vernon, which is aimed very much at the ordinary mounted soldier. [49]

Vernon's schooling focuses on exercises that supple the horse to ensure speed and agility, which seem both practicable and capable of implementation:

> you must use him often to ride the Ring, and the figure eight, first in a greater compasse
> and afterwards in a lesser by degrees: first in his pace, then on his trot and so to his gallop.
> And lastly in full careere, you may teach him this by using your hand, legge and voice,
> for the using him unto your hand you must observe not to use your arms at all,
> but your rist only, this is excellent for facings, as if you would turn him to the left,
> a little motion of the left little finger and a touch of the left leg not using the spur doth it. [50]

This has much in common with Newcastle's basic training methods for teaching suppleness and mobility through circle work, with his refined use of the hands on the reins to encourage lightness and a swift response. These techniques would be sufficient, as it seems very unlikely that in the terrible crush and chaos of battle there would be time to focus on the execution of elaborate caprioles and curvets. Also, while the drama of the capriole, with the horse leaping forward high above the ground, may in theory threaten a man below, even in the refined atmosphere of a riding house, it is a difficult and specialized movement. An additional key consideration in the suitability of the airs of the riding house for the battlefield, must be the time and cost involved in producing the horse and rider combination capable of performing such moves.

As Newcastle expounds at great length the cost and difficulty of obtaining and importing a good Spanish horse (1667: pp.52-53), it seems unlikely that this would be the horse to risk losing in battle, in spite of, or perhaps because of its skill. Even allowing for his claims of a short method of training, to produce one horse that could perform the most modest of airs would take many months, with two or three handlers involved in the training. Then the horses that had the skill and physique to perform the great leaps, the croupades and caprioles, would be in limited numbers of highly expensive animals. Newcastle states that 'It is a Hard thing to find Fit Horses for the Mannage, either upon the Ground, or in Ayres' (1667: p.79) and stresses that 'every Horse is to Chuse his own Ayre, unto which Nature hath most Fitted him' (1667: p.271-271). Nicholas Morgan argues against teaching of the high airs at all, due to them 'tending altogether towards [the horse's] destruction' and being 'a matter rather

---

48   Pluvinel, pp.89-90.
49   *The Young Horse-man, or honest plain-dealing Cavalier,* ed. by John Tincey (London: Partizan Press, 1993), p.11.
50   Ibid. p.43.

of delight than good use'.[51]

A theatrical and active general, such as Newcastle, might wish to inspire his army in the moments before the battle as a figurehead on his superbly trained horse. But unless that horse could then lead a charge at a flat gallop under fire, such a display would be undermined and it is unlikely that more than a few riders would possess such mounts. He may also have had a number of horses with him on the battlefield to allow for casualties which could have included school horses to inspire his men and war horses to lead a charge. This question remains then, as to the nature of Newcastle's irritation at those who speak against the value of the riding house in war training, as he does not advocate training horses to capriole across the battlefield himself. His wider discussions also illustrate full awareness that the high art of the riding house has no place there.

His advice on choosing a horse 'For the War, or for Single-Combat', does not specify a Spanish horse, which he is adamant is the best for the riding house. He is interested more in size and attitude, claiming that 'the Midling or Less Horses is Best for All Things', which include not only war, but 'Hunting-Horses; Horse for Winter-Galloping on the High-Way many Miles; for the Coach, for the Cart' (1667: pp.77-78). It is unthinkable that this all-rounder would be one of his expensive Spanish horses, and he most likely means a good versatile cross-breed, similar to today's hunter. Another clue that such a horse is not a manège horse, is that he suggests geldings rather than 'Ston'd Horses', that is stallions, as most suitable, as they tend to be more placid; a true manège horse would always be a stallion for its fire and presence.

While he advocates his basic method for all horses, the training he suggests for a war-horse does not include any advanced school airs, but rather that 'You should teach him To Leap Hedge, Ditch and Rail […] also to swim' (1667: pp.311-312). However, when he is growing irritated about those who refer to his managed horses as 'danseur & badin', that is 'dancer and prauncer', he argues that they too are versatile without suggesting that the airs of the riding house are transferable to the battlefield:

> […] s'ils avoient quelquels duëls, ou s'ils alloient à la guerre, ils reconnoîtroient leur faute; car ces chevaux là vont aussy bien à la soldade & à passades comme par haut, & les longues journées leur sont bien tost perdre tous les airs qui ne sont proprement que pour le plaisir. Qui plus est, ils en sont beaucoup plus propres à galoper, trotter, tourner, ou autre chose de cette nature, qui est pour l'usage (1658: 'Avant-Propos'). [52]

---

51 *The Horseman's Honour: Or the Beautie of Horsemanship* (London: John Marriott, 1620), p.207. Displays today by the Spanish Riding School of Vienna and the Cadre Noir at Saumur have only a few horses performing these movements, due to the rigorous training required and immense physical strain they put upon the horses.

52 'If those gentlemen were to fight a duel or go to the wars, they would find their error; for these horses perform a journey, as well as they do the high airs; and the long marches occasionally make them soon forget those airs, which are calculated merely for pleasure; moreover, they are much fitter for galloping, trotting wheeling, or any thing else which is

This is the true value of the riding house horse in war: his excellent and solid training which makes him skilful and above all, responsive, even in the face of danger, so that 'I will run him on Fire, Water, or Sword, and he shall Obey me' (1667: p.6). His ability to perform a capriole may or may not be an added bonus if the theory may be put into practice, but his swift obedience and dexterity makes him invaluable. Newcastle's irritation therefore appears, as elsewhere, to be rooted in the common lack of understanding of the art, rather than the need for blind devotion to it. Thus the art of the manège was useful as part of the general education of the officer class for its discipline and overall skill, rather than for specific techniques. Ultimately, it was more about preparing the rider for war and defining his fitness to lead men through his control of his horse. Newcastle's annoyance then at any inability to see the intrinsic value of the work, alongside its beauty as an art form and political importance as a means of display, becomes understandable. It also provides the motivation to add his theories on this art, justifiable entirely in its own right, to those already well-known.

Newcastle's manuals and the complex issues surrounding the riding house illustrate the combined practical, philosophical and personal concerns involved when he came to write. In this book, I will show that the art of horsemanship was a yardstick for aristocratic self-awareness against which Newcastle measured his own life and society. I will therefore explore the manuals as essential in every aspect to an understanding of him as a significant figure of the early modern period, as well as a seminal equestrian writer whose ideas have more resonance with current thinking than might be anticipated.

---

necessary' (1743: p.14).

Chapter 2

'Also he recreates himself with his pen': Newcastle as writer

Language most shewes a man: speake, that I may see thee.
Ben Jonson, *Timber, or Discoveries*

Newcastle's horsemanship manuals are part of a considerable canon of writing, much of it published or intended for publication. This includes plays, introductory verses to Margaret Cavendish's work and public statements issued during the Civil War. There is also a large amount of private correspondence and poetry, as well as his book of advice to the future Charles II,[53] and two undated handwritten manuscripts of notes on horsemanship. In Newcastle's own and a scribal hand, they are a vital primary source in considering the relationship between the two published manuals.[54]

As a poet and a playwright Newcastle was an amateur, producing work of variable quality with typical vigour and enthusiasm. His formal addresses are couched in the hyperbole common at the time while public material moves between authoritative and defensive in style. A romantic spirit fond of bawdy humour emerges though his poems and plays, deep family affection, political aspiration and frustration in his letters and a desire to justify his actions in his public declarations. His horsemanship manuals, however, offer the clearest insight into his motivation because they encompass so many aspects of personal philosophy reflected elsewhere. They also counter the image of him as a dilettante whose 'tincture of a romantic spirit' and liking for 'witty society […] diverted many counsels, and lost many fair opportunities'.[55] The horsemanship manuals are the only texts combining all the elements of his writing, being written for the public but with a deeply personal agenda, including a strong theatricality and the elevation of technique to art.

The key to the success of the manuals as technical guides, however, is Newcastle's talent for putting what is essentially practical into an accessible personal style recognisable from his many

---

53 MS Clarendon 109; subsequent references will be from the transcript included in *A Catalogue of Letters [...] at Welbeck* Abbey, compiled by S. Arthur Strong (London: John Murray, 1903), Appendix 1. pp.173-236, abbreviated to *Letters*. Examples of Newcastle's unpublished material may be found in the Portland Collection, University of Nottingham, PwV23-26, and the British Library Additional MSS 70499.

54 University of Nottingham, Department of Manuscripts and Special Collections, Portland Manuscripts: PvW 21 and PvW 22, subsequently referred to in the text, followed by the folio number.

55 Sir Philip Warwick, *Memoires of the Reign of King Charles I* (London, 1702), p.257.

extant letters and other hand-written documents.[56] The strong impression of his own voice links them to his book of advice to the future Charles II. Like the horsemanship manuscripts, the 'little book' is handwritten with erratic punctuation, digressions and a sense of a lively face-to-face discussion in which the listener could take part if only the speaker would pause for breath.

His conversational style and strong opinions result in texts which are, while undoubtedly arrogant in parts, full of a dynamic enthusiasm. The 1667 manual devotes nine pages to establishing, 'That it is a very Impertinent Error, and of great Prejudice, to think the Mannage Useless', at the end of which Newcastle declares: 'Thus it is Proved, That there is nothing of more Use than A Horse of Mannage'. His proof is usually that he thinks it is so and others of his status agree, including the King, the Duke of York, the Duke of 'Mommorancy', the Prince of Conde and the King of Spain (1667: pp.5-14). Noble birth and sound judgement, for Newcastle, go hand-in-hand.

His self-confidence means he can declare easily that, 'There is but One Truth in any thing; and that my Method is True, cannot be better Demonstrated, than by Experience, which will clearly show, That Mine never misses its End, as All Others do' (1667: p.41). But he also uses irony, humour and precise analysis combined with a strong sense of the reading audience, both in the self-presentation and the handling of the horsemanship aspects:

> But sayes One, Doth your Lordship think, that both your Books would Make me a
> Horseman? I Answer; That they are Written as plainly, and as clearly as Possibly can
> be [….] But whether my Books will Make you a Horse-man or no, though they do as
> much as Books can do, I cannot Tell; for you must have it all in your Head; and it may
> be you will not understand it. But put the Case you do, yet Wanting the Practice, you
> cannot ride Well; and yet no Fault at all in my Books, but in You (1667: p.43).

His method of teaching is also similar in both manuals, though his ideas have developed over time, which supports the material as a working system. He uses repetition as a methodology for experiential understanding, 'Custom having a very great power over Man and Beast' (1667: p.151), and describes each exercise in the greatest of detail, suggesting considerable analysis of each movement before it could be set down. He is aware of the difficulty of describing these exercises both fully and concisely and explains that, 'Vous devez pareillement sçavoir que cét art ne peut étre recueilly dans un proverbe, ou court aphorisme, ou redruit à un syllogisme'. But he recommends his own work, 'puis que je sçay bien, qu'il est tres-bon'(1658: p.271).[57]

---

56   See 53 above.

57   'You ought to be well informed that the art of horsemanship cannot be collected together in a proverb, or a short aphorism […] nor can there be one universal lesson, as many desire in this art'; 'because I certainly know that is very good' (1743: p.132).

The expertise displayed in the technical aspects of the manuals justifies this strong level of personal confidence. Newcastle approaches highly complicated exercises with great precision, so that when teaching the reader how to develop suppleness in the horse, he says:

> Pull the inward Cavezone's Reyn Cross his Neck, not too High, your Knuckles
> towards his Neck, and Help him, with the outside Legg, and Reyn contrary (1667: p.233).

This may well seem incomprehensible to the non-rider but from a rider's perspective, and it is always the rider for whom he writes, this is a subtle movement. The position of the rider's hand allows for 'fine-tuning' of the contact through the bit while riding a circle, and the use of the rider's shoulder and leg to direct the horse's body and encourage it to bend around the rider's inside leg. All Newcastle's exercises are described with this detail and refinement, illustrating his ability as a writer in handling the difficult task of transferring a very practical skill to paper instructions.

A particularly interesting example of this ability is his analysis 'Of the Movement of a Horse in all his Natural Paces', which appears in both manuals (1658: pp.36-37; 1667: pp.145-155). This appears to relate very closely to an analysis of the horse's movement entitled, 'Considerations touching the facility or Difficulty of the Motions of a horse on straight lines and Circular'. This short study, once attributed to the philosopher, Thomas Hobbes, but now considered to be by Newcastle's chaplain, Robert Payne, is one of a number of documents either written or translated by Payne for Newcastle, analysing the science of motion.

Payne's analysis, thought to date from 1635-8, has close similarities in content with the analysis in Newcastle's manuals. However, the stylistic differences indicate an awareness of a reader's need for practical understanding. Relationships between the two remain close enough though, to suggest that Newcastle used Payne's analysis as the basis for his own, altering the perspective for his own purposes and reworking it for accessibility. A close study of both texts also illustrates how Newcastle's handling of the technical aspects of the work arises from close careful attention to the horse in motion.[58]

Newcastle writes in conversational paragraphs throughout both manuals, with headed sections divided into lessons, then subdivided into chapters, each detailing one exercise. He enlivens the complicated technical detail with commentary such as the advice to 'Mark it, Remember it and Practice it if you can' (1667: p.262). However, he begins the practical riding chapters in both with an analysis of the movement of the horse's legs in various paces and airs, using a numbered list, as does Payne in his study. In both manuals and the handwritten manuscript, this material is essentially the same, allowing for the translation of the 1658 into French and a tendency to use less detail in the 1667 text.

---

58   *Letters*, pp.237-240; Timothy Raylor, 'Thomas Hobbes and The Mathematical Demonstration of the Sword', *The Seventeenth Century*, 15.2 (2000), 175-198.

Newcastle's analysis does not correspond with Payne's in terms of the correlation between content and numbers, and overall the focus is slightly different. Whereas Payne is attempting to apply mathematical analysis to the nature of the horse's movement, Newcastle is attempting to explain to a rider how to shape that movement for the manège activities. However, both use this step-by-step approach to facilitate understanding and describe the horse as two halves whose natural posture may be defined as evenly balanced over a straight line. Therefore, every movement takes the horse away from that natural starting position and has a level of difficulty relative to the distance from that initial posture.

Payne states that, 'The most naturall and easy posture of the body of a Horse, at rest, is in a straight line: for in that posture every Horse, standing still, and at liberty, naturally puts himself'.[59] Illustrating this point with a diagram of the standing horse's hoof prints, in the 1658 manual, Newcastle says:

Nous considérons donc premierement la posture en laquelle le cheval est naturellement,
et après comme l'art le doit façonner ; car l'art ne doit jamais étre contraire à la nature
mais doit la suivre, et parfaire. Voicy donc la postúre en laquelle le cheval est
naturellement; car ses jambes de devãt, et celles de derriere, sont d'une distance égale
les unes des autres et sont parallèles, comme vous voyez par cette figure (1658: pp.43-44).[60]

Newcastle's style is more engaging for his readers, in contrast with the scientific language used by Payne. Having established his terms of reference, Payne goes on to discuss the level of difficulty required to move the horse on a circle, arguing that, 'Seeing all such flexure of the body hath in it some difficulty; the greater the flexure, the greater must also be the difficulty; the body being thereby more constrained'.[61]

Newcastle explains this in the context of a manège exercise, so that, 'S'il va terre à terre, au large, quoy que par une ligne il soit prés du centre, néantmoins, à cause de la largeur du cercle, son ply ne sera pas si grand, et il en sera plus à son aise' (1658: p.43).[62]

The chief similarity is in the school of thought, which suggests that Newcastle's theories of horse training appear to be at least partially developed via his fascination with natural philosophy. As a practitioner, his knowledge tests or develops theory to achieve excellence. Thus he apologises if his method 'vous semble à veoir peu court & trop prolixe' but, if shorter, 'vous eust plus retenu dans

---

59   *Letters,* p.237.
60   'Let us therefore consider the natural posture in which a horse stands, and then what art can do to him; for art ought never to be contrary to nature, but to follow and perfect it. I have here given you the natural posture in which a horse stands, having his fore and hind legs equidistant and parallel to each other, as you see in the figure' (1743: p.33).
61   Ibid.
62   'If he goes *Terre-a-terre* large, altho' he seems near the centre of by a strait line drawn, nevertheless, because of the largeness of the circle, his ply will not be so great, and by it he will be more at his ease' (1743: p.33).

les tenebres'. To bridge the gap between theory and practice he aims at a writing style that enables understanding so that 'beaujour luisant à répendre sur vous la clarté de la sçience de la Cavalerie'.[63]

Timothy Raylor suggests that Newcastle requested Hobbes to write a similar study to be incorporated into his next ambitious project after the first horsemanship manual, namely an equally elaborate and comprehensive volume on swordsmanship. Sadly, the swordsmanship manual remained in manuscript and was never completed. However, it is interesting that Payne's essay on the horse 'occupies a position in regard to Newcastle's new method of horsemanship analogous to that of Hobbes' essay in regard to his method of swordsmanship'.[64]

Payne's emphasis on the degree of difficulty involved for the horse also raises the possibility that Newcastle commissioned this analysis as an attempt to understand the horse's progress down to its most basic level, so that he could devise exercises to enable its progress. His insistence upon a balanced system of training, giving equal attention to the right and left side of the horse for equal muscle development would seem to support this possibility. However, both his own best qualities as a writer, and the engaged understanding of his reader require adaptation and redaction of the material. That he is fully able to undertake that adaptation himself illustrates natural writing ability.

While willing to work with experts where necessary, Newcastle was fully confident in his own superiority where horsemanship is concerned. However, he does not patronise his readers and cleverly aligns them with him, through rhetorical questions and by inviting them to make fun with him at poor riders and ignorant 'gallants' who think themselves fine horsemen (1667: pp.5-14). His method and opinions are not presented for discussion or consideration as they are what he believes wholeheartedly to be the best way, based on his long skill and experience. His task as a writer is to win the reader round to his way of thinking, because he considers it to be the best and most valid. The aspiring rider is always 'you' and this direct form of address draws the reader into alignment with Newcastle and opposition with 'them', who are the stupid, the uncommitted, the theorists, the unenlightened.

Newcastle is very much a man with a mission in these manuals. Disturbed that poor horsemanship and shoddy training cast the riding house in a bad light, he is recruiting followers who will aspire to his high standards. In terms of his awareness of himself and his class, the perceptions of the riding house were highly important. While Stephen Greenblatt's concept of self-fashioning focuses on the sixteenth, rather than seventeenth century, many of the features he identifies apply to Newcastle. As a committed royalist, keenly aware of his own heritage, in a situation of exile and dislocation while the locus of his self-definition, the monarchy, was in disarray, it became necessary to his emotional survival to maintain as much of that self-definition as possible. The riding house paralleled 'the cultural

---

63   '...seem not very concise, but too prolix […] might if shorter have left you still in darkness […] you have now a full sunshine to look on you with the splendour of the knowledge of horsemanship' (1743: p.32).

64   Raylor, p.175-178; while unpublished, Newcastle's swordsmanship manuscript is extant: B.L. Harleian Manuscripts MS 5219.

system of meanings that creates specific individuals by governing the passage from abstract potential to concrete historical embodiment'. Therefore, the horsemanship manuals function as 'a manifestation of the concrete behavior' of their author, 'the expression of the codes by which behavior is shaped and as a reflection upon those codes'.[65]

The stylistic features of Newcastle's manuals all support the agenda of raising the profile of the riding house by refining the perceptions of the rider so they become the evidence of its worth. Therefore, he has no hesitation in taking a direct aim at those who undermine the reputation of the art. This refusal to compromise becomes a feature of the writing also and Newcastle opens his first manual by launching at once into an opinionated attack on the stupidity with which many people handle horses:

> Plusieurs personnes rabbaissent l'entendement du cheval infinement au dessous de
> celuy de l'homme, qui neantmoins, par leurs actions, môntrent qu'elles croyent, qu'il y
> a plus d'entendement dans un cheval, que dans un homme (1658: 'Avant-Propos').[66]

Extended rhetorical questions and statements reveal his indignation and make it hard for the reader to disagree with him unless willing to be counted among the stupid:

> But, What makes these Men speak against it? The first Reason is, Because they are
> Ignorant […] But the Main Reason is this: They find they cannot Ride well (1667: p.6).

He uses this bold technique in both manuals, illustrating his astute knowledge of the insecurities that aspiring to a detailed art can trigger, and makes plain that following in his horse's hoof-prints will offer a direct path to success. But he also has the subtlety to assume that his reader is among the intelligent, so that 'Ces choses sont si connuës aux Cavalerizzes, qu'il n'est pas necessaire d'en disputer' (1658: 'Avant-Propos').[67]

His humour lightens the difficult technical detail, creating amusing images to illustrate his point. When discussing whether or not a horse can reason, he argues that seeing the signs of a forthcoming storm, the horse, although 'il n'ait pas ces mots, nuée, obscure, éclair, tonerre', as Newcastle himself does, nevertheless, 'nouse ne laisserons pas luy & moy de nous enfuir sous des arbes pour nous sauver de la pluïe'. He then moves easily back into more serious discussion of the horse's nature, musing that:

---

65   *Renaissance Self-Fashioning: From More to Shakespeare* (Chicago/London: University of Chicago Press, 1980), p. 8-9.

66   'The understanding of a Horse is infinitely degraded below that of a Man by several, who notwithstanding, by their actions, shew, that they believe the Horse to be the more intelligent of the two' (1743: sig. C).

67   'These things are so well known to a complete horseman, that it is needless to say more on the subject' (1743: pp.11-12).

Quelques-uns aussy veulent dire, qu'ils n'one point d'entendement, à cause que les hommes les maîtrisent mais lors qu'un cheval maîtrise un homme, ce qui arrive asses souvent, l'homme n'at-il point d'entendement ? La force maîtrise les hommes aussy bien que les bestes.[68]

Wit and irony alongside philosophical argument help to break up the text and he uses small sayings of his own as a mnemonic. It is easy to imagine Newcastle reminding a rider who is losing his patience with his horse that, 'Il doit toûjours avoir en cét art un homme & une beste en passion, & non deux bestes' (1658: sig. f).[69] The use of readily visualised examples is a great strength of his writing style and enhances the sense of him engaging the reader in conversation. However, while this also appears to contradict his point that horsemanship cannot be reduced to a simple aphorism, when using mnemonics he is helping the rider with small details, rather than attempting to make the whole art 'si court que la devide d'une bague' (1658: p.271).[70]

The humour of his personal insight also leads to good practical advice, as when he refers to breeds of horse, with particular detail being added in the second manual. The Spanish horse had long been the choice of the king and the gentleman, for its beauty, temperament and athletic ability and Newcastle's great love for the varying Spanish types informs much of his writing. However, when he talks of horse breeds, he shows a realistic approach, regardless of his own preferences:

> Now I must Tell you, That there are Good and Badd Horses of all Countries in the World; but there are more Badd than Good, as there are of Men [...] for a Rare horse in any Kind, is a Difficult business to find, I assure you (1667: p.79).

It is this personal yet practical style of writing that transforms the manuals from heavy complicated technical treatises into journals of experience. His wondering observations on the Spanish horse cannot help but raise a smile, when he declares, 'You must know, that of all horses in the World, of what Nation soever they be, Spanish Horses are the Wisest; far the wisest and strangely Wise, beyond any Man's Imagination'. His fascination with this is balanced with the wry comment that, 'I must Tell you, they are not the Easier Drest for that: Because they Observe too much with their Eyes, and their Memories are too Good and so Conclude with their Judgements too soon without the Man'

---

68 'He knows not these words *dark, cloud, lightening, thunder* [...] both he and I notwithstanding take to our heels to shelter ourselves from the rain under the trees'; 'Some too are pleased to say, that horses are void of understanding, because men get the better of them: but when the horse gets the better of the man, which frequently happens, is the man then void of understanding? Force subdues men, as well as beasts'(1743: p.12).

69 'In this act there should always be a man and a beast, and not two beasts' (1743: p.13).

70 'Into as little compass as the poesy of a ring' (1743: p.132).

(1667: p.49). He writes with the recognizable voice of real experience and is not afraid to reveal that he has struggled himself 'and have been very Long learning of this Art of Horse-manship' (1667: p.42).

One of the most quietly humorous parts of the second manual is his account of the difficulty of obtaining a good Spanish horse to found a stud. His practice of addressing his reader as 'you' makes this journey to buy a horse very personal so 'You see that a Spanish Horse is a Dear Ware'. Having purchased the horse for a considerable sum, the new owner must 'Reckon his journey from Andalozia to Bilbo, or St. Sebastien, which is the next Port for England'. This four hundred miles journey would be covered on foot at the rate of ten miles a day, for which the horse would require the company of 'your Groom, and your Farrier at least' to cover the possibility of 'Lameness, Sickness and Death' (1667: pp.52-55).

Following a long sea journey and another cross-country walk to the English estate, Newcastle assures the would-be Spanish horse owner, that 'if he comes Safe to you', and the word 'if' seems significant, 'he will be a very Dear Horse, I assure you.' He adds with resignation, 'These are great truths of the Spanish Horse'. As Newcastle is fond of word play it is also likely here that there is an added touch of humour suggesting that this horse will be 'very Dear' to the heart because he has been 'very Dear' to the pocket. His lengthy telling of this notional journey reinforces the difficulties his readers must expect but the immediacy of this style is also inspirational. When this great man of experience speaks in so personable a way, the reader's own aspirations seem realisable. While Newcastle is undoubtedly addressing those wealthy and privileged enough to have grooms and farriers at their disposal, he is not, however, only addressing those to whom cost is no object at all. He had a history of both expansive spending and resulting debt but his perseverance through difficult financial times seems always to have been motivated by a belief in the real value of maintaining appearances and living up to his status. He encourages his readers to do the same, despite, not regardless of, the expense (1667: pp.52-55).[71]

This conversational style is a strong feature of both manuals, carrying the reader along with the author's enthusiasm. The expansive titles of some of the individual chapters prefigure very long and complex explanations and it is immediately clear that this work is not for the fainthearted. The first chapter of the first manual is entitled:

Réponse à certaines questions, dont la premiere est, en combien de temps on peut dresser un cheval : La seconde, puis qu'un cheval va bien à la soldade pourquoi il n'ira bien terre à terre, à Courbettes, Demi-airs, Balotades, Groupades, & Caprioles?[72]

---

71 The movement of horses to maintain condition and health was clearly an ongoing concern to Newcastle, as PwV 25, fol. 151, contains two different plans for travelling a horse from Welbeck to London, so that it should arrive in good enough condition to perform in the riding house.

72 'Certain Questions answered, of which the first is, In what time a Horse may be dressed? The second, Why a Horse, that goes well upon a March, should not perform the Terre a terre, Curvets, Demiairs, Balotades, Croupades, and

The reader is likely to be a little breathless already and Newcastle's response to these questions allows little time for recovery:

Pour la premier question elle est tres-ridicule, & il est tres-difficile de dire en combien de temps un cheval peut étre dressé ; d'autant que cela depend de l'âge, de la force, des espirits, & de la disposition d'un cheval (1658: sig. A). [73]

There is a strong sense that in opening this book, a galloping horse is released that may well mow the reader down. A glance through the chapter headings alone reveals a confident opinionated author without any pretensions to false modesty. He also, however, reveals a certain innocence that balances his sweeping manner, unconsciously it seems, but effectively. Having stated outright that he is a consummate horseman whose manual contains a full sum of knowledge, he contradicts himself by adding his afterthoughts, with the comment that without them 'il est impossible, à qui que ce soit, de bien dresser un cheval, si ce n'est par hazard' (1658: sig. a). This need to add the last forgotten details adds to the impression of Newcastle as confident, arrogant, naïve and charming throughout both manuals.[74]

The writing style of the second manual has more focus on self-presentation in the context of Newcastle's exile and addresses issues which are implicit in the first manual with regard to his status while in Antwerp. He takes eight pages of the second manual to describe 'the Honour I have receiv'd there', stating that it would 'fill a Volume' to relate them all. Again he reveals himself as cultured and urbane in his courteous references to Antwerp's inhabitants as 'deservedly Famous, for their extraordinary Civilities to Strangers' and his graceful appreciation of the honour and favour of the lords who came to see him ride or invited him to wait upon them. While his flattery of the king can seem self-abasing, as in the promise 'to consecrate, not Books only, but my self, and mine, and all that belongs to us to Your Majesties service', and his arrogance towards those he considers inferior in intellect is uncompromising, the image he creates of himself in his riding house, is one of ease and confidence. However, he also reveals the human concerns anyone might feel when called upon to perform to an audience while recovering from illness, confiding that 'I would obey his Commands, though I thought I should hardly be able to Sit in the Saddle' then adding, 'And truly when he had done, I was so Dizzy, I could hardly sit in the Saddle' (1667: sig. A2-B^v).

Such confessional asides to his reader are effective. He reveals a winning personality as he builds himself up before admitting to just a little frailty. He writes as though to a confidante, so that

---

Caprioles?'(1743: p.15).

73   'As to the first question, it is absurd, for it is very difficult to say in what time a horse may be dressed, because that depends upon his age, strength, spirit and disposition' (1743: p.15).

74   'It is impossible for any Man to dress a Horse well, unless by mere Chance' (1743: p.134).

tactlessness, personal revelation and even gossip can be safely indulged in, as he comments 'Monsieur Founteney, which was either his Nephew or his natural Son; for he gave him All when he Dyed, was also a very good Horseman'(1667: p.5).

Having accepted the invitation to enter Newcastle's riding house, the reader finds himself at once in the exalted company of kings and aristocrats such as King Charles II and the Prince of Conde. References to other notable men are given without explanation, as the expectation is that the noble reader is already familiar with their names (1667: pp.8-9). Also the reader-identity is presumed to be male: the owner, breeder and rider of the manège horse. References to female riders are made to inspire male riders to aspire to higher standards when 'I have seen Women to Ride Astride as well as they' (1667: p.13). Also, while Newcastle is impressed by the Queen of Sweden as 'an Extraordinary Lady [...] in All things', he is quick to point out that she is no judge of horseflesh as 'for the Swedish Horses she had for the Saddle, there was no Great Matter in them'. Her coach-horses, however, bred by the Count of Oldenburg, were 'beyond any Coursers I ever saw' (1667: p.76). He has no doubt that true horsemanship is a male preserve.

While he writes as though to a beginner in ownership, he assumes that the notional reader is an experienced rider in the manège and therefore has social status and a gentleman's education. Though he explains his perfect seat for the rider, he does so only to promote his particular ideas, as 'I suppose most Men know how to get up' (1667: p.203). None of the esoteric terms he uses are explained and definitions are only provided for the high airs, which would not be taught routinely (1667: pp.271-278). He assumes a like-minded reader with a similar level of understanding who seeks further refining skills to those already supplied by noble birth. He then plays upon the insecurities created during times of great political upheaval across Europe by stating his alarm at changing attitudes:

> [...] voire mesme les mecaniques, jusques aux Cuiseniers & Tailleurs (comme aussy
> tous citoyens) s'imaginent de monter à cheval aussy bien qu'aucun Cavalier; combien
> qu'ils croient qu'aucune autre profession, quoy que vile, ne sauroit être apprise en
> moins de huit ou neuf ans (1658: 'Aux Cavaliers').[75]

This rallying cry for horsemen to stand together against the decay of noble arts is a means of reinforcing the hierarchical society in which he believes. Their very name, he suggests, following a precedent set by Grisone,[76] draws them together across the European languages to link them to noble tradition:

---

75   The Appendix contains in full the addresses 'Au Roy de la Grande-Bretagne', 'Aux Cavaliers', and 'A Mes Tres Chers Fils', along with the two poems which are positioned prior to the 'Conclusion au Lecteur' in the 1658 manual. Therefore translations are not footnoted.

76   Blundeville, sig. iv[v].

> Je ne seray pas long-temps à vous montrer comme ce mot Cavalliero en
> Italien est derivé de Cavallo, qui signifie un cheval; & Cavalliero une homme de
> cheval, ou Chevalier; tout de mesme que Equus en Latin signifie un cheval, d'ou est
> derivé le mot Eques, un homme de cheval, ou Chevalier (1658: 'Aux Cavaliers').

He finds it 'une injustice bien grande, & une chose tres-sausse', that 'chacun pense avoir sa provision de Cavalerie tout aussy tot qu'il scait mettre une jambe de chaque de son cheval'. Assuring them that 'Ce n'est pas monter une haquenée de Cambridge à Londres, ou de S. Germain à Paris, qui fait un bon homme de cheval', he reminds them that he is writing 'non pas aux ecoliers, mais aux Maitres' so that his notional reader is among both society's and culture's elite (1658: 'Aux Cavaliers').

    In considering the style and form of the published manuals, the handwritten manuscripts extant in two bound volumes in the Portland Collection offer some useful insights into Newcastle's writing practice. Unfortunately undated, they may at first appear to be the first draft of the 1667 manual as they contain references to the first published manual (PwV 21, fols.60^v, 157^v, 164-165^v,167^v). However, the relationship between them is more complicated. They may be Newcastle's commonplace books on horsemanship covering a significant period of time, or gatherings from such books, with the long-term aim of preparing for published volumes, rather than a dedicated attempt to draft one particular manual. They do not follow the exact layout of either published text, though are generally closer to the first manual in that respect, while much of the material additional to the method appears only in the second.

    As the opening page of PwV 21, with the title neatly written in a scribal hand, is then surrounded by notes and sections 'to followe the laste thinge in this booke', it seems to have started as a 'best copy' but developed into a working notebook, perhaps due to the gathering of material from earlier notes (PwV 21, fol.3).[77] Some of the exercises included appear almost verbatim in both published manuals, for example the analysis of the horse's paces discussed above, while large sections do not appear in either. These include the names of riders whose age is given as evidence of the healthy benefits of the riding house. As Newcastle himself is listed as being sixty four years old, (PwV 21, fol.83^v), this page of the notebooks would appear to date from 1657. Also the reference in PwV21, folio 162^v to breeding horses in England 'when I was ther' and a reference to his financial straits in the present tense (PwV21, fol.158^v), dates at least these pages to the period of exile while PwV 22, folio 5, refers to 'Heere in England', suggesting the ongoing nature of his use of the manuscript books for recording his ideas and plans. One of the strongest suggestions that the manuscripts contain draft material for both manuals is in PwV 21, folios 8 and 87^v, both of which advise on the horseman's seat. The text of folio 8 is found in the first manual, while the text of folio 87^v is in the second.

---

77   PwV 22 is entirely in Newcastle's hand, identifiable though extant letters, including those in PwV 25, and repeats large sections of PwV 21, which is also partially in Newcastle's hand.

As the first manual was published in 1657/8 and a letter from Newcastle regarding its publication is dated 1656, [78] PwV 21, containing much of the material in both manuals, seems likely to predate the earliest arrangements for publication by a year at the very least. The exact relationship between the handwritten manuscripts and the printed manuals would be an entire study in itself but PwV 21 and 22 have a relevant contribution to make in considering Newcastle's writing practice. The manuscripts include lists of noble people who have visited his riding house in Antwerp, and in 1667 many, but not all, of these are placed together in the address 'To the Reader', suggesting a process of revision and redrafting.

There is also evidence of the editing for discretion, so that disparaging comments on French riding in the manuscripts (PwV 21, fol.160) are absent from the 1658 manual and considerably tempered by the time they reach the published text of 1667 (p.4), no doubt with an awareness of the continuing possibility of a French market. The list of horses' names in Italian, French and English in PwV 21, folios 44^v-47, is included in the second manual (1667: sig. Xxxx-Xxxx3^v). However, while the published text adds a list of Spanish names not in the manuscript, it does not retain any of the 'Englishe Names for Horses Proper for Huntinge and Runinge Horses'(PwV 21, fol.46). While this is probably due to Newcastle's deliberate focus on the riding house and his belief that the King should breed horses for the manège, rather than hunting or racing (PwV 22, fol.5), the names themselves are revealing.

Edward Berry identifies a 'bantering, playfully aggressive and stereotypically masculine world' in his study of the hunt, [79] which is suggested by the English names. Therefore, while Nobilisimo, Arogante and Le Paragon are named for their qualities and immortalised in print, sadly the attributes of Glass Ith Arse, Weesell heade and Sauseye Jack are remembered only in the manuscript. The questionable qualities of the English horse perhaps lent themselves more to a homely sense of humour and everyday activities than to the rarified art of the riding house. However, they give a glimpse of the relaxed mood that can only have been possible in the stable-yard when Newcastle called for Meggye with the Lanterne or Shrimpe. Thus the manuscripts offer an insight not only into revision for publication, but also to the life of Newcastle's stables.

Editing for length is seen as the encounter with the Queen of Sweden, discussed above, is written in much fuller detail in the manuscript and unfortunately the rather charming comment that she had 'mee thinkes a greate Lovelines aboute her' is lost (PwV 21, fol.156). Also there is evidence of Newcastle's changing ideas, so that the martingale, a device to prevent the horse from raising its head, while suggested as useful in the manuscripts (PwV 21, fol.77), has a note in Newcastle's hand in the margin which reads 'The martingale Is naughte', and by publication has become entirely 'unuseful'

---

78   PRO SP 77/31, fol.441; printed in *Life*, p.357.
79   *Shakespeare and the Hunt* (Cambridge: Cambridge University Press, 2001), p.117.

(1667: p.315). The manuscripts offer fascinating insights and evidence that the process by which the manuals journeyed from initial idea to published texts was a complicated and thoughtful one.

The final overall style of both published manuals is very similar. Newcastle's presentation of himself as writer and expert is consistent and emphatic, but reflects the different phases in his life at the time of writing. The first manual is divided into four books, broken down into chapters, while the second is in four parts, similarly broken down, although not designated as chapters. Each element of both manuals focuses on an aspect of training, and is then broken down into detailed descriptions of specific exercises.

The 1658 text opens with an engraved title page, followed by a somewhat overwhelming thirty-three subsequent pages of introductory plates, dedications, addresses and privileges. The 1667 manual has only a title page, a two page dedication to Charles II and an eight page address to the reader, giving a retrospective of the author's years in Antwerp. Both begin with an introduction establishing Newcastle as a perceptive and informed forward thinker in relation to ridiculous people who do not understand horses in the first manual, and other trainers in the second. A section discussing breeds, breeding and raising young horses follows. The 1667 manual also includes a number of remedies for treating minor ailments in the horse, and the analysis of breeds is in far more detail. The second section in each considers paces and basic exercises while the third moves into the esoteric territory of the advanced horseman, the 'airs above the ground'. While the first text has thirty-one exercises, the second has only seven, reflecting a general move towards streamlining the process. The fourth section addresses problems and vices that may cause difficulty in training and are similar in topic, although not in lay-out, with the second manual including in this section topics placed among the 'Additions' in the first.

The term 'vice' when applied to horses means habits that reveal resistance, confusion or flaws in temperament and Newcastle addresses each of these potential problems in both manuals. All the chapter headings are technical, for the initiated only and something of a foreign language to the non-horseman, but those of the second manual show less tendency towards detailed summarizing of their content, while more opinions and observation are inserted between the exercises.

The first manual ends with two poems praising the author and his book,[80] followed by the 'Conclusion au Lecteur', summing up Newcastle's aims, expertise and philosophy, while the second manual ends abruptly after a discussion on bitting considerations, with no conclusion as such but followed by the list of 'Excellent names for horses of mannage', cited above. The reason for this is not clear. The list of names as an appendix of sorts gives a sense of conclusion, but it is uncharacteristic of Newcastle to miss the opportunity for the last word in a final note to his readers. This is one of a

---

80   These poems are signed M.D.V., as are the verses in Plates 2, 3 and 4, but who Monsieur D. V. might be, and why he was chosen to write these verses, remains unclear. That they are by Newcastle himself seems very possible but the initials then become confusing. I appreciate the discussions, though inconclusive, on this matter with Trevor Foulds and Adrian Woodhouse.

number of anomalies between the two manuals, about which only conjecture is possible. The second manual equals, and perhaps surpasses, the first in being very readable, with humour, philosophy and personal anecdote woven in to the text. Yet it suffers badly for want of the plates to illuminate the technical detail as well as being decorative and lightening the complicated material of the text.[81]

Another significant difference is that the overall construction of the second is less ordered. While it follows the same general pattern and training programme, it lacks the progressive precision of the first. Therefore, Newcastle deals with the 'helps', his name for the signals given by the rider's body, as well as the artificial aids of the spur and switch, and the handling of the reins all together before the riding section (1667: pp.145-208). The rider or trainer then has to refer back to them when working through the method, which is highly detailed and needs close attention. This appears to be a decision made in the writing process, as Newcastle says that now 'you Know all your Helpes; I will Shew you How to Dress your Horse Perfectly' (1667: p.208), though its value is debatable. A less deliberate feature of the second manual seems to be a certain random quality in the organisation of the material. Therefore, the description 'of the Spanish mules' (1667: p.99, mis-numbered as 95), comes not in the lengthy discussion on various breeds, but after advice on backing a colt. Then the description of the correct saddle and bridle to use comes on page 112, even though the colt's saddle has already been discussed on page 97.

A possible explanation for these anomalies is that by 1667, Newcastle's health was deteriorating. He no longer rode daily, due to his wife's concerns 'that when he had overheated himself, he would be apt to take cold' (*Life*: pp.208-209) and was, by the standards of his day, an elderly man. It may be that the tendency to let his writing be distracted by stray thoughts and digressions, which is evident in the first manual, was less apparent to him as he grew older. That this took place in the writing process is obvious from the chapter in the third section, headed 'This should have been in the second part.' but such omissions are not always redressed (1667: p.320). Thus, while in the first manual, his afterthoughts are all gathered together in the 'Additions', in the second they seem to appear as they occurred to him. However, the introduction, with its anecdotes concerning Newcastle's time in Antwerp has a personable vigour that reveals the writer as still so sure of his method that 'if any man does not like it, it is a great Signe he understands it not' (1667: p.4), and suggest an intellect as sharp as ever.

From both manuals, the reader gains the sense of a strong character in its natural Element. Aside from the technical expertise, it is in this revelation of Newcastle's personality that the manuals are particularly successful. They have a biographical subtext that, though not always fully open to interpretation, reveals the extent to which the horsemanship manuals were interwoven with his life. Changing fortunes, personal philosophy, developing ideas and the vagaries of a long life are all written

---

81 The absence of plates in the second manual will be discussed further in Chapter 6.

between the lines of the printed page. They spill also into other areas of his own writing and that of his second wife, Margaret Cavendish, so that cross-references between their work suggest that horsemanship framed their lives on many levels.

In both manuals, Newcastle refers angrily to those who disparage the trained horse and in his play *The Witts Triumvate or The Philosopher*, gives this attitude to the character 'Caution'. Caution could well be attacking Newcastle himself when he ridicules the man who 'spends a thousand pounds a year in pampered jades like Bankes his horse for to do tricks.' Caution represents those who have no comprehension of the value of horses and horsemanship, disliking horses as 'snorting jades' and despising anything that eats while its master is sleeping. The reference to Bankes shows that Caution does not understand the difference between a trick-horse and a school-horse. The famous counting-horse, Morocco, was well-known but in no way similar to Newcastle's highly skilled manège horses and he disparages teaching 'Tricks and Gambals like Banke's Horse' (1667: p.158). In response to Caution's declaration that, given a horse 'I'll knock him i'the head rather than keep him', Algebra replies 'Sure, sir, horses are both of use and pleasure too, and riding the noblest exercise that is'.[82]

Algebra appears to reflect very closely Newcastle's own stand, that 'In Hunting, Hawking, Bowling [...] and many such things, there is no Use at al but merely Pleasure: But in A Horse of Mannage, both Use and Pleasure' (1667: p.14). That this phrase in various forms is repeated in both horsemanship texts, suggests an ongoing irritation that was annoying Newcastle before he came to write his horsemanship manuals, but which through their publication could be fully addressed. There is also the strong impression in both manuals, as seen above, that Newcastle had received some stinging direct criticism of the worth of the manège and as his most staunch supporter, his wife Margaret Cavendish uses her own work to frame a response.

In *Poems, and Fancies* (1653), predating her husband's first horsemanship manual by five years, she includes detailed references to horsemanship in the incongruous setting of 'A Battel between King Oberon and the Pygmees'. In a poem of 278 lines, Cavendish allows 53 to a defence of the value of trained horses in battle, and as in Newcastle's own references, there is here also the strong sense of responding to a specific detraction of him. She begins line 117 talking of grasshoppers, the 'fairy-horses', performing caprioles then swiftly moves on to a defence of the skilled horsemanship in battle. Her elaborate defence of the criticism levelled against the use of 'horses of manage' is very spirited and takes her away from her fairies completely.

'Some think for War, it is an Aire unfit', she declares and completes her explanation of the nature of the insult by adding 'Many doe think are only fit for pleasure', or, even worse no doubt, 'Unlesse by leaping high themselves can save'. She goes on to display her knowledge of Newcastle's art:

---

82   BL Add 45865, fols.19-20ᵛ; 'Witt's Triumvirate or The Philosopher', ed. by C. A. Nelson in *Salzburg studies in English literature: Jacobean drama studies* (Salzburg: Institut fur Englische Sprach, 1975), lines 230-243.

Besides, all Airs in Warre are very fit,
As Curvets, Dimivoltoes, and Perwieet:
In going back, and forward, turning round,
Sideways, both high and low upon the ground.

She adds that without these skills horses 'May march strait forth, or in one place may stay', which dangers she believes are overcome by training and courage in their rider.[83]

As discussed in Chapter 1, Newcastle does not advocate the use of high airs in battle and Cavendish's choice of movements, aside from the caprioles, perhaps too particularly suited to the fairy grasshopper-horses to resist, focuses on those which gather energy and facilitate swift turns and wheels. Her enthusiasm and eagerness illustrate that both the terminology and the tensions surrounding riding as art were familiar to her, giving an intriguing insight into the importance of the art of manège in the everyday life of the Newcastle household.

While Cavendish had an interest in writing all her life, it was under Newcastle's influence that she began to write for publication and she creates strong images in her work of their daily discussions and time spent writing in one another's company. In her memoirs, she says:

he recreates himself with his pen, writing what his wit dictates, but I pass my time
rather with scribling than writing, with words than wit, not that I speak much, because
I am addicted to contemplation, unless I am with My Lord, yet then I rather attentively
listen to what he sayes, rather than impertinently speak yet when I am writing, sad and
faind stories, or serious humours or melancholy passions, I am forced many times to
express them with the tongue before I can write them with the pen (*Life*: p.306).

His inspirational mentoring of her work is stressed again in *Poems, and Fancies* where she describes herself as a willing acolyte, saying 'There oft I leane my Head, and list'ning harke, to heare his words, and all his Fancies mark'.[84] It is not surprising perhaps then that her beloved husband and his horses should find their way into her own work, especially when she can thereby leap to his defence.

The cross-references between their writings in relation to horses imply not only an interested and supportive wife, but also a cross-pollination of ideas. Newcastle's list of names for 'Horses of Mannage' in the 1667 manual, as cited above, largely refer to temperament. Two that do not however are 'Bell in Campo' and 'Sans Pareil' but these have an additional interest. In Margaret Cavendish's

---

83   *Poems, and Fancies*, pp.182–184.
84   Ibid. p.214.

first collection of plays, published in 1662, 'Bell in Campo' is the title of one, while Lady Sanspareille is the heroine of another.

Lady Victoria, the heroine of 'Bell in Campo', admires the horses chosen by the General of the Kingdom of Reformation, because 'such horses […] are usefull in War […] as have been made subject to the hand and heel, that have been taught to Trot on the Hanches, to change, to Gallop, to stop', all recognisably attributes Newcastle desires in his horses.[85]

The theatricality of the riding house may well have added to the shared interest in writing and strong mutual understanding apparent when they write to and for each other.

Even while insisting that her brain is sufficient stage for her plays, Cavendish 'argues for the edifying function of acting for 'the noblest youths'' and her argument is 'couched within a masculine discourse'. As Sophie Tomlinson points out, Cavendish's use of masculine terminology in prefacing her texts is linked to her fear of the plays, personified as feminine, 'receiving the punitive treatment of a prostitute or public woman'. However, within the tension of her dilemma, she 'views theatrical performance as a mode of self-enhancement, of becoming one's best self, stressing the reciprocity between actor and part' advantages all strongly recognisable from Newcastle's perceived benefits of the riding house.[86]

A more mundane cross-reference is found between Newcastle's remedies for minor ailments in horses (1667: pp.123-143), and Cavendish's description of his discussions on Natural Philosophy with the Dutch scholar, Jean Pierre Van Helmont on the nature of 'radical moisture'. This somewhat esoteric discussion, during which Newcastle expresses his belief that 'the radical moisture is not the fat or tallow of an animal, but an oily or balsamous substance' leads to her asking:

> My Lord's opinion concerning the radical heat: to which he replied that the radical heat
> lived in the radical moisture; and when one decayed the other decayed also; and then
> was produced either an unnatural heat, which caused an unnatural dryness; or an
> unnaturall moisture, which caused dropsies, and these an unnatural coldness'(*Life*: p.137).

This appears to relate directly to his treatment of his horses, as he gives recipes for horses 'over-heated by violent exercise'. The aim of these is to 'Moisten him, because it Dries up all Superfluous Humours which Heat him' and their efficacy may be enhanced by adding 'Wheat-Brann' to his drinking-water to 'not only Cool him, and Moisten him, but also Loosen his Skin' (1667: p.135). Regardless of the difference in today's understanding of physiology and 'humours' to that of the seventeenth-

---

85   *Plays Written by the Thrice Noble, Illustrious and Excellent Princess, the Lady Marchioness of Newcastle* (London: J. Martin, J. Allestrye & T. Dicas, 1662); Lady Sanspareille appears in 'Youth's Glory and Death's Banquet'.
86   'Cavendish and the Fantasy of Female Performance' in *Women, Texts and Histories, 1575-1760'*, ed. by Clare Brant and Diane Purkiss (London/New York: Routledge, 1992), p.141.

century, these recipes and Cavendish's account of her husband's discussion on the subject suggest that Newcastle understood the link between over-heating and dehydration and the need to replenish the horse's body salts, and came to that understanding by careful consideration and discussion.

This seemingly small detail of equine husbandry also illustrates that Newcastle's writing practice was not compartmentalised. His interests in theatre, poetry, science and horsemanship all support and inform one another and appear to have been developed not only in their own contexts but via family discussion. Also, it shows that regardless of Margaret Cavendish's modest insistence that she simply scribbles while he is truly creative, his writing practice is closely interwoven with hers. When Cavendish writes in defence of the riding house, Newcastle allows himself to be represented through her and her belief that 'Your Lordship is an extraordinary husband' would seem to be well-founded, especially in times when a woman writing for publication was a controversial matter.[87] Newcastle, far from frowning upon her enterprise, writes poems of support to preface her work, declaring 'I saw your poems and then wish'd them mine' and in her later works, contributes directly to the main body of the text.[88]

A similar interweaving of writing practice is found in the *Life of the Duke* and the second horsemanship manual, both published in 1667. In the *Life of the Duke* (pp.114-120) and the second manual, (1667: sig. b-B^v), the accounts of the days when Newcastle was feted by the Continental nobility and Charles II rode in his riding house share almost all the material. From the everyday to the fantastic, in small details and bold statements, links may be found between Newcastle, Cavendish, writing and the art of manège.

None though is as wistful as may be found in Cavendish's strange fantasy, *A Description of a New World, called the Blazing World*, first published in 1666.[89] The creation of imaginary worlds is a large feature of her writing and in his poem on this elaborate work, Newcastle praises her ability to 'make a World of Nothing, but pure Wit'. Newcastle and his riding house at Welbeck enjoy a touching cameo appearance in *The Blazing World*, when the Empress of the Blazing World is brought, in spirit form, by her friend and mentor, the Duchess of Newcastle, to watch the Duke train his horses.

Being a woman of great perception, the Empress 'was much pleased' with the art of manège and 'commended it as a noble pastime, and an exercise fit and proper for noble and heroic persons'. Indeed, the Empress is so impressed that she reports back to her husband, who at once 'built stables and riding-houses, and desired to have horses of manage, such as [...] the Duke of Newcastle had'.[90]

Note that upon a single report the Emperor of the Blazing World accepts Newcastle as a role model and desires to follow in his footsteps, unlike those who were managing a new court for King

87   *Philosophical and Physical Opinions* (London, 1655), 'To His Excellencie'.
88   *Poems, and Fancies*, sig. A; *Nature's Pictures* (London: J. Martin & J. Allestrye, 1656), is the first of these collaborations, containing verses by Newcastle among Cavendish's material and songs by him for three of her stories.
89   London: A. Maxwell, 1666. Hereafter, the title is shorted to *The Blazing World*.
90   *The Blazing World and other Writings,* ed. Kate Lilley (Harmondsworth: Penguin Books, 1994), pp. 121, 194, 219.

Charles II without his assistance. Small wonder perhaps, that Newcastle admires his wife's ability to create from wit alone, considering the enormous amount of rebuilding he had to do after the Restoration, in terms of property and reputation. This bitter irony is reinforced when the Emperor of the Blazing World asks 'the form and structure of her lord and husband's stables and riding house'. The Duchess sorrowfully replies that 'they were but plain and ordinary' but 'had my lord wealth, I am sure he would not spare it, in rendering his buildings as noble as could be made'.

Unencumbered by financial constraints, the Emperor shows the Duchess his own stables, 'which were most stately and magnificent', richly bedecked with 'several sorts of precious materials', with 'the walls lined with cornelian', an amber floor, mother-of-pearl mangers and crystal pillars, while the riding house 'was lined with sapphires, topazes and the like'. Even the floor 'was all of golden sand, so finely sifted, that it was extremely soft, and not in the least hurtful to the horses' feet'. This little detail within the sumptuous creation is one of numerous touches which demonstrate that Cavendish has real understanding, as coarse sand is abrasive so could cause brittleness and splitting of the hoof. Contingencies for avoiding this would be very likely to come up for discussion when Newcastle was maintaining his own riding houses. The practical details Newcastle considers so important find their way into Cavendish's fantasy in a manner both valuable to the study of their writing practice and touching as an insight into their marriage. When she relates to her husband the luxury of this other-world riding house he has inspired, and the 'fine horses of the Blazing World', she wishes 'you should not only have some of those horses, but such materials, as the Emperor has, to build your stables and riding-houses withal'. Characteristically, Newcastle replies that, 'he was sorry there was no passage between those two worlds; but said he, I have always found an obstruction to my good fortune'.[91]

Considering modern scholarship on utopian writing by women, Kate Lilley reports that there is a consensus that *The Blazing World* is 'the only utopia-proper by a woman in the seventeenth century' and points out that Cavendish's marriage is 'a partnership which she continually figured as the generative utopian space of her own productivity'.[92] Inevitably then, for Cavendish, Utopia must not only be a place where her own agendas as woman writer are addressed, but where a noble husband may have the fine horses he deserves and keep them in due magnificence.

Further significant personal values and attitudes are reflected in the horsemanship writing and some most interesting comparisons may be made with the 'little book [...] concerning the government of his dominions' (*Life*: p.186) , written for Charles II.[93] This builds upon the advice written when Newcastle was governor and Charles still a small boy,[94] and Newcastle states:

---

91 Ibid. pp.219-221; *Blazing World*, 1994, p.xv.
92 'Seventeenth-century Women's Utopian Writing' in *Women, Texts & Histories*, already cited, p.106.
93 *Letters*, pp.173-236. Subsequent references will be made in the text.
94 Printed in *Life*, Appendix, p.326-330.

Ther Is no oratorye In Itt, or anye thinge stolen out off Bookes, for I seldome or Ever
reade anye, Butt these discourses are oute off my longe Experience, - to presente your
Majestie with truthes which great monarkes seldom heares (*Letters*: p.173).

In the 1667 manual, Newcastle claims similarly that 'I have set down, as clearly as I could,
without the Help of any other Logick, but what Nature hath taught me, all the Observations about
Horses and Horsemanship'(sig. B^v). His own life-experience is always the basis of his expertise. In
horsemanship, long years of studious application to the traditions of the art were disappointing and he
found that 'All was Labour in Vain' until he began to work on his own method, 'For which I have Left
all others'. As in his advice to the future king, he considers the method conceived and devised from
his personal explorations rather than received ideas to be 'as True, as it is New' (1667: p.42). This
conviction as to the unique truth of his ideas is reinforced repeatedly throughout the manuals and a
similar need to be seen as an indispensable authority is echoed in the 'little book'.

The reception he desires from his readers differs greatly, with regard to his monarch he declares:

Iff your Majestie like Itt, I have my Endes with Unspeakable Joye and Contentemente,
Iff you like Itt nott sir, I humblye begg favor off your Majestie, to trogh Itt In to the fier,
that Itt may becoumne a flaminge Sacredfise off my Dewtye to your Majestie (*Letters*: p.173).

Whereas, if his horse-riding readers do not like his book, he knows that 'je suis tres-content en
moy mesme; puis que je sçay bien, qu'il est tres-bon, & meil leur qu'aucun que vous ayés eu jusques
icy' (1658: p.271).[95] Clearly his relationship to his reader is very different, but even in his humility
before his former pupil, he does not claim the work will be unworthy without Charles' approval,
suggesting an ability to keep faith with his own opinions.

In advising King Charles in 'the little book', Newcastle sees direct parallels in the horse and
rider relationship which fittingly illustrates that of king and subjects because of the way it works in
practicality. He offers the same advice to his monarch publicly in the dedication of the 1658 manual,
using parallels of horses to subjects:

[…] un Roy, etant bon Cavalier, scaura beaucoup mieux comme il faudra gouverner ses
peoples, quand il faudra les recompsenser, ou les chattier; quand il fandra leur tenir la
main serree, ou quand la relacher; quand il faudra les aider doucement, ou en quel
temps il sera convenable des les eperonner (1658: 'Au Roy').

---

95   'I shall be content in my own mind; because I know certainly that it is very good, and better than any thing you have
had before' (1743: p.132).

This constant conviction illuminates Newcastle's frustration with those who fail to understand the almost metaphysical undercurrent in the semiotic value of the riding house. This is further illustrated by his view that 'Seremoneye though Itt Is nothinge In Itt selfe yett Itt doth Everyethinge – For what Is a king more than a Subjecte butt for seremoneye'. He thus advises the king to 'Shew your selfe Gloriouslye to your People Like a God' (*Letters*: p.210), recalling the dedication 'Au Roy' in the 1658 manual which enthuses that 'un Prince n'est jamais accompagne de tant de majesté, mesmement sur son throne, comme ill est sur un beau cheval'. This phrase is prefigured in the letter written to Charles in his childhood, explaining to him that nothing 'preserves you Kings more than ceremony' including 'rich furniture for horses' and reminding him that 'in all triumphs whatsoever or public showing of yourself, you cannot put upon you too much king' (*Life*: p.329). This echo of Shakespeare's Henry V is repeated with only slight variations in both manuals as well as the advice book.[96] In 1658, the dedication 'A Mes Tres-Chers Fils' reminds them that 'Les beaux chevaux ornes de riches caparassons, de riches selles […] & de plumes ondoyantes, sont un pompe digne d'etonner les spectateurs avec contentement & plasir'. In 1667, he asks 'What Prince or Monarch looks more princely, or more Enthroned, than upon a Beautiful Horse, with Rich Footclothes, or Rich Sadles, and Waving Plumes, making his entry through Great Cities, to amaze the People with Pleasure and Delight' (1667: p.13).

In a mood of poignant nostalgia, he advises Charles to keep such spectacle alive 'which I assure your Majestie Is the moste Glorious sighte that Can bee seene & the moste manlieste'. Clearly the king should also reinforce this glorious and manly image in his private diversions so Newcastle advises 'your Majestie to Ride your Horses off Manege twice a weeke which will Incourage Noble men to doe the like' (*Letters*: p.223-224). However, it seems likely that Newcastle exposed his own weakness in this longing for the old days. Charles does not seem to have paid much attention to his advice and it is a sad irony that the 'little book' simply reveals Newcastle to be, though shrewd and worldly, also an anachronism.

A final example of stylistic cross-reference between the horsemanship manuals and other published writing by Newcastle may be found in his *Declaration* of 1642, in which he defends his decision to take his armies into Yorkshire and to include Roman Catholics in their number. The content and language of this pamphlet echoes the horsemanship manuals in many respects, not least in revealing Newcastle's acute concern over the image he presents to the outside world.[97] This concern was not unreasonable, especially in the context of Civil War, when maintaining his position would have been vital for a great many reasons to him both as a Royalist, a general and a man with land and family to consider. However, as in the 'little book', that the values and concerns of war and politics are found pre-figured or echoed in his philosophies for the art of the riding house, suggest they were not strategic contingencies, but reflections of his paradigm for life.

---

96   Ed. by T. W. Craik (London: Arden Shakespeare, 2002), Act IV, Sc. I, lines 235-6.
97   *Declaration*, already cited.

Newcastle's writing continually reveals him to be a man greatly concerned at being misunderstood for his actions, even though those actions were often taken with boldness and courage. His correspondence with the Royalist gentry of Yorkshire illustrates a courteous, firm and uncompromising attitude in a difficult time of shortages and caution, set against the need for speed and numbers in arms to fulfil his commission.[98] However, in his *Declaration*, he reveals his indignation and insecurity in a style familiar from the manuals. The use of the emphatic 'I', and the establishing of his authority given 'by His Majesties speciall Command and Commission'[99] is echoed repeatedly in the horsemanship texts. He tends to begin sentences with 'I have', 'I shall', 'I must' or 'I would' when he is expressing either courtesy, indignation, exasperation or defining his knowledge. When drawing attention to his affection and respect for Captain Mazin, Newcastle uses the emphatic 'I' seven times in a paragraph of around ten lines, as he claims Mazin as his own, having raised him from a small boy (1658: p.33). When irritated by over-use of the whip, he declares, 'Je dis donc, que je veus m'en servir, pourveu que ce soit à une necessité, autrement je voudrais la banir du Manege' (1658 : p.10).[100]

In his *Declaration*, similarly he states 'I have great and just occasion' and 'I am confident I have not miscarryed'. He fights his corner by sequential argument, showing the ordered mind that approaches his tasks by logical progression, in the same way that he sets out his training methods. He also presents himself as drawing the confidences of noble men who have been 'to remonstrate unto me their suffering', and 'to desire my aid for the redressing of them'.[101] This prefigures his role in Antwerp, when 'many noble and great Persons' (1667: sig. b2ᵛ) came to see his horses for his skill and guidance. While the situation is very different, he nevertheless presents himself as the focal point when experience, skill and advice are required to counter an unstable current position. He shows the expectation of 'absolute obedience to all my just and lawfull Commandements',[102] exactly as he does from his horses, and offers in his own service to his king. Newcastle shows an implicit acceptance of hierarchy in all he writes, applying it as strictly to himself as to the people and animals he sees as subordinates.

His writing style is also familiar in his use of humour, irony and rhetoric. As discussed above with regard to the horsemanship texts, he lightens the *Declaration* by stating 'I shall retyre my selfe and forces out of your County with much more cheerfulnesse then I conducted them thither'.[103] Once his position of authority is acknowledged, he is more than willing to indulge in amiable

---

98   Ibid. pp.1-5.
99   Ibid. p.3.
100   'I say then, I am for making use of it in cases of necessity only, otherwise I would have it banish'd out of the Manege' (1743: p.19)
101   *Declaration*, p.3-4
102   Ibid.
103   Ibid. p.5.

humour and ease. He cleverly also uses irony to make his detractors appear foolish. Like those who 'because, forsooth, they cannot Ride by Inspiration, without taking Pains' declare it 'worth Nothing' (1667: p.7), he exposes those who protest against his use of 'Recusants', saying 'If there be no Barre in Law against it, then let us examine these pretended grand inconveniences, wherewith (as they alledge), it is attended'.

As seen throughout the horsemanship manuals, he uses a series of rhetorical questions to align his readers to his own view for fear of being classed with these trouble makers. Ending with the question, 'Do our Neighbours of the United provinces reject the auxiliary Regiments under the pay of the French King, because many of them (if not most) are Papists, so long as they are secured of their fidelity to them?' he makes the opposition seem both ridiculous and disloyal, so that 'the point then will not be of their Religion, but whether there they may be trusted in point of fidelity and Allegiance'.[104]

While Newcastle's need to justify his actions any more than his horsemanship manuals may make him seem lacking in self-confidence, his handling of his defence shows a combination of authority, skill and reasonable argument. It also reveals the same style of easy discourse in the appropriate register for his audience as the manuals, suggesting, as stated above, a level of ability sometimes missing from his attempts at more literary styles, such as poetry.

Through the style of his writing in the horsemanship manuals, Newcastle illustrates that they were literally re-creation: of his spirits, his ideas, his enthusiasms, that could not only focus his own morale but that of his peers. The differences between the two manuals in form, structure and paratext reveal much about the way in which they sought to fulfil that possibility and I will explore this further in the next chapter.

---

104   Ibid. p.6.

Chapter 3

'Of the several Authors that have Written of Horsemanship': Newcastle's manuals in the European context

Let us see (as we have purposed) what those excellent authors
that write of this Art have said thereof.
John Astley, *The Art of Riding*

Yet, since by th'Authors happy care and paine
I understood how first to use the reyne.
Ed. R., *The Compleat Horseman and Expert Farrier*

Newcastle published his manuals during a boom time for horsemanship texts. From 1550 onwards, at least twenty different manuals that dealt specifically with riding as an art were circulating across Europe, in numerous editions and translations. These were apart from works on training soldiers' horses or those focussing on athletic and acrobatic feats. However, these early horsemanship manuals could be divided into two types: those that set out the work of a master, and those which followed, imitated or aimed at disseminating the work of a master. The majority came into the second category, being essentially tributes to a great master or his followers. Newcastle however declares that, 'my Book is stolen out of no Book, nor any mans Practice but my own', and is confident that, 'it is the Best that hath been Writ yet' (1667: p.4).

The earliest horsemanship manual to survive is widely accepted to be that of the Greek cavalry commander, Xenophon, written between 440 and 360 B.C. This classical provenance gave the flowering Renaissance art credibility and precedent. It was Xenophon who noted that a horse, when ridden with skill, refinement and gentleness, 'will bound along with proud gait and prancing legs, imitating exactly the airs that he puts on before other horses'. This display behaviour of stallions formed the basis of the art of the riding house, being so attractive to the culture of aesthetics and elaborate display that typified the Italian Renaissance. It offered, as Xenophon had stated so long before, 'a magnificent sight, that looks alert, that is the observed of all observers', a familiar phrase to lovers of Shakespeare, and an insight into the role played by the man on horseback.[105]

Xenophon's text was first published in Florence in the mid-16ᵗʰ century, with the earliest known editions being in Latin and Greek. While it is still seen as the exemplar for the classical tradition, Xenophon's text is notably not about training the horse for display in a riding house situation, but upon the battlefield or in parades and celebrations, with the elements of display being part of the overall self-presentation of the rider:

> If you desire to handle a good war-horse so as to make his action the more
> magnificent and striking, you must refrain from pulling at his mouth with the bit as
> well as from spurring and whipping him. Most people think that this is the way to
> make him look fine; but they only produce an effect exactly contrary to what they desire.

The emphasis on avoiding any violence in the handling of horses is repeated throughout his text because, Xenophon stresses, it will only 'scare them into disorder and danger'.[106] While his work was highly regarded throughout the early-modern period as riding as an art developed, the next significant manual, *Gli Ordini di Cavalcare* by Federigo Grisone in 1550, did not adopt his gentling techniques nor refer at all to his seminal text.

Grisone's techniques were established in the riding school he founded in Naples in 1532. He was not the first to develop training in horsemanship as an art but the fame and success of his school made him the focus of a new generation of riders across Europe. By setting down his methods in print, he established a point of reference for the new art of riding and set a precedent for great horsemasters to immortalise their contributions to the art for future generations. He also established the use of extreme force as necessary, and even perhaps laudable, so that handling the horse and controlling the human passions become combined in the act of riding, giving the exercise a semiotic value.

In the context of renaissance humanism, the assertion of human qualities by the subjugation of the animal could be seen as reclamation of the original relationship intended by God wherein man was to have dominion over the animals and shape nature to his own ends. This may explain Grisone's lack of reference to Xenophon's sympathetic approach, as well as the severity of his own method:

> And do not think that the horse, although he is well put together by nature can do well
> on his own without human aid and true teaching [...] If the horse, whether for
> fear of exertion, or for the mood that he has, or for his infinite haughty nature,
> does not want to come close to the mounting block [...] punish him wonderfully

---

105   *The Art of Horsemanship*, trans. by M. H. Morgan (London: J. A. Allen, 1993), pp.60, 56. See *Hamlet*, Act III, sc. i.
106   Xenophon, p.55.

and without regard with a large stick between the ears and on the head and on every part of the body except his eyes (since he is, thus, incorrigible and very wicked) [...] threaten him with a terrible voice in such a way that the horse, seeing you are determined, will no longer resist you and will approach you like a lamb. [107]

While Grisone stresses also the need to caress and reward the horse, it is evident that he considers severe discipline to be part of the training process. From an entirely practical point of view, it is hard to see how this approach could be useful. Violent discipline is likely to result only in a panic-stricken, craven or resentful animal, which would be the 'effect exactly contrary to what they desire' as suggested by Xenophon. Yet, regardless of the strengths and weaknesses of Grisone's manual, it was the first of its kind and extremely successful. The original Italian text was first printed in 1550 and later editions appeared in 1552, 1556, and 1610, with at least ten French translations between 1559 and 1610, as well as Spanish and German editions in 1568, 1573 and 1623.

Sir Thomas Blundeville's English adaptation appeared in 1560, [108] was revised and expanded in 1565 and had run to six editions by 1609. One of Grisone's pupils, Claudio Corte was brought into England by the Earl of Leicester, then Queen Elizabeth's Master of Horse, in 1565 and his manual *Il Cavallerizzo* of 1562, was translated into English by Thomas Bedingfield as *The Art of Riding* in 1584. John Astley's manual of 1584, also called *The Art of Riding*, contained tributes in the title to 'Xenophon and Gryson, verie expert and excellent Horsemen' and included 'the true use of the hand by the said Grysons rules', although he argues against Grisone's level of violence.[109] Christopher Clifford's *The Schoole of Horsemanship* appeared in 1585, followed in 1593 by Gervase Markham's *A Discourse on Horsemanshippe,* which also both commends and criticizes Grisone's methods and recommends training 'to bee done with all the gentleness and quiet means that may be'.[110] New manuals of the seventeenth century were Michaell Baret's *Hipponomie or The Vineyard of Horsmanship* in 1618 and Nicholas Morgan's *The Perfection of Horsemanship*, which first appeared in 1609 and was reissued in 1620 as *The Horseman's Honour.* From Blundeville onwards, all these English texts are derived in some way from Grisone's methods or are reflections of each other through strong links with the gentleman pensioners, fifty noblemen who, as members of the royal household, were responsible for the provision of suitable horses on formal occasions and included Bedingfield and Astley.

Nicholas Morgan's texts stand slightly apart in having a strong religious perspective which may be summed up by Morgan's argument that only 'the ignorant and pretended Rider proceedeth

---

107   *The Rules of Riding,* trans. by Elizabeth Mackenzie Tobey and Federica Brunori Deigan (Arizona Center for Medieval and Renaissance Studies, 2014), pp. 97; 105
108   Already cited
109   Astley, title page.
110   Markham, (London, 1593), sig. B2v-B3.

to violence'.[111] Morgan gives horsemanship an imperative purpose as, due to man having 'lost all obedience, which by original creation was subject unto him […] now the obedience of all creatures must be attained by Art, and this same preserved in vigour by use and practice'. This echoes the subtext of Grisone's method, even though a new era had brought changes of thought in how this should be practised.

Morgan's work is full of guilt at man's failure. He says, 'I could not find the least jarre and disagreement in the primarie nature of Horses' and argues that man must reassert his authority through considerate treatment and so 'abandon the studye and practice of apish toies and violent helps'.[112]

Markham writes that correcting misbehaviour with the spur must be 'with such gentle bitterness that the Horse may understand it for a help'[113] and there is clearly a conflict in the minds of the horsemanship authors in late sixteenth to early seventeenth century England. In many respects Grisone's ideas were outdated, yet they still served as a precedent due to the deeply held belief that the Italians had a natural authority in the art. However, while a number of manuals reflecting Grisone appeared into the 1620s, the most influential being that of Salamon de la Broue,[114] 'the First that ever Writ of Horsemanship, in the French Language' (1667: p.3) matters took a different turn with the methods of Antoine de Pluvinel.

Pluvinel was a pupil of Giovanni Battista Pignatelli who is widely considered to have been a pupil of Cesare Fiaschi, though this is open to debate. One of the most successful of Grisone's contemporaries, Fiaschi's own manual, *Trattato Dell' Imbrigliare, Maeggiar, et Ferraro Cavalli* was published in 1556 and while Pignatelli left no published work, his influence is reflected in Newcastle's manuals through references to bits 'a la Pignatelle' (1658: p.268; 1667: p.347).[115] According to Newcastle, Pignatelli's three most famous pupils were Pluvinel, de la Broue and St. Antoine, who, 'fill'd France with French Horse-men; which before were fill'd with Italians' (1667: p.3).[116]

---

111   *The Horseman's Honour, or the Beautie of Horsemanship* (London: John Marriott, 1620), p.168.

112   *The Perfection of Horsemanship* (London: Edward White, 1609), pp.2, 53.

113   *The Compleat Horseman*, ed. Dan Lucid (Boston: Houghton Mifflin, 1975), p.21.

114   Salamon de la Broue's *La Cavalerice François* (Paris: 1602), is another text with a complicated publishing history. See Toole-Stott, pp.71-72.

115   Helen Watanabe-O'Kelly, *Triumphall Shews: Tournaments at German-speaking Courts in their European Context 1560-1730* (Berlin: Gebr. Mann, 1992), p.76, cites an unpublished manuscript known in Italy between 1598 and 1627, but it is evident that Newcastle was not aware of Pignatelli as an author at all.

116   Roy Strong differs with Newcastle on this point and refers to St. Antoine as a pupil of Pluvinel in *Henry, Prince of Wales and Englands's lost Renassiance* (Pimlico: 2000) p. 41-42. The lineage through Pignatelli remains the same in either case. Primary source evidence is often lacking or even in dispute, in the lineage of master and pupil. In *The Italian Tradition of Equestrian Art* (Xenophon Press, 2014), Giovanni Battista Tomassini sets out to unravel some of the complexities of names and dates around widely accepted ideas. However, for the purposes of this study, what Newcastle considered to be true is the most relevant consideration.

This rise of the French master began a shift from the perspective that horsemanship was an Italian art, at least on the Continent. Pluvinel's posthumously published text of 1623 marks the beginning of a new era of horsemanship, which ironically returns to the gentler methods advocated by Xenophon. The atmosphere of refined elegance in Pluvinel's method is central to training both the horse and the rider, so violence would be inappropriate on many levels. Hilda Nelson says that for Pluvinel, 'horsemanship is not merely an exercise that shapes an individual's physical prowess, but it also nurtures and reveals an individual's judgement, honour, courage, sense of bienseance, and, even, virtue'.[117] Thus, the assertion of man's dominion comes not through the application of physical pain, but through a moral superiority that does not stoop to degradations of the rider's own nature.

This is highly significant in analyzing the relationship between Newcastle's manuals and those of Pluvinel, and also the differences between Newcastle's own manuals of 1658 and 1667. It also illustrates the way in which the art of the riding house reflected and perhaps even shaped the culture of the court. In 1573, Claudio Corte wrote that 'The professors of this art truly deserve higher praise than those who teach any other art in the world'.[118] Sir Philip Sidney more famously recalls the teachings of his own riding master John Pietro Pugliano, a pupil of Grisone, that horsemen 'were the Maisters of warre, and ornaments of peace; speedy goers, and strong abiders; triumphers both in Camps and Courts'. It seems likely from the steady stream of young men who followed him into the riding house and the success of manuals and authors in their own academies, that not everyone saw the 'strong affection and weak argument' in Pugliano's philosophy.[119]

As young Englishmen left for training on the Continent, so did the Continental masters send their acolytes to England at the request of the nobility, anxious to add this refinement and artistry to their own repertoire of courtly accomplishments. Sidney himself brought Italian masters Romano and Prospero to England and Nicholas Morgan likens the Italian master Alexander's mastery of his horses to Alexander the Great and the famous Bucephalas that 'suffered none to ride upon his backe by flattery or by force,/But his dread lord, that half the world did guide'.[120] The horsemasters may not have had quite such influence as Alexander the Great, but they did move in royal circles. Alexander's arrival in England was at the command of Henry VIII and St. Antoine was 'sent over by Henry the Fourth of France, to teach Prince Henry' (1667: p.2). St. Antoine appears in Van Dyck's famous picture Charles I riding through a triumphal Arch, of 1633, while Pluvinel's relationship with young King Louis XIII is perhaps the most fully illustrated through both the dialogue and images in his manual. The text opens with the King saying, 'let us find out from M. de Pluvinel what is the most perfect understanding of

---

117 Pluvinel, pp.ix.
118 *Il cavallerizzo* (Venice, 1573), sig. b2ᵛ; trans. in Hale, p.234.
119 *Defence of Poesie,* already cited, p.83.
120 *The Perfection of Horsemanship*, pp.21-22.

Horsemanship'.[121] The ensuing discussion and the plates, which focus on Pluvinel himself as much as the King and the horses, show that he is held as an authority and resource in this art, continually overseeing and guiding the riding house activities. If skill in horsemanship showed nobility and grace, those who could train a rider to perfect the art would be highly sought after. In considering Newcastle's attitude to other horsemasters and their work, this high opinion of the horsemaster as knowledgeable creative artiste must be borne in mind. The context in which he developed his own manuals becomes highly significant in the reading of the texts when the cultural influence of the art was so great.

It is evident from the texts published prior to Newcastle's that there was no significant English horsemaster to compete with Grisone or Pluvinel. The men making their mark in the riding houses of England were all Italian, French or Spanish, brought into the country to disseminate the grace and beauty of a Continental skill. While their pupils and followers might go on to instruct or write, the influence was still firmly rooted in the Continental tradition and there is no sense of an English style.

This was clearly of concern to some authors, particularly Nicholas Morgan and Gervase Markham. Morgan's title page declares that his book is 'not invented and drawne from Forraigne Nations, but by long Experience and Knowledge of many yeares practice [...] for the generall good of the noble nation of Great Britaine'.[122] Gervase Markham's manual was issued and re-issued between 1593 and 1610, as part of an enormously prolific body of writing. While he repeatedly claims to be recording 'An Arte never heretofore written by an Author', he titles his 1607 text *Cavalerice*, following the 1593-4 manual *Le Cavalerice François* of de la Broue to whom he refers frequently, and shows the direct influence of Grisone, in common with other authors. However, he is clearly aware of the lack of significant English influence, and seeking to rectify the matter. His text, dedicated to the young Prince Henry, includes also a dedication to the Earl of Worcester who was supervising instruction of the prince, and part of the title is *The English Horseman*. In his introduction he says, 'Almost all English men, whether out of the inconstancies of their natures (which is ever most delighted with new fangled novelties) or out of the bashfulnesse of their modesties, are ever apt to give precidencie and priorities of place to stranger, strange creatures, and strange fashions', even though his own work to some extent proves his point.[123]

While Markham's books were hugely successful, if reprints and number of editions are a measure, his overall influence does not seem to have been great. This may be due both to the derivative nature of his work and to the more 'popular' audience he seems to aim for, Prince Henry notwithstanding, as he includes instructions on 'how to teach them to do trickes like

---

121 Pluvinel, p.15

122 *The Horseman's Honour,* title page.

123 See F. N. L. Poynter, *A Bibliography of Gervase Markham* (Oxford: Oxford Bibliographical Society, 1962), pp.83-115; *Cavalerice or The English Horseman* (London: 1607), p.8.

Bankes'. Even though he addresses his work to 'the Gentleman Readers'[124] who would have the time or resources for horsemanship as a diversion, no man of Newcastle's status would teach his valuable manège horses frivolous tricks. As mentioned in the previous chapter, when Newcastle mentions the famous trick-horse Morocco and his owner Bankes in his play *Witts Triumvate*, he does so to illustrate a lack of understanding of the riding house, perhaps in a deliberate undermining of Markham.[125]

Horsemanship in England seems to have been a concern to many enthusiasts over a long period of time. Blundeville states one of his reasons for his English version of Grisone's manual to have been due to 'what lacke we Englishmen have had, and specially have at this present' so that 'you shall see some that sit on their horses like wind shake redes'. He feels that many English horses are 'so evel broke, as when he is spurred to go forward, he will go backward'. Therefore, 'For redresse of which faultes both in man and beast this booke is chieflye set foorth' so that 'not only by reading, but also by exercise of ridinge, I doubt not but by your spedye profiting therein'.[126]

Despite the enthusiastic response to his book and the proliferation of texts that followed, by 1639, Thomas de Grey author of *The Compleat Horseman* was expressing concern at 'the neglect of the Horse of the Menage, since the applying of our Breed only to Racing'. Interestingly, de Grey sees the interest in 'furnishing ourselves with Horses of speed to runne away from our enemy' to be undermining of the English spirit.[127] As the movements of the manège are based on the natural display of stallions, an additional subtext is apparent in the whole exercise as a display of power when seen by ambassadors and visitors from other countries. The potential of a subtle message in support of the prowess of the English manly spirit may be contained in the riding house but undermined on the racing track, horses for which 'are the most Easily found, and of the least Use', in Newcastle's view (1667: p.80). To those who loved the riding house, the lack of love for it appeared to reveal a lack of manly spirit that did not bode well for England. I will consider this further with particular reference to Newcastle's second manual.

However, to gain a perspective on Newcastle's work overall in the context of the early modern horsemanship manual, an insight into his knowledge of other texts is important. While he does not mention his own training when he relates that 'Monsieur St. Antoine a French-man, was a very good Horse-man, and sent over by Henry the Fourth of France, to teach Prince Henry' (1667: p.5), Margaret Cavendish adds the detail that he was sent 'to the mewse to Mons. Antoine, who was then accounted the best master in that art' (*Life:* p.134). Newcastle's own knowledge is therefore related in a direct line to Grisone, entirely through his own practical training as a boy and regardless of his

---

124   *Cavalerice*, title page.
125   *Witts Triumvate or The Philosopher*, already cited.
126   Blundeville, sig. A.iii.
127   London, 1639, sig. b2^{1v}.

choice of reading matter.

While he says in his second manual that he 'Read all their Italian, French, and English Books, and some Latine ones; and in a Word, All that hath been Writ upon that Subject, Good and Bad' (1667: p.41), deciding exactly which texts of 'All that hath been Writ' Newcastle was familiar with poses difficulties. Various editions of the Blundeville text were available and are fairly consistent when compared with those of Pluvinel. Blundeville's original translation appeared in 1560, and he admits to freely adapting the text because of the frustration he had in 'having to follow so doubtful phrases, and manners of speaking, and so confused an order of writing'.[128] There were numerous editions of Pluvinel's work in circulation issued between 1623 and 1640 to which Newcastle could have had access. Not all were authorised and R.S. Toole-Stott highlights some of the problems this causes later analysis. Of the first edition in 1623, he says, 'This is most difficult book to collate, the plate numbering [...] differing from copy to copy'. The number of plates in different copies varies from sixty-one to eighty-three, with some being duplicated or left out and variations in the date being added to the printed title. The second edition is dated 1624 but irregularities in pagination are still present and the 1626 edition has the same plates as the 1623 edition but is unauthorized. The 1625 edition is considered to be the definitive version by Mennessier de la Lance, because it was edited by Pluvinel's friend and confidant, Rene Menou. Yet this in itself becomes a problem because identical passages are found in Menou's own work, so accurate authorship is hard to establish. This edition is said to be based on Pluvinel's own manuscript, but it does not contain all the original plates, and has some additions, while the verses in honour of the author are missing. While it is difficult to be precise over the provenance of each text, Menou, as Pluvinel's acolyte, may be assumed to have perpetuated his ideas as Grisone's pupils did in their manuals.[129]

However, establishing a provenance of ideas becomes difficult when between the author's seminal work and the reader there are so many obstacles of language, presentation, translation and adaptation. Newcastle was writing to his father in 'schoolroom French'[130] at the age of ten, and so his command of French as an adult may well have been sufficient for him to fully enjoy and appreciate Pluvinel and French editions of Grisone. However, in 1671, his friend, Jacques de Solleysel, pointed out to him that the translation of his second manual into French was poorly done, suggesting that Newcastle himself did not possess sufficient knowledge to recognize the flaws. Whether or not he read Italian fluently, and so could have read Grisone in the original is debatable. British Library Harleian MS 6796 contains two short works translated from Italian by Robert Payne, Newcastle's chaplain. As his brother Charles read Latin and French and his correspondence with mathematician John Pell suggests that he read Italian also, it is unlikely that these translations were for his benefit. Sir Charles

128 Blundeville, 'To Sir Robert Dudley'.
129 Toole-Stott, pp.92-95.
130 Trease, p.24

Cavendish wrote to Pell in 1645 that Hobbes' English Optical Treatise was 'in English at my brother's request',[131] and Newcastle commissioned an English translation of Galileo's *Dialogo* from Joseph Webbe.[132] Overall, the available evidence suggests that Newcastle preferred his reading material to be in English regardless of his level of knowledge in French and Italian.[133]

Newcastle opens his second manual with a chapter entitled, 'Of the severall Authors that have Written of Horsemanship, both Italians, French and English'. This is a comprehensive list: Grisone, Claudio Corte, Laurentius Russius,[134] Cesare Fiaschi, Pasquale Caracciolo, Piero Antonio Ferraro, Salamon de la Broue and Antoine de Pluvinel (1667: pp.1-5). He then goes on to 'anatomize' Grisone and Blundeville, mentioning in passing the writing of Markham and de la Gray (1667: pp.17-37), though no other English writers at all. He considers that Grisone 'Writ like a Horse-man, and a great Master in the Art' (1667: p.1), even though, as mentioned above, Blundeville, in translating the work from the Italian found it hard to read and follow, Grisone being 'a better doer, than a writer'.[135] Claudio Corte, Newcastle acknowledges as 'an Excellent Rider' but dismisses him as an author, saying 'I think, that, very much of his Book is stolen out of Grisone' (1667: p.2). Corte's book, as mentioned above, was issued in 1573 and translated into English in 1584 by Thomas Bedingfield. As he was a pupil of Grisone, it is perhaps unsurprising if Newcastle recognised the hand of the master in the work of the pupil, whether he read the work in the original or in translation. Laurentius Russius' *Hippiatrica Sive Marescalia* dates from 1462, but was first printed in 1490 and ran to several editions, including a French edition of 1610.[136] Newcastle dismisses him as 'none of the Best, With Horrible Bitts' (1667: p.2) and indeed he is an early example of the more primitive tradition that recommends extreme violence:

> the rider will carry an iron bar, three or four feet long and ending in three well-sharpened
> hooks and if the horse refuses to go forward, he will dig one of these hooks into the
> horse's quarters and draw him forward; alternatively an assistant may apply a heated
> iron bar under the horse's tail, while the rider drives the spurs in with all available strength.[137]

Cesare Fiaschi was also a pupil of Grisone and his book was never translated into English,

---

131   BL MS Add. 4278, fol.223v

132   BL MS Harl. 6320.

133   I am grateful to Dr. Noel Malcolm for sharing his research on this topic with me.

134   Although Newcastle calls him 'Cussius' (1667: p.2), both his overall spelling of the name and description of the book make it probable that he means Laurentius Russius, whose work includes an alarming array of fierce bits.

135   Blundeville, sig. i.

136   F. H. Huth, *Works on Horses and Equitation: A Bibliographical Record of Hippology,* (London: Bernard Quaritch, 1887) p. 4.

137   Translated in W. Sidney Felton, *Masters of Equitation* (London: J. A. Allen, 1962), p. 23.

although it did appear in French. While Newcastle's comment that 'he meddles with Musick' (1667: p.2) seems derisive, later in the same manual he comments that 'There is not man, that hath not a Musical Head, that can be a good Horse-man, because all Horses go in a just and Musical time' (1667: p.297). However, Fiaschi's musical advice is dismissed and he skims likewise over all the other authors and books he mentions. There is a tension evident in his discussion between riding practice and writing style, especially when translations are involved. Newcastle repeatedly refers to riders and writers in the same sentence. This seems largely because most of the early manuals were Italian and the interest led to the importing of Italian riders. Therefore, in terms of available resources for the Englishman, riders and writers had a comparable influence, which Newcastle recognizes. Also he comments that many of the best riders 'never Writ' (1667: p.3). Clearly, a writer's style could be excellent even while his method was derivative while an excellent rider's poor writing might detract from the understanding of his method.

To be successful in Newcastle's opinion, the work needed to be well-written and innovative, with full evidence of riding ability, and he is continually disappointed in this respect. Even de la Broue, potentially interesting as 'the first French-man that ever Writ in that Art' (1667: p.3) fails to impress, and Newcastle was not alone in criticising him for deriving his methods from Grisone.[138] De la Broue's book receives more detailed attention from Newcastle than some, which suggests that he had devoted some depth of study to it, but he sums it up as, 'very Tedious, many Words for little Matter'. He also comments that 'La Broue, to seem wiser than he was, and to make up a Book, divides a Circle into so many parts […] that it confounds a horse more'. This appears to link directly to his comment in the address to horsemen in the first manual that he will not 'produce an entire book on how to divide a circle into several sections' (1658: 'Aux Cavaliers'). Pluvinel, although 'no doubt but he was a Good Horse-man' receives very little attention, as his method is 'absolute Routine' and 'hath spoyl'd more Horses than ever any Thing did' (1667: p.5).

His analysis of English writers is limited, aside from detailed references to Blundeville, to the briefest derisory mention of Markham who is 'but Blundeville with other Names' and 'De la Gray', who is also 'but Blundeville, with some New Medicins that are but indifferent.' Thomas de Grey is distinguished only for the dubious honour that his ideas on breeding are 'the most Ridiculous thing that was ever known Writ'. He ends this dismissive address of the English contribution by saying 'And thus for our English Authors, of whom I have told you the Truth' (1667: pp.32-33).

Overall, Newcastle's attitude suggests first hand familiarity with the texts, including translations. However, rather than detailed study, his knowledge seems to be of particular features, such as the 'long discourses' (1667: p.2) in Carraciolo's *Gloria del Cavallo*, which runs to over a thousand pages. He reveals a general tendency to locate derivative material and then dismiss the whole text. This is

---

138   Toole-Stott, p.72.

unsurprising and there is a great sense of frustration in his manner over the lack of innovation which makes it clear that he considers the originality of his own approach to be a necessity for the future survival of the art.

In 'The First Part' of his second manual, the chapters of which are unnumbered, he explains 'How I found Out my Method in the Mannage; And that it is The only Way to Dress Horses'. He lays out his riding background, which includes having 'Rid with the Best Masters of all Nations' and 'heard them Discourse at Large, and Tried their several Wayes', along with reading their books. He remained however dissatisfied and 'all that while I thought still, All was Labour in Vain; and that there was something not Found out, which They and their Books Mist'. With renewed vigour and enthusiasm, he then applied himself to 'consider so Seriously, and Study so Earnestly' every aspect of the art until 'at last I Found this Method, which is as True, as it is New, and is the quintessence of Horse-manship: For which I have Left all Others' (1667: p.42).

The key to this innovation is his firm but non-aggressive insistence that 'the Horse follow my Wayes, and Obey me'. 'I seldom Beat them,' he says, 'but when I meet with great Resistance, and that Rarely'. His new understanding seems to be based largely on the calm assertion of his will upon them, which he describes as 'Force' and in response 'they Obey willingly, for the most part; and however, all Yeeld, and Render themselves at last' (1667: p.42). This reflects an understanding of a horse's acceptance of confident leadership that is part of its nature as a herd animal and commonly understood today. For Newcastle, however, it represented a point of departure from other writers, thus he feels justified in claiming total originality, regardless of his place in the lineage of riders that goes back to Grisone.

This casts a light upon the differences between his two manuals, the way in which he approaches both Pluvinel and Blundeville and why it is Blundeville, the translator, rather than Grisone, the author, upon whom he focusses his attention. As discussed in the previous chapter, while Newcastle's method remains very similar in his two manuals, in all other respects they are very different. Close attention to these differences gives an insight into the hidden agenda behind them.

While Newcastle's first manual of 1658 was published in French, it was not written in French but 'Traduit de l'Anglois de l'Auteur en Francois par son Commendement' (1658: Title page). His possible motivations for this are many. Queen Henrietta Maria was French and the language was spoken widely at the English court, at that time in Continental exile. French was also the traditional language of chivalry and had connotations of gentility and refinement. It was not though, the original language of horsemanship, which was Italian. However, French was the language of Pluvinel, who had become the acknowledged horsemaster after setting up his academy in Paris while Newcastle was still a boy, taking up the place long held by Grisone.

It is entirely in keeping with Newcastle's character, that he would align himself with and yet still challenge the centre of excellence in his chosen field by publishing his work in French. By 1658 he was living in Antwerp, not knowing if he would ever be able to return home to England, with no significant role to play in the court-in-exile and in need of worthwhile occupation and perhaps some means of generating income. His horses and skill in their training offered him a context in which to locate and actualize himself, with the potential for some discreet gentlemanly financial arrangement were he to share that expertise with others. This could only be attempted on the grand scale suited to his status, so he settled in the former home of the artist Rubens, entertained the Continental nobility and set out to produce the most comprehensive and lavish horsemanship text yet to be written. However, if he wished to establish himself as the supreme European horsemaster, he had to contend with Pluvinel's memory and manuals.

Pluvinel died in 1620, and the editions of his manuals started appearing in 1623. By the 1650s, a similar situation existed in France to that in Italy and England, where Grisone's manual had been expanded upon, adapted and assimilated into other texts. Therefore, Newcastle does not devote much attention to the Grisone derivatives in his 1658 manual, aside from his arch reference to de la Broue. Instead he focuses his attention on carefully, and largely respectfully, superseding Pluvinel. He refers to him gracefully in passing, as a way of affirming his own views, for example mentioning that 'Le grande Maître en c'ét art, Monsieur de Pluvinel, en fait soit autant' (1658: p.268).[139] They shared much in terms of ideals and attitudes and Newcastle would most likely have become the next great horsemanship author without any manipulation of his readers through natural progression. However, though fully confident of his own superiority, he nevertheless takes no chances and while his first manual does not analyse the work of other masters, there are parallels to Pluvinel's manuals throughout.

His aim seems not so much to rival Pluvinel in this first manual, the only criticism being a caustic indirect comment about fashion (1658: 'Aux cavaliers'), to which Pluvinel pays considerable attention,[140] but rather to tacitly acknowledge areas of his thought while aiming to transcend them. The layout of Newcastle's book is quite different from Pluvinel's and they have a different focus overall, and yet there is a strong suggestion of unspoken reference to the earlier text that can hardly fail to go unnoticed by anyone who has seen both. Newcastle appears to be demonstrating a like mind to that of the previous great master, while discreetly emphasizing his own higher social status and independent ideas.

The engraved title-page of Newcastle's first manual is very similar to that of Pluvinel in design. Rearing horses, heraldic devices and architectural features focus attention on the authors' credentials and bear little similarity to any significant earlier manual, while the quality of the plates in both texts marks a new level of detailed sophistication, reflecting courtly grace and style. Pluvinel's plates emphasise the ease and respect of the relationship he shares with his young protégée, King Louis XIII, at the age of 16.[141]

---

139 'Likewise that great master of his art, Monsieur De Pluvinel, said the same' (1743: p. 131).
140 Pluvinel, pp.15-16, plate 2.
141 Ibid. pp.17, 33, 34; examples of Pluvinel's plates may be found in Appendix 3.

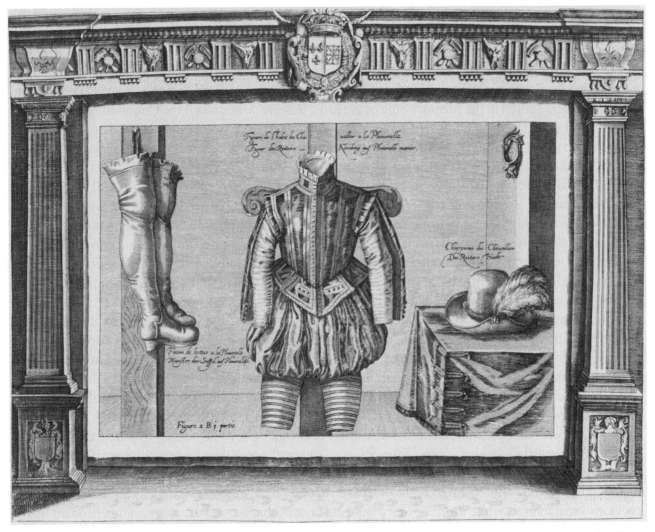

'Figure de l'habit du Chevallier a la Pluvinelle' from Antoine de Pluvinel's *Le Maneige Royal* 1626

The king leans forward to hear Pluvinel speak, his hand resting on the horsemaster's arm, or looks over his shoulder to ask Pluvinel's advice. Pluvinel stands alongside his chair to explain an exercise or leans over him in an air of confidence-sharing, to illuminate the young man's understanding. The delicately tender and protective attitude of these plates suggests a degree of trust that implicitly elevates Pluvinel's status.

By 1658, Newcastle no longer had the ear of a king in this way but establishes in the dedication

Title plate from Antoine de Pluvinel's *Le Maneige Royal* 1626

that he was the 'premier Gouverneur de Votre Majeste' and that 'j'ai eu l'honneur de Vous mettre le premier a cheval dans le Mannage'. He states that 'je n'en puis souhaiter de plus sur-eminent' than to have served the future monarch during this most formative time of his life and establishes his own perspicacity in noting 'quelle abondance de fruits verteux Elle nouse apporteroit en son age plus meur' (1658: 'Au Roy'). The two plates depicting Charles II and Newcastle as victors in battle are exactly the same except that one has Charles' head and one has Newcastle's. When viewed in a comparative sense with those of Pluvinel alongside Louis XIII, it can only be read that while the French king absorbs

The young Louis XIII (seated) asks the advice of Monsieur de Pluvinel
from Antoine de Pluvinel's *Le Maneige Royal* 1626

Pluvinel's knowledge, the English monarch assimilates Newcastle's.

Having established this close relationship, Newcastle then sets himself out as independent. His riding house plates are not full of courtiers, pupils and admirers, as Pluvinel's are and there are no other riders except Captain Mazin, Newcastle's Master of Horse and protégé, who fully understood this new method having been trained by Newcastle from boyhood (1658: p.33). Newcastle stands alone in skill, a foreigner on the Continent, developing the skills he has learned from a noble equestrian heritage by establishing his unique approach. The plates depict him as a man of high status, influential in the education of a monarch who, unlike Pluvinel, never carries his own hat.

In the Pluvinel text, Monsieur le Grand suggests that 'if it please Your Majesty one day to visit his stud farm, he will observe, as we have many times, how the foals, large and small, run joyfully after their mothers […] take now and then a good demi-volte […] and sometime go up in the air as though they are doing a courbette'.[142] It is, however, Newcastle's own mares and foals that are illustrated in Plate 12 of the 1658 manual, which could well have been drawn from Monsieur Le Grand's description. Newcastle does not need to look at the king's horses to 'confirm the opinion of Monsieur de Pluvinel that the various airs come naturally to horses and that nature gave each Horse his own particular air'.[143] He is master of his own fine estates, all of which are beautifully illustrated, and can observe his own stud to confirm that 'si donc le Cavalier suivoit la nature, il sauroit mieux les approprier à ce à quoi la nature les a eveés, de sorte qu'ils seroint des bon chevaux' (1658: p.6).[144]

Therefore, he need not set out to rival Pluvinel, but, rather more gracefully, pick up his torch and offer innovations within a great tradition. Pluvinel appears on horseback infrequently in his plates and even then remains on the sidelines to guide the action. This may reflect his health at the time the plates depict: when Louis was sixteen, his horsemaster would have been fifty-six, somewhat elderly by seventeenth-century standards. Newcastle, however, directs Captain Mazin then takes over the riding to demonstrate the advanced stages of training. This athleticism at the age of sixty-five, which he had reached by the time his first manual was published, further reinforces the active nature of his ongoing contribution, especially as Pluvinel had died at the same age. Pluvinel's role as mentor to the young king may also have made a central position in the plates inappropriate. Newcastle's plates, however, show him as central in every sense.

Pluvinel and Newcastle have much in common as horsemasters. They both understand that the rider's attitude influences the horse's confidence so he must have 'a pleasant expression'[145] or 'le visage gay et réjoüy'(1658: p.36). [146] They agree that the rider should never demand 'more from a horse than half of what he is capable',[147] and so should 'reduisés-le au petit pas, mélant le douceur avec les aides & châtiment' (1658: 'Avant-Propos').[148] They share an overall philosophy that requires that

---

142 Pluvinel, p.32.

143 Pluvinel, p.32.

144 'if the horseman studies nature, and the dispositions of his horses, he would know better how to appropriate them to the uses for which they were created' (1743: p.17).

145 Pluvinel, p.26.

146 'a countenance pleasant and gay' (1743: p.30).

147 Pluvinel, p. 24.

148 'reduce him by degrees, mixing gentleness with helps and corrections' (1743: p.14)

horse and rider be treated with respect and dignity, without ever compromising human dominance.

Newcastle opens his first manual with an essay on the intelligence and reasoning capacity of the horse, which he clearly feels is under-rated. His irritation that 'il y en a, qui tout aussy tôt qu'ils sont desses un jeune cheval tout à fait ignorant du Manege, pensent qu'en le battant & éperonant ils en feront un cheval dressé dés le premier matin' (1658: 'Avant-Propos'),[149] shows his expectation of thoughtful riding. Pluvinel spends some time discussing the 'judicious horseman' and describes how by gentle handling he overcomes the recalcitrant horse, Bonnitte, so that 'It did not take long for him to understand what I wanted of him'.[150] He is more subtle than Newcastle in his criticism of others, but he is not addressing his peers as Newcastle is, so must needs be more circumspect. Referring to the rough handling considered necessary by others to tame a difficult horse, while Newcastle outspokenly declares that 'je desirerois donc qu'on ne crust pas le cheval plus capable que l'homme, qu'on appelle raisonnable' (1658: p.2),[151] Pluvinel more carefully states 'I was touched to the quick by this judgement'.[152] Newcastle feels that patience and knowledge (1658: 'Avant-Propos') are the essential qualities of a horseman; Pluvinel chooses grace and judiciousness,[153] but their descriptions of these qualities in practice are very similar.

While Newcastle's manuals are focused on training the horse and Pluvinel's prime concern is the training of the rider, they are of like mind in the treatment of the young pupil. Newcastle devotes Chapter II of his first manual to criticising bullying masters who verbally abuse or 'ont leurs pochettes pleines de pierres à leur jetter' and treat their students 'd'une façon hautaine & insolente' (1658: p.8),[154] while Pluvinel 'condemns those riding-masters who shout at their young pupils and menace them'. Pluvinel believes that the young pupil must be allowed to make mistakes and learn from them,[155] while Newcastle says, 'Enseignés donc premierement à vôtre écolier ce qu'il doit faire, le luy repetant souvent avec beaucoup de patience, ou il n'apprendra jamais'(1658: p.9).[156] From these points of contact, Newcastle presents his own method, much of which is technically and philosophically very different to Pluvinel's. Therefore, his text not only keeps pace with the changes in attitude and practice, but contributes further innovation. It serves to establish him as a contender, a man of great experience in the art of riding horses, whose aristocratic lineage and personal holdings were lavishly illustrated for the

---

149   'There are some people, who, as soon as they have got upon a young horse, entirely undressed or untaught, fancy, that by beating and spurring thy will make him a dress'd horse in one morning only' (1743: sig. C).

150   Pluvinel, pp. 21, 22.

151   'I wish people would not require more capacity of a horse than of a man, whom they stile rational'(1743: p.16).

152   Pluvinel, p.22.

153   Ibid.

154   'fill their pockets full of stones to throw […] in a haughty and imperious manner' (1743: p.18).

155   Pluvinel, p.xii.

156   'First of all teach your scholar what he should do, repeating it often to him in a mild manner, or he will never learn' (1743: p.19).

benefit of his Continental readers. He effectively takes his English heritage into exile with him through his manuals and lays out his credentials, as well as his expertise.

Once he returned home to England, matters were different and this is reflected in the second manual. One of the few nobleman still in England who openly retained a keen interest in the riding house through the *inter regnum* was Newcastle's son-in-law, the 3rd Earl of Bridgewater. Small wonder then that Newcastle, knowing horsemanship was flourishing on the Continent where he himself had been lauded as an innovator, should on his return home be dismayed. Interest in this most noble of arts had disintegrated, leaving it largely out of fashion or where it survived, relying still upon the 'old Authors'. The weight of ironic derision in this term, which he uses throughout the 1667 manual, seems to grow with each repetition, so that the whole of English horsemanship seems bound helplessly to the past.

Not so, however, as Newcastle set out to revitalize the art single-handedly by publishing a second manual in English in 1667, though a more modest enterprise, with no privileges, plates or line drawings at all. It is also dedicated to Charles, now restored to his throne, but focuses only on Newcastle's devotion to his king, rather than any past relationship between them. It also, for those who can read the message, points out that he feels a little overlooked in his 'solitary Country Life' (1667: sig. b).

This second text opens with an address 'To the Readers' and sets out to illustrate the courtesy with which the Continental equestrian community treated Newcastle during his exile. His countrymen are made aware that he has been treated with respect while abroad and that he honoured this by publishing his first manual in French. However, he would not have them feel neglected, so stresses that 'I now for the more particular Satisfaction of my Country-men print this second Book, in English' (1667: sig. b). He may have been criticized for publishing in French and sought in the second book to redress the balance and widen his audience. It is equally likely that he felt overlooked and out of favour, part of a lost regime, and was seeking a way to re-establish his expertise in defining standards of gentlemanly aspiration. In this respect, there is a similarity between the manuals, as each was published at a time when his public profile had changed due to politics and circumstance. His opinion of himself as the great master who superseded the 'old authors' still favoured in England was well founded. He had returned home as the only Englishman to have made any impact upon an art long seen as Continental and provides evidence by describing in eight pages of great detail 'my only private Riding-House at Antwerp' and the 'Honour I have receiv'd there'. Apart from the personal satisfaction he evidently gains from the acknowledgement of Don John of Austria, the Marquis of Seralvo, Marquis of Caracena and 'the Prince of Conde himself' amongst many others, he points out the 'Commendations that were given to Horses and to Horsemanship' which were, of course, 'very proper in this place.' (1667: sig. b2ᵛ – p.1ᵛ). If the Continent, that model of fashion and style, values horsemanship, he seems to ask, then why does the English nobleman either overlook it, or use antique methods? By mentioning noblemen from several regions of the Continent, he demonstrates that the art is alive and flourishing there, then backs up his message by his reference to Charles II as a fine horseman. Here, however, he was on lost ground, as by this time, in 1667, Charles II had lost all interest in the riding house and it may be that in writing his manual, Newcastle simply reinforced himself as a relic of his king's past.

He evidently did not anticipate this when he wrote and addresses his second manual with a fierce vigour, by attacking the problem he sees in the English reliance on earlier writers. His lack of patience with Blundeville, and the other authors he dismisses are that he sees them as derivative, either of Grisone, or Grisone through Blundeville. He seems highly irritated by Blundeville whom he acknowledges as 'a fine Gentleman, Well Travelled, an Excellent Scholler, a Good Translator, and puts things into an Excellent Method', but 'Tyed himself too much to Old Authors' (1667: p.31). By the time Newcastle came to write, Grisone's original manual was over one hundred years old and his irritation that a century later horsemen were still relying on his text and those derived from it is unbounded. However, Blundeville himself was long dead, so Newcastle's annoyance, which may have been understandable towards a contemporary relying heavily on the past, is initially bewildering.

When Blundeville introduced the English translation of Grisone, the original text was still very new, so his work would have surely been a revelation to his countrymen. The way in which subsequent texts focus around and develop from Grisone and his students is more by way of tribute than plagiarism, as Blundeville had started something of a trend. Yet by Newcastle's time, all the resulting texts had been made archaic in both method and philosophy by the influence of Pluvinel. However, until Newcastle, no author had made a serious attempt to bring the English manual up to date. While the provenance of ideas from 'old authors' underpins much of the philosophy of the early modern period, Newcastle was not alone in feeling irritated at a total reliance on them and echoes his friend Ben Jonson's belief that 'Nothing is more ridiculous then to make an Author a *Dictator*, as the schooles have done *Aristotle*'.[157] In ridiculing Blundeville, Newcastle goes to what he sees as the root of the problem.

Having opened his second manual with his observations on previous authors, none of whom has impressed him greatly, Newcastle devotes nine pages, rather than the four paragraphs in the first manual, to those who 'think the Mannage Useless'(1667: pp.5-14). This venting of general spleen on the state of riding and horsemanship manuals is leading up to an attack against the only rival author who receives any serious level of direct attention from him. While 'Old Grison' is mentioned in the overview of authors, 'his translator, Mr. Blundeville' is not mentioned at all at first but then has a sixteen page chapter devoted to a detailed analysis of his manual (1667: p.17).

While Newcastle uses the familiar contemporary term 'anatomized' to describe this analysis (1667: p.17), 'vivisected' would come closer to the nature of his attention. He is merciless with

---

157   *Ben Jonson: A Critical Edition of the Major Works*, ed. by Ian Donaldson (Oxford University Press, 1985), p. 76.

Blundeville, attacking him throughout as 'Foolish', 'mightily Deceived', 'Mistaken', 'very Ridiculous' and using 'Tormenting ignorant Follies' and methods which are a 'Horrible Folly' and 'Abominable' (1667: pp.17-23). Having ended his initial diatribe, 'And thus much of Mr. Blundeville's Riding', he launches with renewed vigour on the very next line into an attack on Blundeville's advice on breeding, which is 'Unnatural', and 'Ridiculous' at the very least. He focuses on destroying Blundeville's credibility, saying he 'did not Understand', that his bits 'are very Ridiculous' and his methods 'Abominable'. He is also disparaged as superstitious and full of 'Tales to Tell to Children, rather than to Men of Reason and Discretion; all Mountebank-ship and Fooleries'. The energy Newcastle expends in undermining Blundeville on these points is considerable. He has little patience for superstition, and it seems that he considers anything he views as folklore to be perpetuating an outdated approach to horsemanship, as bad as thinking 'Squirts, Fire, Whelps, Hedge-hoggs, Nailes, and I know not what' will encourage 'a Resty Horse' to be calm (1667: p.18).

His first great attack on Blundeville is followed by his declaration on 'How I found Out my Method in the Mannage And that it is the only Way to Dress Horses' as discussed above. He goes on to a far fuller discussion of horse breeds than in the first manual, occasionally lapsing back to attacking Blundeville, then a very comprehensive discussion on saddling and presenting the horse to its best advantage. This leads into advice on shoeing, stable management and home-remedies for minor illnesses. The 'Second Part' (1667: p.145), which addresses riding the horse, does not begin till almost half way through, while in the first manual, Newcastle is discussing training within the first thirty pages. Also, while he addresses his subject as fully as in the first manual, the number of exercises overall is fewer and in less detail, with additional material in terms of observations and discussions. As discussed in the previous chapters, Newcastle's age and lifelong tendency towards distraction from his main point are a consideration here, but so are his intended English readers.

In the material on breeding, remedies and presentation of the horse, he is offering the content favoured by Blundeville and other English authors, which seems to distract him from his overall intent. Blundeville's second manual, as well as expanding his first to include 'all the precepts' of Claudio Corte,[158] also adds sections on diet and diseases. Thomas Bedingfield, Nicholas Morgan, Christopher Clifford, Markham and Thomas de Grey also have comprehensive sections on health and husbandry, while John Astley includes a 'short discourse of the [...] Trench, and the Martingale',[159] equipment Newcastle does not mention at all in the first manual but which he disparages in the second as 'to no Purpose at all' (1667: p.314). As discussed in the previous chapter, Newcastle's manuscript contains notes on this form of bit and head restraint, which he later decides are obsolete. If he intends to refer tacitly to Astley's text, it may be the case that initially he meant to offer his own methods for

---

158   *The Fower Chiefyst Offices belongyng to Horsemanship* (London: Wyllyam Seres, 1565-66), sig.A3ᵛ.
159   Astley, title page.

equipment still used in England, but upon reflection decided outdated methods should be dismissed.

Thus, as Newcastle's first manual echoes Pluvinel, in a way which comes close to a tribute, the second appears to attempt to be familiar to English riders, but at least partially to disparage the traditions they embrace. He goes so far as to mention plans he has for a subsequent book 'on Marshalry and Shooing' (1667: p.33), another area of interest addressed in great detail in English texts.

Therefore, new light is shed on the differences between his two manuals by seeing them both as direct products of the time of writing, representing not only specific moments in the development of Newcastle's method but also in the history of the horsemanship text. With his characteristic enthusiasm and passion, he aims in both to stir up the love of horsemanship, 'comme étant un exercise tres-noble' (1658: 'Avant-Propos'), for 'Pleasure and State' (1667: p.13), assuring his readers that 'messieurs les railleurs' (1658: 'Avant-Propos')[160] are as nothing beside the high opinion of the 'many Noble great Persons, who did me the favour to see my Mannage' and included 'several worthy Gentlemen, of all Nations, High and Low-Dutch, Italians, English, French, Spaniards, Polacks, and Swedes' (1667: sig.b2ᵛ-p.1ᵛ). Undoubtedly this desire is borne of his own love and faith in the art. But there is a deeper need and urgency present also when both texts served to define times of great conflict and upheaval for him, perhaps offering an emotional stability when all that he relied upon for personal identity was highly insecure.

---

160   'as an exercise that is very noble'; 'sneering gentlemen' (1743: p.14).

Chapter 4

'The Epitome of Horsemanship':
Newcastle's Method 'Anatomized'

When first, my lord, I saw you back your horse,
Provoke his mettle, and command his force
To all the uses of the field and race,
Methought I read the ancient art of Thrace,
And saw a centaur, past those tales of Greece;
So seemed your horse and you both of a piece!
Ben Jonson, 'To My Lord Newcastle'

The first cause of Absurd conclusions I ascribe to a want of Method.
Thomas Hobbes, *Leviathan*

Newcastle's manual are complicated and political at many levels, with an underlying philosophy and personal agenda as discussed already. However, to focus on them solely as a vehicle for political and personal ideals would be to undervalue them. The horsemanship manuals are about 'fitting every Horse according to his Nature, Disposition, and Strength'(1667: p.349). Therefore, regardless of all else Newcastle's two manuals set out a complete system for training horses, showing between them consistency, development and growth through experience.

To gain an understanding of Newcastle's purpose and method, it is essential to understand the raw material with which he was working. Even though long domesticated, the horse remains by nature a prey animal whose instinctive reaction to danger is flight. It is also a herd animal, which readily accepts leadership, finding safety and comfort in accepting and knowing its correct place in relation to its social group. This way of approaching life is not unlike Newcastle's own and it is not surprising that he felt such an affinity with the horse.

Much of the relationship between horses within a herd hinges around the acceptance of the herd structure. The lead stallion or matriarchal mares will drive out any young horses, usually colts, which are troublesome, because this behaviour upsets the balance of relationships and makes the herd vulnerable to predators. In a domesticated environment, the relationship between horse and rider is dependent upon a similar acceptance of the place of each in the 'herd' their interaction creates. So when the horse initially and periodically attempts to test the boundaries set by the rider or handler, it is effectively checking its own safety. Therefore, the rider should 'Be not discouraged if your Horse do Oppose you, for it shews Strength, Spirit and Stomach'(1667: p.199). If the rider/handler does not respond with confidence, then the horse can no longer rely upon that leadership and may become dominant or anxious, depending upon its temperament. In this case, neither party is safe.

While modern equine psychology attempts to define the nature of this relationship, those who have handled horses have always worked within its parameters. The way in which the horse is trained to cooperate is loaded with information about the rider or handler to any knowledgeable observer. In the highly competitive world of the early modern nobility, the symbolism of the dominant stallion was implicit in the image of the man who has obtained the submission of his mount. Thus the monarch or nobleman on horseback displayed something essential about his own nature through this ability. Newcastle's method establishes him as the leader by skill and the horse's acceptance of his will, offering a more subtle message than the cruder methods advocated by earlier writers.

To ride the horse so that it can display its beauty is a highly skilled activity, as the rider must not hinder the horse's freedom of movement. The power in a horse comes from its haunches and the further back the centre of its balance, the more weight it will carry on its haunches. This frees the front legs to manoeuvre and move with lightness, which makes for an efficient use of the horse's energy, and 'is our main Business and Work' (1667: p.334). It is also essential for the advanced movements towards which Newcastle worked his horses. Much of the modern understanding of the movement of horses comes from the advent of photography, which enabled close analysis of each stage of a step. That Newcastle had begun to uncover this depth of knowledge is evident from the technical accuracy of his descriptions, and also of the plates, which can only have resulted from many hours of detailed discussion with the artist.

While Pluvinel demonstrates a comprehensive personal understanding in his method, he does not explain how others may achieve the same result in such detail. Pluvinel's text is primarily an account of how he works and how riding a horse can make a man; Newcastle's text is about how 'you', the reader, can put his method into practice, and how training a horse can make a man. Pluvinel's text is as much, if not more, about the young rider as the horse, to address 'what one must do in order to become a perfect Horseman',[161] whereas Newcastle states in the dedicatory address to Cavaliers that he writes not for students but for masters (1658: 'Aux Cavaliers'). His method is at times less readable for this very reason, but it is more use in the practical application, which establishes the text as seminal in the progressive history of horsemanship manuals. His illustrations are the first to break the exercises down into stages that precisely depict the detailed instructions of the text, while Pluvinel's focus on the courtliness and gentility of the overall picture the horse and rider present. These two important

---

161   Pluvinel, p.15.

horsemasters each have their own agenda and the differences in their method reflect the passage of time.

As Newcastle advises the use of both his manuals together (1667: sig. b2ᵛ; pp. 43, 93, 112), I will use this approach in analysing his method. This will also extend to consideration of the plates from the first manual, as Newcastle refers the reader to them in the later text. He advises that 'There is in my French Book, Circles and the Prints of Horses Shoes, to shew how his Legs should Go; there is also exact figures of all Postures, and of all Actions, both of Man and Horse, and more cannot be'(1667: p.43).

Newcastle divides his method into four progressive sections from the breeding of a suitable horse, through its youth, backing and on through the various levels of training. This is the general pattern used by most authors, from Xenophon onwards, though some start with a mature horse, or do not deal with the preparation prior to the arrival in the riding house for early training.[162] Like others, Newcastle offers advice on dealing with 'vices', which are resistances to training due to unease in the horse, rather than lack of understanding, and trouble-shooting exercises, while the plates illustrate the most important exercises broken down into stages.

Having offered comprehensive advice on choosing and breeding suitable stock, Newcastle lays out his training method for a young horse. He includes more detail on preparation prior to riding than earlier authors due to his understanding that the raw material is highly important, and this is his first innovation as he completely rejects the idea that the early rides will involve taming wildness.

While Pluvinel talks of the horse's 'extreme displeasure' and having 'occasion to be angry'[163] at the first attempts to ride him, Newcastle states that if his reader follow his early handling methods, 'il ne sera point extravagant, ny ne se couchera, & n'aura pas plûsieurs actions revesches, ordinaires aux jeune chevaux' (1658: p.30).[164] He advocates a gentle, unhurried handling when preparing for backing due to the understanding that a horse put under great pressure will either panic or settle into a resentful or cowed acceptance. The chances are that the rider would feel the backlash from this at some point in the future.

Blundeville says, 'Although you may begyn to handle your horse when he is full ii. yeares old and upward, yet it were better to tary until he be iii. yeares and a halfe old'. By this time a horse is well developed in its mind and body and is far more of a physical challenge to a handler than a weanling if it refuses to co-operate. While 'Grisone would in no wise have a young horse to be ridden at the first with any bit, for feare of marring his mouth', if the horse will not respond to coaxing towards the mounting-block for the first ride, then the rider should 'rate him with a terrible voice and beate him yourselfe with a good sticke upon the heade betwixt the eares'.[165] Thomas Bedingfield's comment that the rider should 'beware in anie wise to strike the horse upon the head, and cheeflie betwixt his eares, for so he may easily be slain' suggests that perhaps some horses never reached the next step of the training. However,

---

162   Pluvinel, p.21; Blundeville, sig. Aviiiᵛ.
163   Pluvinel, pp. 32, 39.
164   'He will not be wanton, apt to lie down, or be guilty of any extravagant actions common to young horses'(1743: p.27).
165   Blundeville, sig. A8ᵛ-Axᵛ

Bedingfield, translating Claudio Corte, goes on to recommend a servant 'with a wispe of fire' behind the horse if it will not walk forward. This uneasy balance between concern for the horse's safety and methods of coercion that are highly dangerous for all concerned arises repeatedly in these early manuals and calls into question their practicality.[166]

While Pluvinel's treatment is more refined than earlier texts, Newcastle's manual is the first to stress that laying the groundwork reaps rewards later on. He advises that weanlings should be kept together, accustomed to casual daily handling in the pasture and the stable and treated 'in all Kinds, like the Older Horses', so that riding becomes simply the next step. He recommends a routine of 'doing the same Thing every Summer, and every Winter' and suggests that the fillies who will be kept for breeding are backed for riding, as well as the colts, 'For, being thus Gentle, [.......] if They or their Foles, be Sick, or Hurt, you may easily take them Up for the Farrier to use his Skill to Recover them' (1667: pp. 97-101). This common sense approach makes dealing with the horse safer for handler and horse alike, and changes the training process from an ordeal to a progression.

Once the riding has begun, this progressive method continues and Newcastle advocates steady steps over a period of days, rather than intensive training, so that 'le Cavalcador luy place le plus qu'il pourra la teste & peu à peu' (1658: p.31),[167] working slowly towards the desired carriage. While Pluvinel says that in the second lesson 'I begin by making the horse's head resolute and steady', he does not explain how this is to be done.[168] Newcastle devotes considerable detail to explaining how, by the use of a firm but sensitive hand and circling exercises, the position of the head will be achieved. The use of exercises 'upon Large Circles', which are reduced as the horse becomes more supple, ensures that the hind legs must reach further under the horse's body. The horse will therefore develop supple strength, moving towards the ideal of lightness and elegance by bearing more weight on the haunches and giving relative freedom to the forehand. With a light hand on the rein, in time the horse's head will lower as its back rounds. The rider should 'give him no other lesson than this, until he be very Supple on the Shoulders upon his Trot' because all the early training is to ensure that 'the Foundation of all things in the Mannage' is secure and well-established (1667: p.208-209).

Newcastle's constant emphasis on the use of simple bits stresses that more severe bits do not put a horse upon his haunches, but on the forehand or behind the bit, meaning that he will tuck his head in to avoid contact at all. This illustrates an attention to the horse's anatomy that becomes a key feature of Newcastle's method and is significantly more sophisticated than that shown by earlier writers who 'shew themselves full of Ignorance, and Simple People, to imagine, That a piece of Iron in a Horse's Mouth can bring him Knowledge' (1667: p.343).

---

166   *The Art of Riding [...] written at large in the Italian toong, by Maister Claudio Corte*, trans. by Thomas Bedingfield (London: Henrie Denham, 1584), pp. 96-97.

167   'The rider must take care to manage his head by degrees' (1743: p.27).

168   Pluvinel, p.39

Many of the early Italian manuals devote a large proportion of the text to effective bits, with Grisone's including over fifty full page illustrations of different styles to choose from. Many of these are exceptionally severe in their action, and the sheer number of choices indicates a problem area. This suggests that the importance of a full use of the hind legs and back to achieve good head carriage was not fully understood or, at least, valued, even though the use of circles in training was already established.

Newcastle's argument is always that a good rider will not need to resort to such remedial methods, in agreement with Pluvinel who uses 'only about a dozen different mouthpieces which will take care of different kinds of horses'. He recognises that different shaped mouths may require different shaped bits and like Newcastle favours the bits 'a la Pignatelle' for their relative simplicity.[169] Newcastle goes into further detail on the purpose behind bitting and explains that the main factor is not the bit but 'the Art of appropriated Lessons' (1667: p.349). Like Pluvinel, Newcastle uses the term 'apuy' which means 'support', referring to the ideal known today as having the horse 'on the bit' or in 'self-carriage'. This means that there is a subtle relationship between the bit and the rider's hand along the rein, without the horse leaning or pulling. This makes the horse's movement much softer and gives the appearance of effortlessness, but like dancing or swordsmanship, represents many hours of training. Newcastle illustrates his awareness that a horse, like a child, learns most readily in short varied lessons. He advises that the rider should always 'laissés-le toûjours en sa force'(1658: p.32),[170] allowing the horse to rest before growing too tired to retain what it has learned. This is in direct contrast to earlier methods that rely on exhaustion in the horse to achieve compliance.[171]

As Newcastle is writing for masters not students, it may seem strange that he troubles himself with the rider's position. Any rider who needs this most basic of advice would surely be unable to cope with the advanced technical work that follows. He highlights, however, that there is much bad riding, even amongst those who consider themselves to be horsemen and ridicules poor practice mercilessly:

> This Cavalier Seats as far Back in the Sadle as he can, his Leggs stretcht as far
> Forward before the Shoudlers of the horse, with his Toes out, that he Spur him in
> the Shoulders; and Stoops in the Back, which they call a Comely Seat; not Knowing
> How to hold the Bridle in his Hand, nor Ghess at any Helps at all (1667: p.9).

Thus, he provides basic advice, as well as advanced technique, both for the reputation of his art, his belief in the posture he uses and also so that the rider will remember to address his own contribution to the working partnership (1667: p.9).

---

169   Pluvinel, p.149.
170   'leave him at last as vigorous as you found him' (1743: p.28).
171   Blundeville, sig. Cvii-Di^v.

The rider's seat influences every move the horse makes and Newcastle's parody contains the exasperation of the expert at unconscious ineptitude. Therefore, his initial concern is that the rider's position should not hinder the horse's movement. The alignment of the body, 'his Leggs being straight Down, as if he were on Foot, his Knees and Thighes turned inwards to the Saddle', enables a secure position which is essential 'for a Horse-man hath nothing but those two with the Counterpoize of his Body to keep him on Horse-back' (1667: pp.203-206). Corte's advice, through Bedingfield, is a little different and recommends that 'from the knees down let you legs be loose and at free liberty'.[172] As he then goes on to warn against the rider's legs tipping him too far forward or backward, it would seem that this method had its difficulties. Newcastle is aiming for an independent seat with a secure, deep, long-legged position so that the horse may move freely while the rider's lower leg is able to support, control and encourage its movement. The rider's posture on his horse should help create common, rather than individual, centres of gravity as if 'they had but one Body, and one Mind, like a Centaur' (1667: p.13).

His emphatic belief that the rider's legs should be 'not too far from the Horse's Sides, nor too near, that is, not to Touch them' is to prevent the horse being bumped and touched by mistake, as the aim is to teach it that every touch of the legs is an instruction (1667: p.204). This means that the rider's balance keeps him upon the horse by moving with the animal, rather than clinging to the reins or gripping tightly with the legs, in contrast with Pluvinel who advises that the rider's knees 'be squeezed with all one's strength'. Pluvinel's advice aims to make it 'impossible for the horse to inconvenience [the rider] nor make him lose his good posture'. This may reflect the formality of an earlier style or that Pluvinel is more interested in the young rider, who is perhaps not yet secure in his position, than the young horse. He does stress that if 'he is trying to school the horse', he may need to use different aids and change his position.[173]

Newcastle's advice that the rider should be 'Free and with all the Liberty in the world as […] in Dancing *A la negligence*' (1667: p.205) is very apt, as it illustrates both the harmonious interaction of horse and rider and the understanding that form and freedom go well hand in hand. The rider whose expression reflects confidence will transmit this through the relaxed ease of the riding position and so transmit calm leadership to the horse, which will be calm and responsive as a result.

As a final preparation for training, both manuals include very similar versions of the lengthy and somewhat bewildering discussion of 'all the Natural Paces, and Actions of a Horses Leggs' (1667: p.145), possibly inspired by the work of Robert Payne, as discussed above. In the first manual, for the purposes of illuminating a very complex discussion, Newcastle uses diagrams of hoof prints to show the positioning of the horse's feet. The second of these seems to suggest that the horse has six

---

172   Bedingfield, p.34.
173   Pluvinel, pp.26-27.

legs (1658: p.44; 1743: p. 33). However, the first diagram illustrates a natural stance, followed by the movement of the horse's forelegs to one side then the other of a notional circle, called a 'volte', which is the smallest circle a horse can travel with its feet making two parallel tracks. Thus one foreleg moves inside the volte and is not illustrated and what the diagram is actually illustrating is this movement to both left and right. This illustrates the level of horsemanship to which Newcastle is aspiring, with floor patterns to show precise positioning as well as general direction. His method enables the rider to communicate with the horse directly through its acute sensitivity to touch and this awareness of the capacity for subtle response in the horse makes him an innovator.

This innovation also extends to training the rider to a subtle understanding. A rider who can feel where each hoof is on the ground at any given moment can achieve a much greater level of precision. To begin to feel, the rider must understand what is happening beneath him and the discussion on 'Natural Paces', while undoubtedly difficult to follow, is attempting to translate feeling into text in a very new way. While Newcastle uses humour to enliven the technical detail in his image of the would-be acolyte, manual-in-hand upon his horse, he is reminding his reader that his method can be used exactly as written, in a fully practical way. Therefore, 'Now that you are on Horse-back, Know how to sit, and Know all your Helpes; I will shew you How to Dress your Horse Perfectly' (1667: p. 208).

Before the rider can start to follow Newcastle's exercises, he must first understand the workings of his cavesson, the great technical innovation of Newcastle's method. Surprisingly, in neither manual is this equipment given the hyperbolic attention one might except from a man so quick to praise his own new techniques. Although the cavesson features consistently throughout the method, its initial introduction is casual. It is nevertheless emphasised as a vital piece of equipment which 'is to Stay, to Raise and to make the Horse Leight; to Teach him to Turn, to Stop, to Firm his Neck, to Assure and Adjust his Head, and his Croup, without Offending his Mouth' (1667: p.156).

The use of a cavesson noseband with reins tied to a pillar had a long history by the seventeenth century and Newcastle refined and developed this method. In using the rope tied to a fixed point or points, the horse learned by experience that it could not leap beyond the length of the rope, but without any damage to its sensitive mouth. Over time it would refine its movements to avoid working against the rope so the desired precision would be reached. Then the bit would be introduced and the horse moved on to the next level of training. It would then, in theory, respond similarly by not pulling against the rider's hands but accepting the light check of the bit. Newcastle takes this idea and puts the reins of the cavesson into the rider's hands, passing them through rings on the noseband, rather than fixed points, and then rings near the rider's knees. The horse cannot tear the reins from the rider's hands, because its strength is diffused through the rings by the rider's knees. Thus the rider's control of the reins is much more sensitive and refined than tying them to a pillar, which Newcastle does not introduce until much later in the training, when the horse has already learned to respond to pressure.

The rider is thus in the position to use pressure and release on the reins, beginning with slight lateral and vertical flexion which may be increased as the horse understands and grows more flexible. While there is potential for disaster here, Newcastle is not writing for the inexperienced, as he makes clear in his address 'Aux Cavaliers'. He also claims that 'je puis luy commander d'avantage avec deux doigts en cettre sorte qu'on ne fera des deux mains en l'autre' (1658: p.47).[174] Therefore any danger of over bending or anxiety on the horse's part could easily be remedied and because a light touch was sufficient, the overall refinement is greater.

E. Schmit-Jensen says, 'Newcastle has often been criticized for this extreme flexion of the horse's head and neck, but it is obvious that he knew how to employ it advantageously'. He adds 'it is clear that he also succeeded in suppling the horse's back', noting that 'once the horse's back functions properly, everything else in training becomes comparatively easy'.[175] Newcastle advises the rider not to have the rein too long or short 'car l'un ou l'autre perd les forces du Cavalier' (1658: p.48).[176] If the rein were too long, the neck would not flex sufficiently to work the horse's muscles, but if too short, then the horse would be inclined to simply bend at the neck, whereby control of the hindquarters is lost and the benefit of the exercise lost.

This is not the same as the draw-rein, a much older device, which pulls the horse's head down with equal pressure on each side through the bit-rings. Newcastle calls this the 'Perpendicular-Line' and having explained that it 'works extreamly upon the Curb […] to pull his Head Down', he says emphatically, 'This I never use' but that he 'thought fit to Tell you what it is, and the Effects of it' to illustrate the difference from his own technique (1667: p.175).

Newcastle's method takes the principal of the draw-rein and uses it laterally instead of vertically, from the cavesson rather than the bit, and only ever in one hand, rather than forcing the head down with two. The impact upon the horse is completely different as any equipment such as a draw-rein ultimately forces the horse into the required position, thereby undermining the aim of self-carriage. This is because it encourages the horse to 'go horribly upon the shoulders, though their Heads be Down', rather than engaging the hind-quarters which, as Newcastle is fond of saying, 'is the End of all our Labour, and the Quintessence of our Art' (1667: pp.265-266).

In using the cavesson in the exercises that follow, Newcastle flexes the horse's neck so that its head is turned toward the shoulder, changing sides regularly to ensure that muscle is developed equally. His cavesson teaches the horse to flex laterally with mobility between the jaw and neck, rather than the jack-knife flexion between the shoulder and the lower-neck. The purpose of this is to create a finished, that is fully trained, animal which is supple through its neck and shoulder and ultimately

---

174   'I have greater command over him with two fingers in this method than with both hands by the common method' (1743: p.35).

175   Introduction to Allen facsimile of *General System,* 1743, already cited, p.2.

176   'The power of the rider is diminished'(1743: p.35).

through its back. This is very difficult for the horse due to the construction of its spine, which is a fairly rigid structure to support the heavy contents of the body. If the spine were more flexible, it would not be possible to ride the horse but training works towards the maximum flexibility possible. Most of the spinal movement is in the neck and tail areas and the apparent bending of a horse upon a circle is due to the mobility between the cervical vertebrae, the movement of the rib cage and the freedom of movement available to the front legs, which can adduct and abduct in relation to the body. This is best observed by watching a horse attempt to reach around to scratch its own back, a very awkward movement which illustrates just how little flexibility there is between the shoulders and the croup. Indeed while there is a very small amount of lateral movement between the thoracic and lumbar vertebrae, there is none in the sacral area, and this is one of the reasons that horses engage in 'mutual grooming', where each scratches the other's back. There is no other author prior to Newcastle who uses a method such as this, and it suggests a close understanding of the way the horse's spine works, perhaps arising from the work with Payne.[177]

Clearly the technical aspects of the manuals are hard to follow to the non-rider, but a level of understanding is important to appreciate their value as practical working documents. The training plates (numbers 14-29; 36-37) in the first manual follow the text, illustrating in accurate technical detail the points that Newcastle makes. They demonstrate the practical application of the method in a way that is helpful to the lay-person, as well as the rider. The plates begin with the perfect seat of the rider (Plate 14), and then illustrate key points in the progressive training method. Marginal notes in the text in the first manual direct the reader to the correct plates and some of the plates have a page reference. By following the training method in the text with reference to the plates, both their technical accuracy and the way Newcastle uses them to clarify the detail in the written instruction becomes clear.

The first stage of basic training, once the young horse is at ease with a rider and moving forward willingly is 'to Supple his Shoulders [...] for that is the Foundation of all things in the Mannage' (1667: p.209). These lessons develop confidence, flexibility and self-carriage and lay the groundwork for the next stage. Newcastle starts by explaining how to use the cavesson for the most benefit then details a series of lessons with great precision. In Plates 15 and 16, the horse has a bit in its mouth but is being ridden from Newcastle's cavesson. Captain Mazin holds the cavesson reins with 'les ongles de la main droite en haut, & le petit doight vers l'épaule' (1658: p.48), using the subtlest flexing of the rider's hands to influence the horse's movements.[178] This is particularly clear in the Plate 15 exercise, 'Trot a Droite'. Although the back of Mazin's hand is towards the reader, it can be seen to be turning slightly upwards.

---

177   See Peter C. Goody, *Horse Anatomy: A Pictorial Approach to Equine Structure* (London: J. A. Allen, 1983), for a detailed but accessible analysis of the horse's body.

178   'with the nails of your hand directed upwards to the left shoulder' (1743: p.41); In the 1667 manual, pp.176-177 the position of the hands is dealt with in great detail in the explanation of 'helps', but then not addressed in the individual exercises. This loses some of the clarity of the earlier text but reflects the overall style of the second text.

Turning the hand so that the finger nails are upwards brings the rein under a different tension than if the hand is straight, but without the rider shortening its length. He is encouraging a rounding of the horse through light pressure on the cavesson via the rein, rather than forcing it with brute strength. This is also clear in Plate 15, where the horse's shape is rounded and driving forward from the large muscles of the haunches, with the different paces illustrated to show the progression of the exercise. The slight rotation of the hand adds more subtlety of movement than a direct lift. It also enables the rider to move the reins without needing to lift the arm from the elbow, simply rotating it at the wrist, which 'Works the same Effect' (1667: p.166). The purpose of this movement is to flex the horse laterally at the neck, encourage suppleness throughout the body, and prevent the horse from falling onto its forehand and effectively pulling itself forward, rather than carrying its weight on its haunches. This difference has a considerable effect on the ability of the horse to move elegantly and efficiently. All the exercises in Plate 15 illustrate using this principle at the walk, the trot and the *galop*, showing that the rein remains a very similar length throughout, while the horse is balanced and Mazin's arm remains in position.[179]

The rider's legs are positioned to help the horse curve through the body. Therefore, once the horse's neck is correctly positioned, Newcastle instructs that the rider 'doit aider son cheval doucement de la jambe droite, ce qui mettra la crouppe dehors, & en mesme temps travaillera les épaules, mais nõ plus que la moitié de la crouppe ; car l'autre moitié est perduë, puis que le Cavalier n'en at aucun sentiment' (1658: p.48).[180] His belief that at any one time the exercises can work both the horse's shoulders, but only one side of the croup is a little confusing. By the very nature of the horse's physique, every movement affects the whole body to some extent. Newcastle seems to be focussing here on the tendency of the hindquarters to drift outwards so that the outside rear hind can work with less effort. If the rider were to attempt to keep the hindquarters in position with the outside leg, this would influence the rider's body alignment, which is crucial in maintaining the desired position. As the rider's outside leg is bringing the outside shoulder in, and the horse's inside foreleg passes in front of and crosses the outside foreleg due to the direction of travel, then both shoulders will work efficiently. His instruction that the rider should 'bring in your outward Shoulder moderately' (1667: p.177) when the horse is working the circle, reinforces the importance of the body as an aid, as the turn inward would influence the rider's weight and pelvis position, which would influence the horse's response. This capitalises on the horse's instinct to seek leadership. When the horse is sufficiently educated and

---

179   The term 'canter', referring to the three-beat pace that is the natural progression from the trot was not used in the riding house in the early modern period. This pace was known as the *galop* (also spelled *gallop*). In the manège, the sprint speed of the true gallop would be inappropriate in terms of available space and the aim of graceful dance-like movement, while the two-beat trot and four beat walk do not offer the moments of suspension and dynamism which the *galop*, or canter, exploits.

180   'He should touch his horse gently with the right leg, which will force his croup outwards, and work his shoulders at the same time, but only half of his croupe, the other being lost the rider having no feeling of it'(1743: p.35).

the rider suitably competent, a close unity is achieved. Therefore, a change in the rider's position will encourage the horse to maintain the unit in balance and adjust its position accordingly for its physical and psychological comfort.

A development of this use of the cavesson and the circles is the movement known as a 'shoulder-in', whereby the horse's shoulders move off the parallel track with its hind quarters so that it makes either two or three tracks, rather than one, depending on the degree of the angle. This is another of Newcastle's innovations, a movement not used in this manner before his time, but one taken up and refined further by the 18th Century French master, François Robichon de la Guérinière, to whom it is often attributed. The significance of the shoulder-in is largely to do with the development in expressive lateral movement, especially in the hind legs. Michael J. Stevens considers that 'this exercise is one of the most useful available to the trainer. It supples the shoulders, encourages engagement and strengthens the hocks [...] as the horse is made to curve his body round in front of the inside hind leg so that this hind leg does more than its usual amount of work and is the prime limb for propelling the horse along'.[181]

Newcastle devotes considerable detail to discussing the position of the horse's feet and, in the first manual, uses diagrams of concentric circles to illustrate the tracks made by the hooves. He is working for precision and concerned that the rider should not achieve an appearance of correctness while failing to actually achieve the true suppleness desired. This is shown especially well in walk and trot exercises in Plate 15, where it may be seen that the horse's raised hind foot will step down just inside the track of its forefoot on the same side.

This plate also shows the rider's use of weight and focus assist the horse to maintain the correct position, as discussed above. In the exercises where the horse is travelling to the right, that is, on the right hand, Mazin's body is turned slightly into the circle, most clearly in 'Au pas a Gauche' and 'Trot a Droite'. In the exercises on the left hand, this is evident from the visibility of his left elbow. Therefore, the rider's seat bones and body alignment follow the direction intended and the horse will naturally follow because all its instincts are to carry weight upon its back in the most balanced position. It will also follow the rider's body language and tend thus to focus its own attention, either physically or visually depending on the exercise, in the direction of the rider's gaze. While Mazin appears to be looking straight ahead in 'Au pas a Droite', the horse is not as close to the pillar he is using for reference, as in 'Au pas a Gauche', where he looks into the circle. Therefore, it appears that in 'Au pas a Droite', he is moving the horse into position by directing his focus that way.

Plate 15 follows the principles of suppling through the walk, trot and *galop*, with hoof prints on the ground illustrating the path the horse will take in completing the exercise. The pillar in the walk exercises is to enable the horse to keep its position and the horse is worked on both hands, that is to the right and left, to aid even muscle development. In the first manual, he repeats the instructions for

181   Michael J. Stevens, *A Classical Riding Notebook* (Buckingham: Kenilworth Press, 1994), p.62.

each exercise on both hands, while in the second he simply instructs the rider that 'For the Left-Hand […] do in everythyng, as I told you before for the Right-Hand' (1667: 284-285). This is part of his movement away from the step-by-step approach of the first manual, and while not always helpful, in this instance is an effective way of streamlining the text.

Plate 16 moves the horse to the next level, as it works off the circle, though still using the cavesson reins. The images in this plate are particularly useful in showing the progression through one exercise at the trot and *galop*, as explained in detail in both manuals (1658: pp.48-58; 1667: pp.208-213). This illustrates one of Newcastle's main methods of progression, namely to bring the horse to a place where it naturally wishes to move to the next stage. When trotting, the horse will reach the point where he is 'so Leight, as he offers to gallop of himself' (1667: p.209), as this is the next natural gait. He is then ready to move on to performing the exercises at the *galop* without any additional pressure being put upon him.

If the images in Plate 16 are viewed from the centre to the outside of the plate in both phases of the exercise, it may be seen very clearly that Captain Mazin is preparing the horse to turn and go in the opposite direction. His weight is further back in the images to the outsides of the plate and he prepares to turn his body, thus shifting his weight to encourage the horse to take more of its own weight on the haunches and pivot, allowing the forehand freedom to change direction. It may also be seen that the hand holding the flexed position of the head has moved higher and slightly closer to his body. The hand to the outside of the turn is on the reins attached to the bit, and will use them to support the horse's neck and shoulder through the turn. These first training plates establish that the images are not simply an approximation of the movement, part illustration, part decoration, but a highly technical and accurate depiction of the exact nature of the horse and rider relationship to accomplish a complicated exercise.

Newcastle does not illustrate his method of stopping the horse, as it is straightforward to follow in the text. He again uses attention to detail to ensure that the horse is inevitably going to work on lightness and bring its haunches underneath its body. This is highly important as 'to make him Capable of all Justness and Firmness in all sort of ayres, and Mannages; Depends absolutely on the perfection on the Stop'. Obtaining a firm halt may be done by teaching the horse to go backwards and will help 'to put him on his Hanches; to Accommodate, and Adjust his Hinder-Feet' as when being asked to stop, the horse must drop its hind quarters a little, applying its natural brakes, in a similar way as it would to go backwards. The rider should 'put your Body Back to put him upon the Hanches', to assist in this, and remember with a young horse to 'Stop him but seldom; and when you do, Stay him rather by Little and Little' until he is stronger and more balanced. Without due care in this 'you will give them such a Crick and Taint in their Back, as they will never Recover it' (1667: pp.210, 220, 238).

After working the shoulders and establishing a secure balanced halt, attention moves to the horse's croup or hind-quarters, with the exercises illustrated in Plate 17. It is more difficult for a horse to supple its hindquarters, due in part to the huge muscle bulk, which would be increased by the work on the haunches that Newcastle advocates. The muscles in a horse's hindquarters are the source of its forward motion, therefore to abduct and adduct them takes effort. Newcastle's lessons to supple the croup all work on the crossing of the feet, which he explains in detail, particularly in the first manual:

> Le cheval va icy en passager ou *Incavallare*, qui est croiser une jambe sur
> l'autre : mais parce que le cheval est sur l'action du trot, en laquelle ses jambes
> se remuënt en croix, il met, ou croise le bras de dehors par dessus celuy de
> dedans, & au mesme temps il avance la jambe de dedans ; le mouvement
> suivant, il avance le bras de dedans, & croise la jambe de dehors par dessus
> celle de dedans. Ensorte qu'en cette action, en lacquelle il remuë ses jambes en
> croix, il est impossible qu'il croise le bras & la jambe de dehors en mesme
> temps, par dessus le bras & la jambe de dedans, mais il les croise l'une par
> dessus l'autre chaque second mouvement (1658: p.62).[182]

While it may be difficult to read this section without envisaging the horse in a complicated knot of its own legs, at its simplest explanation, Newcastle is saying that a horse moves its legs on the basis of opposed diagonals. The reason for his somewhat bewildering use of detail is so that the rider understands the positioning of the legs in order to achieve the required end. If the horse is worked incorrectly, the muscle development will not be suitable for the more advanced manoeuvres to come.

Plate 17 illustrates that the lessons for working the horse's croupe encourage the horse to move the hind legs laterally, as well as forward and back, enhancing his athletic ability. The capacity to cross the hind legs when travelling directly sideways or on a circle, makes a great difference to the range of movement of the horse, but takes a considerable amount of practice. Newcastle is aiming to enable the horse to free up this motion, through a range of specific exercises. These start by using the wall as a psychological barrier to prevent forward movement, with the horse working at a right angle to and along it, its neck flexed in the direction it is travelling. This is less restrictive than if the barrier were physically provided by the rider's hand, via the bit.

---

182 'A horse in this action passages, which is, to lap one leg over another; but because he is on the action of the trot, in which he moves his legs crossways, he places or crosses the outward fore-leg over the inward and at the same time he advances the inward hind-leg; the next step he advances the inward fore-leg, and crosses the outward hind-leg over the inward, so that it is impossible for him in this action to cross both his near-legs at the same instant over his off-ones; but he crosses them one over the other every second movement'(1743: p.41); *Incavallare* is accepted Italian terminology in the riding house from Grisone's time, meaning 'to lap one thing over another'; see also 1667: p.222; Blundeville sig. F7ᵛ.

Plate 17 illustrates this to the right hand side of the page. The horse is required to cross its legs directly to the side, whereas in the next stage, on the left hand side of the page, the exercises around the pillar, the legs are moving on a circle also. The circle is much more difficult, hence the more straightforward use of the wall until the horse understands its task. Newcastle focuses on making the desired movement easy and any other difficult, so that the horse's natural inclination enables success.

The images in Plate 17 again show in Captain Mazin's position how the weight and body alignment of the rider assist the horse by turning in the direction the horse is moving. In the 'Au pas a sa Longeur a Droite', the crossing of the left hind foot in front of the right hind may be seen very clearly. The floor patterns show that the horse is turning in a small circle in its own length, that is around a fixed notional centre. The pillar is used in much the same way as the wall, so that each time the horse encounters the pillar, to avoid it, it will correct its position, supported by the rider's aids. The rider must use the 'Inward Reyn, and Outward Legg' (1667: p.222), effectively balancing the horse between the rein and the leg. It may be helpful to consider that a horse is sensitive enough to feel a fly land on its skin. This sensitivity can be dulled by rough handling but Newcastle is focused on retaining this quality to enable the final polished work on a fully trained horse to be so refined that the audience cannot see the cues given by the rider. He advises that the rider should 'not help every time, but (in Musical time), according to the time of the horse' (1667: p.291). This advocacy of intermittent stimuli, the 'helps' or in modern terms 'aids', in time with the rhythm of the horse's pace, is more effective than constant pressure which the horse's brain will eventually ignore. He will then become unresponsive to hand or spur, 'for then he will not Care for them no more than a Stone or a Block' (1667: p.185).

The next progression is the terra a terra, literally 'ground-to-ground', a rocking-horse motion, where the horse moves forward and sideways slightly, illustrated in Plate 18. Newcastle frequently uses the term synonymously with the *petit gallop* (1667: pp.228, 230, 231), which is helpful in defining the movement as similar to a highly collected canter, indicating the perfect balance of the horse and rider partnership. Newcastle is aware that this is a complicated exercise and in the first manual refers back to previous line diagrams 'de peur de vous énnuyer de plusieures repetitions'.[183] In both, he allows for small steps of progress, illustrating his points with analogies to illuminate the points he is making. When discussing the physique necessary in 'Leaping Horses', he illustrates that muscular strength and ability do not necessarily go together by saying:

> Take one of the Guard, the Strongest Fellow that is, and I will bring a Little Fellow
> that shall Out Leap him many a Foot: yet that Strong Fellow would crush that

---

183   'lest I should offend you by many repetitions' (1743: p.56). The spelling of terra a terra varies between the different editions.

Little Fellow to Death with his Armes: So 'tis not Strength but Disposition fits
Horses for Leaping (1667: p.277).

He moves on through the fourth and fifth division of lessons very swiftly in comparison with
the earlier exercises, as the horse is much more advanced in its training and he is now moving towards
riding off the long-shanked bit, which operates on the basis of leverage on the horse's poll and jaw. The
plates illustrate this important progression, which is reinforced by the detail that Newcastle himself
now rides, it being appropriate for the master to take over the instruction of the most advanced airs.

In light hands, use of the shanked bit is a refined and precise method. However, in untrained
hands, it is capable of putting the horse's head in a vice-like restriction. This is why the detail of
the loose reins in Newcastle's plates, as well as those of Pluvinel, illustrates the understanding that
the weight of the rein on the branches of the bit should be sufficient contact. Ann Hyland, whose
authoritative work on the history of the horse in war involves considerable practical exploration,
says that when using a Tudor period bit that although 'used harshly the thin chain would have been
painful,' her Arab stallion 'went extremely well in this bit, but he was on a loose rein, as were the
horses shown in Newcastle's work.' The bit Hyland used in this experiment was very similar to the
bit shown in the centre in Plate 39.[184]

All the earlier lessons are moving towards the step whereby the cavesson is removed and
the horse is worked off the bit alone, having achieved sufficient flexibility and strength to hold its
posture without the assistance of the training-aid. Newcastle is careful to add exercises by which
'vous connoîtrez asseurement si vous l'avez bien travaillé sur les premieres leçons, ou non' (1658:
p. 96).[185] This is crucial if the horse is not to be over-challenged, and to ensure that the precision of
each exercise is accurate to prevent injury or, perhaps worse to the early modern rider, loss of face
in performance (1658: p.97).

Plate 20 illustrates the horse working off the bit and Newcastle takes over for the advanced
stages of the training. The rotation of the wrist is especially clear in 'De pas a Main Gauche de
la Longeur' as Newcastle's fingers are visible; similarly in the 'Terre à terre a Main Gauche'. Also
note that in both terra a terra images, Newcastle uses his body position to direct the horse, looking
over his shoulder, thus putting weight on the seat bone in the direction of movement. The backward
movement of his weight in doing this acts as a brake without him touching the horse's mouth, so that
it is effectively rocked back on its haunches which will not interfere with its self-carriage. He also uses
the rhythm of the movement 'car le petit gallop divertit le cheval, & les cadences de terre à terre le sont

---

184   *The Warhorse 1250-1600*, p. 8-9; Bitting is a complex and technical subject with considerable implications for the
horse's comfort and the training process. For an accessible further explanation, aimed at riders, see Greg Darnell, *A Bit of
Information* (Colorado: Western Horseman Inc., no date).
185   'You will be able to judge absolutely whether he has been worked right upon his first lessons, or not'(1743: p.57).

obeïr à la main & aux talons, & lors qu'on le remet au petit galop, il obeït à la main aux talons : aynsy on le rendrea cheval parfaitment obeïssant à la main & aux talons' (1658: p. 96).[186] This is natural and relaxing to the horse so its desire to work at that pace will enable it to quickly learn the 'helps' which signal the pace at which it is comfortable. He goes into greater detail on this point in the first manual and in the second says 'And thus Working with the Bitt, Produces many Excellent things, for Terra a Terra, as I have particularly set down afore' (1667: p.171). As at this point in the second manual he has dealt only briefly with the terra a terra, he appears here to refer his reader back to the earlier text. The precision with which the plates illustrate the detail of the terra a terra, where the gestures of the rider's head, position of his body and depiction of his fingers are all accurate, goes far beyond any earlier manual in illuminating the method.

The final lessons in this advanced groundwork are all to 'finir un cheval parfaitement dans le Manege' (1658: p.112)[187] and 'to put them upon the Hanches, which is the Master-Piece of our Art' (1667: p.269). This indicates that the basic training is perfected and the horse is fully able to undertake displays in the riding house, including the 'demy-airs', which are the intermediate moves in which two legs remain upon the ground, as opposed to the airs above the ground in which all four feet leave it. The terra a terra is a key feature of these exercises, as it approaches the airs above the ground in its motion without demanding too much of the horse. As this first challenging and complicated stage of the training draws to a close Newcastle is at pains to point out that 'il faut plus de papier à écrire ces leçons, & plus de temps à les lire qu'à les practiquer' (1658: p. 116).[188]

Newcastle's athletic training works alongside his understanding of horses as thinking, feeling creatures. His knowledge of the horse's anatomy enables him to train in a very specific way, allowing for the animal's intelligence and ability to recognise subtle signals of weight and pressure from 'the Hand and the Heel, which makes them all Perfect [...] and never Fails me' (1667: p.004).[189] With this method, he assures his reader that once a horse is sufficiently mature, 'having both Understanding and Strength' so that he will 'learn much Sooner and Better', then 'I can [...] Make him a Ready-Horse in three Months'(1667: p.202). The horse must be of 'si bien dispose', reiterating the point made earlier that not all horses are suited for this intense training, which illustrates that his approach is not mechanical, but based on each horse's strengths and abilities. Moreover, the horse must be in good hands. If those hands are as capable as his own, or Captain Mazin's, then his reader is unlikely to fail with any horse at all. Newcastle reinforces this by reminding his reader in the first manual

---

186 'For the gentle gallop pleases the horse, and the times of the Terre-à-terre make him obey the hand and heel; and thus he is made perfectly obedient to both' (1743: p.57).

187 'to perfectly finish a Horse for the Manege'(1743: p.65).

188 'it requires more paper to write these lessons, and more time to read them, than to put them into practice'(1743: p.67).

189 The 1667 manual has additional pages, numbered 001-040, inserted between pp. 342 and 347.

that he uses this method with continual success himself and that he has seen Captain Mazin succeed with a variety of horses:

> [...] soi foibles, soit forts, mediocres, de toutes humeurs, de toute nature, & de disposition differente, chevaux Hongres, Cavalles, des grands & gros chevaux, chevaux de taille mediocre, petits chevaux, & bidets, chevaux de tous pays, comme chevaux d'Espaigne, Pologne, Barbes, Turcs,Neapolitains, Roussins, Danois, & de touts sortes & diverses especes de chevaux de Flandres; pour les chevaux mélez (1658: p.117).

He adds, with unconscious irony, that Mazin failed only with those that fell sick, went lame, or died in his hands.[190] This strange mixed-bag of horses, including mares and ponies, perhaps for feisty ladies and boys to learn on, all benefited, he claims, from his new method, though he does not mention how Captain Mazin coped with what seems a heavy demand for his skills.

In preparing for the highly advanced moves, not suitable for all horses, Newcastle explains that the rider must 'in all Ayres follow the Strength, Spirit and Disposition of the Horse and do nothing against Nature; for Art is but to set Nature in Order, and nothing else' (1667: p.271). Choosing the air for which the chosen horse has a ready aptitude is emphasised many times and this illustrates why, in performance, a number of horses are used in turn, each displaying special skills 'unto which Nature hath most Fitted him' (1667: p. 272):

> I Rid first a Spanish-Horse, call'd Le Superbe, of Light-Bay [...] he went in Corvets forwards, backwards, sideways, on both Hands; The second Horse I Rid, was another Spanish Horse, call'd Le Gentry [......] No Horse ever went Terra a Terra like him, so just and so easie [...] The third and last Horse I Rid then, was a Barbe, that went a Metz-Ayre, very High, both Forward, and upon his Voltoes (1667: sig. c^v-c).

In this advanced training, he goes back to working the horse in hand, this time around the pillar. The use of the single, rather than double pillars is another significant change between Newcastle's methods and those of Pluvinel. He ends his final section of lessons in the 1658 manual with 'Discourse sur les deux piliers (1658: p.235), which effectively undermines this key method of Pluvinel's training, though without any mention of his rival's name. His argument is that two pillars are restricting and

---

190 'proper disposition'; 'the weak, the strong, those of moderate strength, of all humours and natures, and of all different dispositions; Hungarian horses, mares, great large horses, middle-sized ones, little ones, poneys, horses of all countries, Spaniards, Polanders, Barbs, Turks, Neopolitans, Danes, all sorts of Flanders horses and horses of mix'd breeds' (1743: p.67). A more satisfactory translation of the 1658 'Hongres', in the context of this paragraph, would be 'geldings'.

make the horse dependent upon their support. Experience and observation are always the basis for Newcastle's arguments and he believes that one pillar allows the novice horse support without restriction, thus encouraging freedom of expression in the horse's athleticism.

This is illustrated in Plate 24, where the horse is worked in hand to prepare for the curvet. Blundeville describes this movement as 'a continual prauncynge and dauncynge uppe and downe stil in one place, and sometime sydelynge to and fro, wherin the horse maketh as though he would fain runne'.[191] It has changed greatly over the years and today is a series of leaps forward on the hind legs. It is also 'that motion which the Italians call Corvette or Pesate',[192] so that the terms are sometimes used interchangeably in the early modern manuals. This can also cause difficulties in analysis, as images of the curvet and pesade in practice resemble a modern levade, as discussed in Chapter 1. Newcastle says, 'if you raise him high, and he does not advance it is a Pesade and not a Curvet', thus distinguishing between the two, whereas Bedingfield uses the terms synonymously. For Newcastle, however, the pesade is still a dynamic movement, unlike a levade, as he uses it every few steps upon a circle:

> Raise him as high as you can, and Hold him there Gently […], and Walk him away
> again, and Raise him again, and do this all along the Volto, and this is a right
> Pesate (1667: p.018).

This is because he believes that making a horse work in place without forward motion of any sort must be used with caution because it can make the horse restive and impatient, due to the dynamic gathering of energy in the movement. As he explains 'the Ayre of Corvets gives a Horse Patience with Discreet Riding' but 'I have seldom seen that Discreet Riding'(1667: p. 272).[193]

In Plates 23 and 24, training for this movement begins in hand so that the horse can learn without the weight of the rider, being prompted by taps from the poinson, a short stick with an iron point at the end of it. This simulates the aids given once the rider is in place, so the handler should 'le piquer doucement de son petit poinçon à l'endroit des éperons' (1658: p.133).[194] A second handler taps the horse on either side of the shoulders with a switch to shift its weight backwards and raise the forehand. Newcastle explains that the single pillar is useful here because, without the restriction of the second pillar, once he understands the movement, the horse 'go upon his Voltoes perfectly […] which

---

191   Blundeville, Book II, sig. M2.
192   Bedingfield, p.46.
193   The pesade as described by both authors cited is a dynamic preparation for forward movement, rather than a maintained position, and, while offering the same suggestion of perfect balance and control as the levade, also implies a gathering of energy. Therefore, I would suggest that the semiotic value of the familiar fine art image of a rider on a horse performing a pesade is as much about his own dynamism as about his ability to control the horse's energy.
194   'prick him gently in the spurring place'(1743: p.71).

I never saw but this Way' (1667: p.280). Note that the groom holding the rope tied to the pillar has it looped around twice. This means that should the horse panic, the rope can be released quickly, but if the horse simply puts up some resistance, the rope cannot be pulled through the groom's hands. This is yet another illustration both of the subtlety of Newcastle's method and the accuracy of the plates, which offer good working practice, not an idealised or unrealistic expectation.

Plates 25 and 26 illustrate the progression through the advanced training exercises. Newcastle advises that 'you must put your Body a little Forward' (1667: p.207) when working in airs where the horse raises the forehand, so that the addition of a man's weight on his haunches does not restrict its freedom of movement. The plates and the text of both manuals continue to work in this detailed, precise way and once the foundation of the curvet is established, the high airs, although exceptionally difficult to perform well, are built one after the other with relatively little additional information being designed for the advanced horse. However, it is also likely that Newcastle chooses to withhold his most important secrets to maintain his uniqueness, 'for, to make them go in Perfection in all Ayres as I can, were too much and too great a Miracle'(1667: p.48).

The less exalted rider's position may require some moderation in the high airs, so that he does not inadvertently 'rather make the horse fling himself forward than make a regular leap'. To ride a horse performing the high airs requires great skill also, for safety and grace so that 'when you Raise him, instantly put your Brest out, which makes your Shoulders go a little back (though insensibly) to the Beholders' (1667: p. 295). The rider should never forget that this is a performance art with the need to appear before an audience in complete harmony with a horse whose skill attests to the rider's own grace and dedication.

In both manuals, Newcastle includes a section on 'all the FAULTS & ERRORS THE HORSE Can commit; with the Vices, and Horse's Sins in the MANNAGE', including 'How to Cure him' (1667: p. 299). Vices in this sense are errors or perceived disobediences that reduce the effectiveness of the method and these remedial exercises revisit earlier stages of the training and anticipate ways in which the horse may develop bad habits. They offer a number of exercises for each 'vice' both to refocus the horse and also for riders who 'en voiant, imitent & penser monter à ma mode' (1658: p.202).[195] Newcastle is aware that riders, like their horses, may try to take the easy way out in training, so explains why following his method without fully understanding or taking the time needed for precision will not work. His indignation comes through strongly at 'many presumptuous Fellows, as Ignorant as they are Presumptuous that Laughing, say, They will make any horse a Leaping-Horse' (1667: p.317) or attempt to 'faire choses impossibles & contre nature'.[196] Although it is clear throughout his training that Newcastle is strict with his horses, and tolerates no rebellion, he believes 'more Horses are Spoil'd

---

195   'by seeing imitate, and imagine they ride as I do' (1743: p.103).
196   'perform impossibilities, and things contrary to nature' (1743: p.104).

by ill Riding, and are made Vitious, than by Nature' (1667: p.308).

Faced with a 'resty' horse, Newcastle advises that 'Il faut un peu le forcer, mais pas long-temps; ca on le rendroit pire'. As his method throughout advocates, the rider must assert himself, but not attempt to intimidate the horse which can only result in panic and injury to both:

> Je n'ay point encore vue que la force, & la passion aient gagné quoy que ce soit sur
> un cheval ; car le cheval aiant moins d'entendement quele cavalier, sa passion en
> est plus forte , tellement qu'il l'emporte toûjours sur le Cavalier, ce qui fait
> qu'aucune violence n'a d'effet sur luy (1658: p.205).[197]

He advocates brisk use of the spurs, with a cool head rather than temper, for all resistances, 'for this Remedy never fails' (1667: p.307). The rider must 'leave not Spurring of him […] until he Obey you: […] and if he Obey you in the least Kind, Cherish him, and make Much of him' (1667: p.185). Pluvinel does not devote any particular attention to vices but does recommend a similar method to Newcastle in explaining that 'the horse will know that if he does not move he will be pricked, and that if he moves he will pricked neither by the valet nor by the little stick'. This 'serves as the rowel of a spur'[198] in the same way as Newcastle's poinson, and relies upon the same principle that the horse is taught to move away from pressure without being terrified or tormented.

This is in sharp contrast to methods by earlier authors, the most infamous being Grisone's 'shrewed catte teyed at the one end of a long pole' to be thrust 'betwixt his thyes so as she may scratch him' and the 'shirle crye of a hedgehog beinge strayt teyed by the foote under the Horse's tayle'. According to Blundeville this method was efficacious in making a horse belonging to the King of Naples that refused to go forward have a sudden change of heart and unsurprisingly 'he had as much a do afterwards to kepe him from the contraye vice of running away'.[199] The seemingly unconscious irony in these violent methods is that obviously they do not move the horse from an attitude of resistance to one of compliance. Remove the suffering hedgehog and once the horse has calmed down, the likelihood is it will be just as 'restie' again and probably also afraid of hedgehogs. The more thoughtful methods of Pluvinel and Newcastle are forceful reinforcements of their basic training, rather than extravagant gestures of domination. While unconcerned if he should draw blood from the horse when it is being rebellious, Newcastle also advocates swift rewards for compliance 'that he may see you

---

197   'He must be forc'd a little, but not long, because force will make him worse'; 'I have never yet seen that force
and passion have prevailed the least upon the horse: for the horse having less understanding than his rider, his passion is
so much the stronger, which makes him always get the better of the horseman, and shews that violent methods will not
do'(1743: p.105).
198   Pluvinel, p.69.
199   Blundeville, sig. E.ii[v].

have Mercy as well as Justice, and that you can Reward, as well as Punish'(1667: pp.184-185).

Newcastle's work in the riding house spanned youth to old age, when he would watch his equerries work, even when he had become too frail to ride himself. It is therefore unsurprising that his methods should change and progress over the years. The two manuals of 1658 and 1667 offer a useful illustration of the changes in ideas that happened over one decade. He does not ever explain or indeed refer to his changes in ideas from one manual to the next, except to refer readers of the second to the illustrations or further detail in the first and his belief that using 'both together' is the best way to proceed.

Most of the changes come in the early stages of the horses' life and training, suggesting they were making such swift progress that he found he could refine his techniques further. While in the first book, he suggests weaning between Michaelmas (September 29) and Christmas, by the second he is more specific in suggesting Martelmas (November 11). The earlier text suggests that for exercise the young horse may be walked in-hand 'au Soleil & à l'air dan quelque cour, ou quelque lieu palisse, affin qu'il s'ébatteent & recréent leurs éspris'(1658: p.27).[200] By the second, Newcastle has refined his methods so that on 'a Fair Day, let them then go Out in some Inclosed Yard, to Play and Rejoyce themselves' (1667: p. 94). This most likely reflects upon, with the passage of time, the discovery that even in a loose-box, young horses grow restless and are less likely to be troublesome to handle, or to hurt themselves through exuberance, if they are allowed out to play together when the weather is fine. The reason for 'this Housing every Winter' is to keep the horse with a fine coat and an appearance suitable for the manège. Living out all winter, the horse would grow a long coat and Newcastle does not approve of this, asking 'Is there any Thing in the World Looks so like a Bear, and so Ill-favouredly, as a Colt in Winter upon a Common, and stands as if he had neither Life nor Spirit?'(1667: p.95). In-wintering, however, requires attention to boredom and high spirits, 'good and fresh Litter for them, good Sweet Hay, and Wheat-bran, and good Oats' (1667: p.94) and the two manuals show how his ideas for best practice change with his own experience.

When it comes to riding the young colts, the first book recommends a quilted saddle at first, or one made of chaff or straw (1658: p.26), but by the second 'such a Saddle as you ordinarily ride Horses of Mannage in' (1667: p.94) is considered suitable. It may be that the change in management to increase activity has made the young horses more tractable, or that experience has shown that a horse which has been well-handled discerns little difference between an ordinary saddle and a lighter one of straw.

---

200   'In fine weather walk them in the sunshine about your court, that it may comfort and cherish their spirits' (1743: p.25).

Both the detailed way in which Newcastle progresses through his method and the remarkable precision of the plates in the first manual are innovative. The level of attention to the finer points of each exercise argues strongly for a long and careful working process in the preparation for publication, involving the artist, writer, horse and rider in detailed experimentation. The exercises are similar in both manuals and some are exactly word for word the same, though the layout is quite different.

In the second Newcastle focuses more attention on explaining the operation of the bridle, which may suggest that he had been asked questions that lead him to feel more detail was needed. He also reorders the second, so that the 'helps' are understood before the rider starts the training. Both of these revisions suggest that Newcastle assumes his readers have some familiarity with his method, and that he attempts to make it more accessible, though the success of this is arguable. However, without the greater tendency to digression, as discussed in the Chapter 2, it may be that the through line of the second manual would be equally clear, but it is also possible that the creative process involved in preparing text and plates to complement one another added to the clarity of the first text.

There are fewer exercises in the second manual overall, and more advice and opinion in some respects with less detail in others. However, the basic techniques are essentially the same, showing progression and development when they differ, rather than any radical change of direction. This suggests that Newcastle worked in a focused and personal way, little influenced by other ideas he must have experienced during his exile, due to the Continental interest in the art and during encounters throughout his life with other enthusiasts.

Therefore, his overall method is entirely practical. His advice on breeding and choosing a horse, his early handling recommendations and his gradual introduction of riding address the need for a sound, safe and manageable horse at every step. His advanced training introduces his innovative cavesson as a refinement of earlier techniques. He understands that the horse learns by repetition but that different horses may need different exercises and that while strong leadership is important, so is gentleness and a humane approach. The plates enable his reader to see the text in practice and understand the need for precision and excellence, as they are both technical and inspirational. Even though they are lacking in the second manual, he refers his reader back to them, seeing them as crucial. Practicality is all, and provides the evidence that 'my Method is True', which 'cannot better be Demonstrated, than by Experience, which will clearly show, That Mine never misses its End' (1667: p.41). He invites the reader to put him to the test, for he believes there is 'no other Philosophy but trying' (1667: p.28).

Chapter 5

'**Après l'homme le cheval est le plus noble animal':**
Newcastle and the horse's mind

Why maister of whome should you bee afraide,
I am able to justifye as much as you say.
Morocco to his master, Bankes,
Maroccus Extacticus

For it is a false assertion that the sense of man is the measure of things.
Francis Bacon, *Novum Organum*

Newcastle introduces his 1658 manual with a lengthy discussion on the horse's intelligence and powers of understanding, using the work of contemporary philosophers Thomas Hobbes and René Descartes as points of reference. In the 1667 manual, he reports that visitors to his riding house declared, 'my Horses were such, that they wanted nothing of Reasonable Creatures, but Speaking' (1667: sig. b2). Not only the texts of both manuals but also the letters of dedication and the engraved plates of 1658 reveal a carefully considered and consistent stance on the horse's nature.

In the 1658 introductory discussion, Newcastle declares that:

Nous n'avons que deux choses pour dresser un cheval parfaitement, qui sont, l'esperance de la récompense, & la crainte du châtiment, lesquelles gouvernent le monde. Et nous ne sçavons pas que Dieu ait autre chose pour éguillonner son peuple a la vertu, que la liberalité de ses salaires infiniz, & l'horreur des peines preparées à leur forfaits (1658: 'Avant-Propos').[201]

This analogy sets out his philosophy both for the training of the horse and the behaviour of the man towards it and forms the central motif for all that follows. As an ardent royalist, believing

---

201 'There are but two things that can make an accomplish'd horse, *viz.* the hope of reward, or the fear of punishment, which all the world are influenc'd by; and as far as we know, God has no other means of exciting his people to virtue, but by the largeness of his infinite rewards, and the terror of the pains that are prepar'd for their crimes'(1743: p.12).

passionately in the hierarchical model of leadership typified in the monarchy, Newcastle's relationship with his horses supported and underpinned all he believed in. As he states repeatedly, it is his practical experience that qualifies him to make these observations for the benefit of others. Also, he assumes a riding readership, who will not only share his love of the riding house but also understand that 'Il n'y a rien de semblage par pais, ou aux recontres publiques, soit pour l'usage, soit pour l'honneour' (1658: 'Mes Tres-Chers Fils').

Locating the nature of both usefulness and honour had changed from the earlier manuals. The art of the riding house elevated each rider to authority over a creature easily able to kill him by superior strength. Attempting to subdue that strength by sheer force was, in Newcastle's view, inviting not only danger and violence as a response, but also reducing the man to the level of an animal. Instead, to work with the horse and gain co-operation by means of strong but moderated authority reinforced the image of the rider as an artist, whose skill and perception made him the natural leader.

Newcastle argues that through interaction with the horse, man can experience a relationship that gives him the responsibilities and power that echo God's relationship with mankind. To Newcastle, winning the horse's trust goes essentially with a firm discipline, but does not imply indulgence, as he always insists that 'Fear doth Much; Love, Little' so the horse 'must Fear me, and out of that Fear, Love me, and so Obey me.' This is akin to the fear man feels for God, so is linked with respect, the acceptance of authority and the expectation of swift but just punishment, 'And thus they will Chuse the Reward and Shun the Punishment'(1667: p.196).

While he does not explicitly discuss the reclamation of a relationship lost with the Fall, this is implicit in his interest in establishing an appropriate relationship between man and the horse which counters the violent means proposed by others. Thus, infuriated by Blundeville's methods, he declares, 'He would have Us to Strike a Horse with a Cudgel or Rod, between the Ears, and upon the Head; which is Abominable, though he thinks it a Rare Secret.' (1667: pp.22-23). While Blundeville's advice always starts with a quiet approach, coaxing and 'continually cherishing him with your hand', if the horse does not understand or co-operate then beating him violently until he submits is the next step. To Newcastle, it is not the beating that offends so much as the pointlessness of it, because more thoughtful ways yield better results. Underestimation of the horse's intelligence reveals the limitations of man's own in a way that proves him unworthy of standing for God in this way.

To some extent Blundeville's expectation of the horse's understanding demands a reasoning power far more human than any argument put forward by Newcastle. With a horse that attempts to lie down crossing water, a 'natural disposition incident to that horse which is foled under the signe of Leo', he advocates four 'footmen with cogels' so that:

When the horse beginneth to lie down they may be readye to leape upon him and with the help of the rider to force him to ducke his heade downe under the water, so as the water may enter into his eares. Not suffering him to lift up his head again a good while together but make him by main force to kepe it stil under: continuallye beating him all the while with their cogels berating him with loude and terrible voices. That done, let him onelye life up his head to take take breath & aire. During which time cease not also to beat him still upon the heade […]

This should continue for some time, though Blundeville suggests not too long 'otherwise it were disorder', and then be repeated upon subsequent days until 'you shall see it will make him forget his lyinge downe and to pass through quietly', though adding a cord tied to the horse's testicles which 'the rider may straine and let go according as he see occasion', may be efficacious. Aside from the shock to modern sensibilities of this advice, its practicality is severely doubtful and injury inevitable to rider, horse and cudgel-bearers. However, what is most significant here, is that Blundeville believes that the horse will learn from 'the greefe' of the drowning along 'with the other corrections' that it should 'leave this vice'.[202] Thus he expects the horse to use deductive reasoning to conclude that the instinct to lie down causes the drowning.

Newcastle's approach, however, is to use spurs to drive a recalcitrant horse forward, based on his awareness that the horse's instinct to move away from pressure overcomes all other instincts. His method reveals an evident understanding of stimulus and response and the nature of a flight animal that simplifies the training method and makes it safer for all concerned. The specific mention of using spurs on 'a Horse that Falls down upon the Ground, or in the Water' (1667: p.307) suggests a deliberate counter to Blundeville.

His irritation at methods that will make the horse 'Ten times Worse' (1667: p.19) seems rooted both in the desire to 'dresser un cheval parfaitement' but also frustration at the way in which man reveals his own shortcomings by beating and spurring a horse that is 'tout à fait ignorant du Manège' (1658: 'Avant-Propos').[203]

Through insight into the horse's mind, not as that of an equal, but certainly as that of a thinking creature, Newcastle believes that man himself shows independence and courage. A right relationship with his horse ennobles man by giving god-like authority over a creature whose own worthiness of spirit and intelligence reflect the rider's skill.

Man does not rebel against God if he trusts God's judgement and wisdom, and if he rebels through needless arrogance, that judgement and wisdom will assert itself righteously. When man shows similar judgement and wisdom, he too will be served without rebellion. If a young or ignorant

---

202 Blundeville, III, sig. D.i.ᵛ; the desire to roll in water and mud is instinctive to many horses, regardless of their birth-sign, and is to do with scent and the maintenance of their skin in a healthy condition.

203 'make an accomplish'd horse'; 'entirely undressed or untaught' (1743: pp.12, 11).

horse, or one with a passionate spirit does rebel, 'un bon Cavalier ne doit jamais se mettre en cholere contre son cheval, mais le châtier san le fâcher comme un espece de Divinité au dessus de luy.' Like God, the horseman must mete out justice tempered with dispassion. Then the horse will 'prendra tout en bonne part, & ne se fâchera jamais' (1658: 'Avant-Propos').[204] Newcastle states that it is fear in man that refuses to allow intelligence to horses, and that an inconsistent or poor rider 'shall Spoil your horse, let him do what he will; because he wants Art' (1667: p.199). This is an astute statement, showing an underlying insightfulness into man's need for intellectual as well as physical domination.

Once this relationship is established, the rider must be free with praise and sparing with punishment, without ever losing that respect. It is important always that the horse should know when it has done wrong and when it has redeemed itself by compliance so 'when they do Well, I Cherish and Reward them'(1667: p.198). While he has little good to say of previous authors in general, on this subject he agrees with them:

> Pluvinel, and most of the Great Masters in Horse-manship, Praise always
> Gentleness, and Flatteries, and making much of the Horses, either by Clapping,
> Stroking them, or speaking Flatteringly unto them, or giving them some Reward to
> Eat: And Pluvinel sayes, One ought to be a Prodigal in Caressing, and making
> much of them, and a Niggard in Corrections, and careful not to offend them; and
> that there is not other way to Dress Horses but this (1667: p.197).

The idea that a horse appreciates 'cherishing' was not new and Newcastle's ideas on the matter are little different to those of other writers, though he shows less emotion than either Thomas Bedingfield or Nicholas Morgan. While Bedingfield suggests that the rider should aim to 'make him be in love with you', [205] Morgan is by far the most indulgent in his advice, due to his feeling that through the Fall man is responsible for any disobedience in the horse. He claims that it is wrong 'to punish him for ignorance' and that given kindness and consideration the horse 'with a sweet smile inherent in nature and expressed in countenance' will 'seem[eth] naturally to fawne on you to gaine your love'.[206] Pluvinel believes that 'horses can obey and understand us only through the diligence of caresses [...] But when they behave badly one must chastise them vigorously'.[207]

Morgan aside, no author suggests that love precludes firm chastisement, and it is one of the anomalies of the Grisone method that his followers believe that discipline that is little more than

---

204 'put himself in a passion with his horse, but chastise him with a kind of divinity superior to him [...] take all in good part , and never be offended' (1743: pp.13-14).
205 Bedingfield, p.95.
206 Morgan, *Perfection of Horsemanship*, pp.63, 69.
207 Pluvinel, p.43.

gratuitous violence can go alongside an easy relationship with a horse that loves its master and its work. The difference between Newcastle and the earlier texts is that 'a bold stroke' comes after a patient attempt because he realises that a confrontational approach 'Astonishes the Weak Horse [...] makes a Furious horse Madd; makes a Resty Horse more Resty [...] and Displeases all sorts of Horses'. The alternative however is not 'to Sit Weak [...] but to Sit Easie', in the understanding that 'The Horse must know you are his Master' (1667: pp.207-208).

This hierarchical relationship is at the heart of Newcastle's method, born of his upbringing and his genuine belief in the royalist model of love and respect for the divinely appointed ruler, and responsibility towards those below one's own status. While perceiving the life of horses as a hierarchy is anthropomorphic and underestimates the complexity of the equine herd as we understand it today, it is in keeping with life as understood by the nobleman of the seventeenth century. Horsemanship both parallels and contributes to the philosophy for Newcastle. By understanding the potential for training in the horse, man reinforces his own role, laid out by God, as having dominion over the animals, but as a benign master, working with the essential nature of the creature and using force only as a last resort in the face of rebellion as it is 'so dangerous a thing to have a Jade' (1667: p.308).

This does not suggest an indulgent approach to the horse, but rather one which sees that 'l'entendement le plus foible est toûjours le plus passionné' so that the horseman degrades himself if he 'pique son cheval en le mâtinant'.[208] Like God, the man can reserve punishment for those times when the horse tests his authority and then must 'avanturer d'entreprendre trop sur luy pour le reduire'. But also, extending God-like forgiveness, when the horse submits, 'il faut incontinent se descendre & le caresser'. He recognises that faced with a horse that is very resistant, the rider must take time and 'reduisés-le au petit pas, mélant le douceur avec les aides & châtiment (1658: 'Avant-Propos').[209] Here, as God trains his people to acceptance of his loving wisdom, so the rider trains the horse to accept him as a wise authority, not a violent aggressor.

Even the more primitive tradition followed by Blundeville advises the rider to 'conceyve with yourself, that you and he have as it were but one body. And that you both have but one sence and one will.' The horse-rider relationship is most effective when the horse acknowledges the rider as taking the role of herd leader and rebellious behaviour is the animal's instinctive way of testing that leadership, so the rider must sit 'boldlye, and without feare'.[210] Once the horse accepts that the rider will provide a relaxed but confident lead, the horse's body language then reflects that of the rider. Therefore, a calm and focused rider will result in a horse with similar qualities, which clearly reflects back the self-possession of its rider and thus becomes evidence of it. This lends itself well to the God/

---

208 'The weakest understanding is always the most passionate'; 'spurs his horse rudely' (1743: p.13).
209 'venture a bold stroke to reduce him'; 'you must alight that moment and cherish him'; 'Reduce him by degrees, mixing gentleness with helps and corrections' (1743: p.14).
210 Blundeville, sig. B.iii – iiiv.

man, king/people parallel because it is natural rather than coerced and like God's people and the king's subjects, the horse is easier in itself when handled and ridden by a strong but fair rider.

The horse is the appropriate vehicle for the demonstration of this relationship in Newcastle's eyes, due to its natural intelligence. His acknowledgment of the horse as a creature having 'Imagination, Memory and Judgement' (1667: p.219) means training is elevated to a subtle and artistic process, not simply one using force to overcome a powerful animal. However, as 'le fameux Philosophe Monsieur de Cartes'(1658: 'Avant-Propos'),[211] declares that animals do not think, he feels the need to counter this argument.

While he allows that some horses are 'vitious' or try 'Jadish tricks', he also states that 'the worst natured Jade in the world […] is much easier Drest […] than a Horse that has been Spoil'd by ill Riding' (1667: p.311). He argues repeatedly that the reason and understanding of a horse is comparable to that of a man in that it can be seen to learn, to remember, and to understand. He also points out that 'Si on gardoit un home, dés sa naissance, dans un cachot jusques à l'âge de vint-ans, & qu'apres on le mît dehors, on verroit qu'il auroit moins de raison que plusieures bestes qu'on a dressées & elevées'.[212] This is a particularly important comment in the light of the great interest at the time in the cases of wild children while the Wildman, as explained by Erica Fudge, 'figured in a number of ways – as ape, demon, savage. Irish native, New World native – to represent a border figure which made concrete the fear of descent into the animal'.[213]

During the years of exile, through interaction with Descartes, Hobbes, Sir Kenelm Digby and Pierre Gassendi, among other intellectuals, Newcastle and his brother, Sir Charles Cavendish, maintained their cultural interests. For Newcastle to interpret the intellectual issues of the day through his experience in the riding house is entirely in character. Focusing on speech, the key point of conflict in arguing against the reason of animals because, according to Descartes 'speech is the only certain sign that thought is hidden in the body',[214] Newcastle suggests that, 'ce qui est cause que les hommes parlent, & non les bestes, ne provident d'autre chose que de ce que les bestes n'ont pas cette gloire & cette vanité qu'ont les hommes'. He also points out that 'nous voions que la raretés choses produit fort peu de langage en plusieurs Indiens' (1658: 'Avant-Propos'),[215] suggesting that he compares Descartes and Hobbes in his analysis of the horse's mind.[216] Associating the need for speech with our acquisitive nature, he argues that:

---

211 'the famous philosopher DES CARTES' (1743: p.12).

212 'If a man was locked up from his birth in a dungeon till the age of twenty, and afterwards let out, we should see that he would be less rational than a great many beasts that are bred and disciplin'd' (1743: p.13).

213 Fudge, *Perceiving Animals*, p.58.

214 *Meditations and Other Metaphysical Writings* ed. Desmond Clarke (London: Penguin Books, 2003) p.174.

215 'The reason why men speak, and not the beasts, is owing to nothing else, but that the beasts have not so much vain-glory as men'; 'we see that the rarity of things among many *Indians* occasions their using language very little' (1743: p.12).

216 *Leviathan*, p.408

D'abondant, les bestes ne se divertissent point en bracelets, en bâgues émaillées,
ni en infinies bagatelles de cette espece, mais elles suivent simplement la nature,
sans avoir si grand nombre de phantômes & de poupées en l'espirit que les
hommes, dequoy ils ne se soucient pas (1658: 'Avant-Propos').[217]

There is a strong irony here, as Newcastle's own life was very full of such trappings of
human nature, with horses always among his expensive luxuries, and his humour at man's expense
does not preclude laughing at himself. However, the idea that 'reason' and language go together
relates to the suggestion that the horse does not think at all, whereas Newcastle's experience teaches
him otherwise, 'Let the Learned say what they Please' (1667: p.219).

He knows that all men do not see what to the horseman is obvious and he recognises also,
with his keen ability to cut through sophistry, that this is because 'tant ils ont peur de leur monarchie
rationale'(1658: p.13).[218] He echoes Hobbes' opinion that 'this is incident to none but those that
converse in questions incomprehensible, as the Scholemen'.[219] Through experience, not theory,
Newcastle knows that a horse learns well by repetition and gradually increasing difficulty when
guided by a confident hand. Therefore, his methods are based on routine and gradual progression
designed for the level of understanding of which the horse is capable.

The similarities between his advice on horses and that on the handling of courtiers in both the
1658 dedication and his 'little book' of private advice to the future Charles II suggest his insights into
human nature too. As a committed royalist, Newcastle's assertion that 'Monarchy is the Govermente in
Cheef off the whole Bodye Poletick, In all Itts partes, & Capaseties by one Person only' is in no way
surprising. That this should filter into his treatment of horses to whom the lead stallion in the wild or
rider in captivity fulfils a similar role, explains one of the keys to his success with them. With horses,
as with all subjects 'familiaretye breedes Contemte', so the method Newcastle advises Charles to adopt
with his militia, nobles and common people is the same as that he uses on his horses:

I Shoulde wishes your Majestie to Governe by both Love and feare mixte together as
ocation serves – having the power which Is forse and never to use Itt butt uppon nesesetye. [220]

With the horse he believes that, 'Love is not so sure a Hold, for there I Depend upon his Will;
but when he Fears me, he depends upon Mine' (1667: p.196). He echoes this in advising Charles

---

217 'Therefore the beasts do not amuse themselves with bracelets, enamel'd rings, and innumerable baubles of that
kind, but follow nature simply, without having, like men, their heads crouded with a multitude of thoughts and business,
of which horses are not solicitous'(1743: p.12).
218 'so jealous are the schoolmen of their rational empire' (1743: p.13).
219 *Leviathan*, p.44.
220 *Letters,* pp.182, 201, 203.

against allowing undue familiarity, even amongst those closest to him, declaring 'iff theye doe nott mende putt them oute'.[221] This is particularly interesting in this context as a young horse being presumptuous towards the lead stallion risks being driven out of the herd to fend for itself. Surviving without the favour of the king is equally difficult for the courtier. He also understands the nature of challenge implicit in over-familiarity towards the monarch, which, allowed to pass, can only suggest weakness. His rules for fair and effective government are along the same lines and his precedent is consistent throughout the advice book and the horsemanship texts.

The 'little book' declares, in words close to those found in both manuals:

> thatt kinge that can nott punishe, & rewarde In juste time can nott Governe, for ther
> Is no more to Governe this worlde butt by Rewarde & punishmente, - & Itt muste bee
> don In the verye nick off time or Else Itt Is to no purpose, - Wee knowe no more [than]
> that God Almightye hath butt Rewarde & Punishmente both for this worlde & the nexte. [222]

The reference to 'the verye nick of time' is especially interesting, for he advises as discussed in the previous chapter, that as soon as the horse obeys, the rider should dismount and 'cherish him', while with pleasing courtiers the king must 'Cale them to you & cherishe them for they deserve itt'. However, this should not be seen as humanising the horse but rather an astute understanding equally applicable to horse and human: neither rider nor king can be 'well Setled In your Sadle' unless the relationship with the human or equine subject be clearly defined. [223]

In the dedication to the 1658 manual, Newcastle lays out these parallels clearly:

> Qui plus est, un Roy, etant bon Cavalier, scaura beaucoup mieux comme il faudra
> gouverner ses peuples, quand il faudra les recompenser, ou les chatier ; quand il
> faudra leur tenir la main serree, ou quand il faudra la relacher ; qaund il faudra les
> aider doucement, ou en quel temps il sera convenable de les eperonner. Il ne faut
> jamais les monter jusques a leur faire perde l'haleine, ou bien ils deviendront retifs,
> & rebelles, ou (comme l'on dit) ils prendront la bride aux dents, & s'emporteront;
> mais il faut plutost les traiter doucemet, & ne prendre que la moitie de leurs forces,
> affin qu'ils puissent etre gaillards, & faire toutes choses de leur bon gre, & avec
> vigeur (1658: 'Au Roy').

---

221   Ibid. p.211.
222   Ibid. p.221; 1658: sig. f; 1667: p.198.
223   *Letters,* p.213, 211.

This illustrates that Newcastle does not simply see the horse/courtier parallel as a metaphor, but believes that the herd-nature of humans parallels that of horses to such an extent that the riding house becomes a suitable training ground for the future monarch. As man against God and the people against the king, the horse may rebel as, 'nor doth the Horse love Subjection, nor any other Creature' (1667: p.200). However, while 'They will strive all the Wayes possibly they can, to be Free, and not Subjected [...]when they see it will not be' and that they can live at ease by accepting, 'all Yeeld and Render themselves at last'. This ultimate acceptance, 'willingly, for the most part' (1667: p.43) is crucial and a moment of lasting change in the process of training.

The recognition of the right to leadership by virtue of strength and presence, natural to the horse, is no metaphor to Newcastle, but a parallel that reinforces all he believes in and his personal needs in life. A key strength of his work is that he offers treatment of the horse that runs true to his whole philosophy for a hierarchical society. While God, the monarch and the horsemaster need to inspire love and fear, by implication those emotions become desirable in the subject, human or equine. An unpublished poem 'On the best of kings' in Newcastle's hand in the Portland Collection declares, 'Wee all doe love thee, yett we feare they rodd, Nott love for feare, butt feare for love, like Godd'. This suggests a need for God or the monarch which reflects exactly the natural instinct of a horse for leadership in order to be at ease in relation not only to its herd, but also to its personal space. Therefore, that Newcastle himself took on that leadership role when riding his horses, placed him in the precise position to them that he desired for himself. His poem to Charles continues, 'Live for thy owne sake, live for ours, for thyne, Oh live, for God's sake, universe, and myne'. [224] There is desperation in this impassioned plea for Charles' life that precisely parallels the fear a horse would experience when separated from the herd through which it gains its safety and comfort.

Newcastle's understanding of the mind of the horse seems to derive from recognition, though it seems unlikely that he would have perceived this himself. But evidence of his behaviour towards his monarch, his family, his servants and his horses all suggests a consistent approach of respect within his understanding of hierarchy. His style implies the quality known today as 'passive leadership', which is not in fact passive at all but denotes a supreme confidence in the ability and right to lead, which inspires others to accept and follow. This method works extremely well with horses and humans but was perhaps compromised by Newcastle's desire for 'glorious slavery' in his relationship with the monarch. If Newcastle's belief that the horse 'puisse sçavoir, & par mesme moyen, penser à ce qu'il doit faire' (1658: Avant-Propos')[225] is neither metaphor nor a self-indulgent anthropomorphism, it may then be questioned as to how he arrives at his view. While he is not the first to consider the horse's mind as active and intelligent, his close analysis of the way that mind works is a step forward in the development

---

224   PwV25, fol. 1.
225   'may know, and even think upon what he ought to do' (1743: p.12).

of the horsemanship manual. While Pluvinel observes 'anger, despair and cowardice', all very human emotions, in his horses, and seeks to overcome them by 'coolness of mind',[226] Newcastle's training is based on the belief that his Spanish horses are 'strangely wise' (1667: p.49). Pluvinel knows that a frightened horse is a dangerous horse and he aims to calm and reassure it by a gentle approach. Some horses in the plates accompanying his manuals are blinkered and the text explains that he sometimes rides them thus blindfolded because 'horses learn better when they cannot see and are […] less inclined to be distracted'.[227] Like the hood on a falcon, the blinkers would keep the horse quiet, but suggest an unpredictable creature, not able to stand or work quietly without the denial of a sense. There are no blinkered horses in Newcastle's manuals and his advice on rendering them calm and tractable begins when they are weanlings. This ensures regular contact with human handlers without any pressure upon them, so that by the time they are old enough to begin training 'they will Lead, and be as quiet as any Horse' (1667: p.97). As a thinking creature, the young horse learns that man will not harm him, which eases the training process to avoid what Pluvinel describes as 'the extravagancies of an unreasonable animal'. There is a suggestion that while Pluvinel's approach is quiet and gentle, the early rides on a young horse may well resemble a rodeo. In time, this wildness will be overcome as the horse realises the man is persistent, but this approach involves considerable 'perils' to both horse and rider. [228]

As Pluvinel moves on from the belief that the horse's natural fear of man can be beaten into a submissive state, so Newcastle then progresses in understanding that the natural fear itself can be overcome by allowing the horse's mind time to assimilate what it is experiencing. When Newcastle describes the Barb as being 'of a good Disposition, excellent Apprehension, Judgement and Memory' (1667: p.53) he knows through experience that a horse is not generally aggressive, learns quickly and can work with a degree of independence and retain what it has learned. He knows that horses have will, motivation and character, and understands how to work with these qualities, rather than seeing them as something to be broken.

To illustrate his methods of training, Newcastle frequently draws an analogy with the teaching of a school-boy because to him the parallels are self-evident. 'What Judgment' he asks 'can one give of a Little Boy, what Kind of Man he will Prove?' Similarly, attempting to judge a horse by 'Marks, Colours and Elements' is worthless and as a child's skills will be learned as he grows, with a horse 'Ride him, and Try him […] is the Best Philosophy to know him by' (1667: p.104). Attempting to force learning by 'the diversity of Bitts' can be effective 'no more than a Book in a Boyes Hand, can at first, make him Read' (1667: p.343). Thus, 'Horses learn nothing but by Custom, and Habit, with often Repetitions to Fortify their Memories'(1667: p.218). He draws the analogy to the learning boy repeatedly in both texts, primarily in relation to unrealistic demands on the young horse. In the opening

226   Pluvinel, p.ix.
227   Ibid. p.102.
228   Pluvinel, p.ix.

paragraph of the first manual, he says, 'Je voudrois bien demander à de tels stupides & lourdaus, si en battant un garçon, on l'appendroit à lire sans luy môntrer ses lettres auparavant ?' (1658: 'Avant-Propos').[229] The likening of the horse to the boy illuminates Newcastle's perception of the horse's reasoning ability as like that of a young mind, full of natural potential but requiring training.

Plate 12 in the 1658 manual is glossed, 'Les poulins', that is 'the foals', and it is evident from the short tails that all the horses in this plate are youngsters, yet many are executing moves which appear to be those of the mature horse in advanced training. However, these are not manège horses practising, but young stock demonstrating the natural propensity for agility the rider will educate into the art of the riding house. They show too that the airs are based on the natural behaviour of display.[230] As discussed in Chapter 3, this point is made in Pluvinel's manual also, when the young king is advised to watch the foals in his stud farms playing in the fields. Although Plate 12 is in many respects a fantasy, as while the airs do relate to mating rituals, no horse performs them with such stylised precision, the point that Newcastle will 'Perfect Nature by the Subtilty of Art' (1658/1667: title page) is being made. This aim of shaping what is natural is behind the analogy with the schoolboy and the necessity of patience and humanity in the learning process is apt because unnecessary force and violence are counter-productive.

Newcastle also uses analogies to illustrate that horses, like men, may have different roles and useful purposes that reinforce the hierarchy :

> Lors qu'ils s'agit de faire une Republique, affin que les homes puissant vivre
> ensemble, ceux qui font des plumes à metre sur la teste de ces moqueurs-là, sont
> aussy utiles dans la Republique pour les maintneir & leurs familles, & servent
> autant aux autres hommes pour vivre les uns par l'aide des autres, comme sont
> ceux qui vendent le bœuf & le mouton ; car tout tend à vivre, ;es uns par l'aide
> des autres, sans se faire tort ni offense.

As there are different types of men who may all contribute to society, so there are different types of horses with different styles and purposes in the riding of them:

> Quant au cheval dressé, quils appellant danseur & badin, s'ils avoient quelques
> duëls, ou s'ils alloient à la guerre, ils reconnoîtroient leur faute ; car ces chevaux là
> vont aussy bien à la soldade & à passades comme par haut, & les longues journées
> leur font bien tost perdre tous les airs qui ne sont proprement que pour le plaisir.

---

229 'I would fain ask such stupid people, whether, by beating a boy, they could teach him to read, without first showing him his alphabet?' (1743: p.11).

230 This is well documented behaviour. See Lucy Rees *The Horse's Mind* (London: Stanley Paul, 1984), p.115.

Qui plus est, ils en sont beaucoup plus propres à galoper, trotter, tourner, ou autre
chose de cette nature, qui est pour l'usage (1658: 'Avant-Propos').[231]

He illustrates a practical situation in which men and horses play their part according to their
talents and expands on this point further in his opening chapter. His lengthy exposition of talents which
some possess and some do not, may be summed up in the sentence, 'Je voudrais bien sçavoir si tous
ceux font profession des letters sont parfaits en toute sorte de sciences?' So, where horses are concerned:

> [...] si le cheval est proper à aller à la soldade, mettés l'y: ou si son naturel le porte
> à aller à Courbettes, il faut l'y metre: tout de mesme à demi-air, Passades, terre à
> terre, Groupades, Balotades & Caprioles : s'il n'est propre à aucume de ces choses,
> mettés-le à courir la bague : s'il n'y est propre, mettés le à aller par la ville (1658: p.6).

Not all men can be preachers, or musicians or artists and not all horses can be skilled in every
possible use for them.[232]

However, he is emphatically not advocating an equality of service to the state, even between
men. There is no suggestion that the service of the man who makes feathers to put in his master's
hat is equal to that of his master, merely that he is also useful in the smooth running of society. The
feather-maker will be able to earn his keep, maintain his family and bring money into the community.
Furthermore, the horse does not serve the state, the horse serves man and that man has responsibility
for ensuring that his own and the horse's service is fitting for their skills (1658: p.5). Therefore, the
nature of the human/animal relationship is expressly illustrated further, as the horse's usefulness is in
the hands of the man.

Newcastle's observations and years training horses taught him that they learn much as a child
does and his nature was not to despise that but to work with it as a resource. His approach suggests an
observant, relaxed and liberal nature, as evidenced in other aspects of his life and his upbringing when

---

231   'When a commonwealth is to be form'd, that men may live together in society, those who make feathers to put into
their masters hats, are as useful in the republick, for the maintenance of themselves and families, and for the good of the
community, as those who sell beef and mutton; for the tendency of the whole is to live by aiding one another, without
wronging or offending any body'; 'As for a managed horse, which they call dancer and prauncer; if those gentlemen
were to fight a duel, or go to the wars, they would find their error; for these horses perform a journey, as well as they do
high airs; and the long marches occasionally make them soon forget those airs, which are calculated merely for pleasure;
moreover, they are much fitter for galloping, trotting, wheeling, or anything else which is necessary'(1743: p.14).
232   'I'd fain know, whether all those, who makes learning their profession, be themselves perfect in every science'; 'If
the horse is fit to go a Travelling pace, let him do it; if he is naturally inclined to make Curvets, he must be put to it; and
so of the Demi-Airs, Passadoes, Terra-a-terre, Croupades, Balotades, and Capriols, If he be not fit for any of these, put
him to run the ring: if he be not cut out for that, use him as a drudge to go of errands'(1743: p.16-17).

'his father being a wise man, and seeing that his son had a good natural wit, and was of a very good disposition, suffered him to follow his own genius' (*Life*: p.193).

It was perhaps as much his character as his philosophies that suited him for innovations in the understanding and training of horses. Studies of his life support this view. Katie Whitaker says 'he was in fact a hugely likeable man who took delight in pleasing other people – easy and affable in his manners, rarely standing on the ceremony his high social position allowed him.'[233]

Lucy Worsley's study of life at Welbeck Abbey under Newcastle reveals 'a uniquely fluid and quarrelsome character at odds with those of more conventional households', wherein his second wife and daughters wrote with 'a freedom in behaviour and self-expression that was unusual for their century'.[234] This ability to allow self-expression to those in his demesne may well reveal a great deal about his attitude to his horses and his desire to understand them as thinking creatures. For, regardless of an instinct to liberality, his belief that 'Familiarity breeds Contempt [...] and does no Good' indicates that any threat to his leadership would be swiftly quelled like the rebellious horse, that must 'Acknowledge me to be his Master, by Obeying me' (1667: pp.196-197).

A serious challenge to his autocratic role would be unlikely and within the relaxed relationship evident between him and his second wife, she writes that 'I rather attentively listen to what he says, than impertinently speak' (*Life*: p.306) and that she learned only of decision to move their household when he had 'already given order for wagons to transport our goods' (*Life*: p.131). Similarly, when writing playfully to his children, he signs himself 'Your loving and in this your obediente father'.[235] His love was assured, his obedience however, was an indulgence. Within that context, his daughters especially relied upon him and looked to him for leadership, as 'an intellectual liberator' who had encouraged their writing, 'giving them a control of words and thoughts that would enable them to be themselves'.[236]

This encouragement of his daughters and his second wife as writers and his unconventional household in general, suggests that while he may have felt insecure at court, within the extended family encompassed by his estates, he felt at ease. Without any insecurity in his personal identity, he could write in an introductory verse to Margaret Cavendish's first publication *Poems, & Fancies* (1653), 'I saw your poems and then wish'd them mine' (sig. A1). He could approach his horses so as that they will 'be Pleasant, lively [...] and take Pleasure in you, and in the Mannage', while aiming nevertheless that they should 'follow my Wayes and Obey me (1667: pp.39, 42). His treatment of his horses then becomes an aspect of his patriarchy, which extends to everything living under his command. Within his personal domain, as willing and obedient subjects, they received the benefits

---

233   Whitaker, p.67

234   'An Habitation not so Magnificent as Useful': Life at Welbeck Abbey in the 17th Century', *Transactions of the Thoroton Society of Nottinghamshire*, 108 (2004), p.123.

235   PwV25, fol. 21.

236   Whitaker, p.86

of his relaxed rule. Nick Rowe's description of him as a patron illustrates a similar idea so that 'his indulgent temperament appears to have offered encouragement while opening up possibilities of expression and allowing some degree of licence, rather than narrowly dictating terms of approach.'[237] Keith Wrightson stresses, however, that in all aspects of paternalism of this sort, 'Such relationship stemmed from the existence of permanent inequalities and were based on the recognition of the power of one party and the dependence of the other. Moreover they were conducted on terms largely, though not wholly, defined and determined by the relative superior'.[238] That this attitude should extend to every living creature in its perceived place reinforces it at every level, so that the ability of the horse to recognise his leadership becomes not only a measure of its own reasoning capacity, but also evidence of its master's patriarchal power.

The plates in the 1658 manual are rich with classical imagery and offer an insight into Newcastle's attitude towards his horses. This heightens and stylises many of the points he makes in the text. In the classical tradition, the horse is far beyond the unthinking machine suggested by Descartes, or the brute perceived by early humanists to be overcome by force. Artists were fully aware of the imposing picture made by a man, especially a king, on horseback and Newcastle asks his reader frequently, 'What can be more Comely or Pleasing, than to see Horses go in all several Ayres?' or, 'As for Pleasure and State, What Prince looks more Princely or more Enthroned than Upon a Beautiful Horse […]?' (1667: p.13). Far more effective surely, to be so gloriously mounted upon a creature of intelligence than an unreasoning brute.

The presentation of his horses in the plates becomes part of the overall philosophy Newcastle puts forward. He implicitly reclaims the classical imagery of the horse as a noble partner, reasoning and intelligent, but over whom man maintains divinely appointed superiority. This takes on an additional significance in the context of a time when he was detached from any significant political power, from his home and from all he had aspired to prior to the Civil War. He did not need to argue for the English aristocracy in his efforts to establish himself as a great horsemaster to his Continental audience. He did need to assert himself as having a powerful and effective contribution to make to the shaping of the gentleman, despite his own personal dislocation.

Newcastle's views on the horse's mind are consistently supported by reference to his practical experience. While he regards horsemanship as a 'science' in the sense that it is a skill requiring expertise and intellectual application, it is primarily an art for its aesthetic qualities. The 'reasonable creatures' quote (1667: sig. b2) may be misinterpreted as anthropomorphism but the use of human analogies is a way of helping the reader understand. The manuals were written for the educated nobility so even where they relate to political ideals, they were aimed at readers, including Charles II, who would

---

237 *The Cavendish Circle*, p.94.
238 *English Society 1580-1680* (London: Routledge, 2003), p..65.

understand the points Newcastle was making. Both were also aimed at gentlemen recovering from long periods of disturbance and change. Therefore, the relationship Newcastle puts forward as appropriate between man and horse is an affirmation of the social structures he retains faith in.

The engagement with the horse's mind, not as something beastly to be subdued, but as an intelligence to be managed, offered the opportunity to transcend the violence of the battlefield while still asserting the qualities of the refined soldier. Newcastle writes from practice, his readers could apply or reject his advice also from practice: clearly it is often easier and more appealing to latent human aggression to dominate a creature though force. As Keith Thomas says, 'it is impossible to disentangle what the people of the past thought about plants and animals from what they thought about themselves', which ultimately means that 'man's attitude towards the horse mirrored his attitude towards his fellow men'.[239]

Therefore, Newcastle's contribution to the discussion on animals in the early modern period is grounded in his personal experience of the horse as a creature that learns and remembers. The way in which he uses that experience is based on his royalist understanding of hierarchy and his personal nature, which is well-documented as being 'very acceptable to men of all conditions'.[240] The horse and the riding house are not metaphors for life in Newcastle's manuals; they are parallels to it and illustrate the validity of all he believes in. There is nothing more affirming of his own status than 'to see so Excellent a Creature, with so much Spirit, and Strength, to be so Obedient to his Rider, as if having no Will but His' (1667: p.13).

---

239   Thomas, p.16.
240   Clarendon, vol. III, p.382.

Chapter 6

'A strange conceit of a Great Master': Newcastle's plates as virtual reality

And beside the skyll in horses and in whatsoever belongeth to a horseman,
let him set all his dylygence to wade in everye thing a little farther then other menne,
so that he may bee knowen almong al menne for one that is excellente.
Count Baldassare Castiglione, *The Book of the Courtier*

Newcastle's 1658 manual is distinguished by the forty-two double-folio sized copperplate engravings printed from original designs by Abraham van Diepenbeeck.[241] The high quality and detail lavished upon these illustrations ensured that they are still regarded among the most significant sets of illustrations in Diepenbeeck's prolific output of drawings and designs. The overall production of the book made it exceptional, illustrating the status of the author, despite his straitened financial circumstances at the time. Newcastle had to accept the help of court agents, Sir Henry Cartwright and William Loving and wrote in 1656, 'I am so tormented about my book of horsemanship as you cannot believe, with a hundred several trades I think, and the printing will cost above £1300'.[242] This date suggests the long-term nature of the project and Newcastle's agitation suggests also his close involvement with the production process.

The plates were produced from Diepenbeecke's drawings by a team of eight engravers, an unusually large number, with two or three being more usual.[243] The urgency this implies is supported by Toole-Stott's survey of extant copies of the text. All the manuals he examined 'have the numeral 'I' added in MS. to the date of the printed title which (before the addition) was 1657. The engraved title is always 1658.' He suggests that, 'the complete work with the engraved title was not published until 1658, but […] copies with the printed title were ready and in circulation in 1657. Possibly, the work was held up for the completion of the engraved title (which is an inserted leaf)'.[244] Katie Whitaker adds to the impression of the great enterprise involved in preparing the text as a just acknowledgement of all that

---

241   See Appendix II.
242   Printed in *Life*, p.357.
243   I would like to thank Adrian Woodhouse for sharing his insights and research on the production of the plates and his expertise on the Cavendish estate architecture and heraldry with me; See Johns, p.434-492, on the art and practice of the engraver.
244   Toole-Stott, p.84.

Title Plate

Newcastle's status demanded:

> Unlike his plays, which appeared anonymously, William intended to publish this more aristocratic work under his own name. Wanting a title page at once impressive and socially correct, he consulted the most senior English herald, Sir Edward Walker, the Garter King-of-Arms, still with Charles II's court in exile.

No doubt he was particularly pleased to have confirmed that 'there were precedents that entitled William as a marquess and a knight of the Garter, to take the courtesy title of prince'.[245]

The great roll-call of his titles actualises the belief put into words by Margaret Cavendish that 'tis a part of Honour to aspire towards a Fame'.[246] It also follows the philosophy laid out by Hobbes that 'Scutchions, and Coats of Armes hereditary, where they have any eminent Priviledges, are Honourable' and give evidence for a man that the 'Value of him by the Common-wealth, is understood, by offices of Command, Judicature, publike employment; or by Names and Titles, introduced for distinction of such value'.[247] Newcastle was therefore honour-bound to assert his status because such assertion helped to maintain social order, the alternative to which was anarchic destruction.

In the overall presentation of Newcastle through his manuals, the plates have a significant role, as well as supporting the technical agenda of the text. However, if they are viewed as a 'conceit' in themselves, their various layers of meaning become part of a whole. His use of horsemanship as a means to this end supports the argument that 'representations of power and a vivid shared aesthetic combined in fine breeds of horses' so that 'their circulation and appreciation were integral parts of imperial bids for recognition'.[248]

The manual begins with the elegant title plate expounding in full detail Newcastle's impressive lineage, including all his titles relating to pre-war offices. The two rearing horses, the heraldic devices and the attending cherubs, all direct the eye to the claim that this is the text of a both new and extraordinary method for horse training, hitherto undiscovered, and authored by the thrice noble and very puissant 'Prince Guillaume Marquis et Comte de Newcastle'. Having been introduced, as it were, in this title page to the author, the reader then becomes Newcastle's guest through the plates that follow throughout the manual. The opportunity to reveal his cultured taste, architectural innovation and significant land holdings, denied him in his exile, becomes possible through this device, along with - most importantly—the personal stamp of his individuality.

The invitation to accept Newcastle's hospitality is in the preamble of plates 1-5, which establish his identity as English Lord and royalist general. In the original text of 1658, these are positioned between the engraved title page and the dedications, so that the first impression made upon the reader is visual. This initial impact is crucial as Newcastle's ability to offer the courtly welcome of his true home made his assertion of himself as a horseman of European expertise and importance more assured. In his study of Newcastle's last great building project, Nottingham Castle, Trevor Foulds points out that after the Restoration Newcastle believed that 'his social position, titles and extensive lands reinforced by his experiences on the continent while in exile [...] supplied a continental dimension that legitimately put him on the same level with

245   Whitaker, p.208.
246   *Poems, and Fancies*, sig. A4.
247   *Leviathan*, pp.52, 48.
248   Jardine and Brotton, p.151.

Plate 1

continental dynasts such as the families of Conde and Bourbon'.[249] During his time on the Continent, he makes a similar claim for dynastic superiority though the plates of his first horsemanship manual for the benefit of those whose recognition he would use to re-establish himself on his return home.

Plate 1 has the strong image of Newcastle as General, ordering the battle, which rages in the field below. With the legend 'LA BATAILLE GAIGNEE' [sic], that is 'The Battle Won', beneath the

---

249 'This greate House, so Lately begun, and all of Freestone': William Cavendish's Italianate Palazzo called Nottingham Castle', *Transactions of the Thoroton Society of Nottinghamshire*, 106 (2002), p.86.

feet of Newcastle's horse, the features of the scene are consistent with the genre of scenes of battle and the plate overall recalls contemporary portraits of significant generals and royalty. The impact of Newcastle in the foreground overseeing command of his troops is standard iconography for emphasizing the puissance and status of the depicted leader. Similarly his abilities are reinforced by the detail of his army surging forward to mow down the injured and dying from the opposing side. Newcastle's cavalry appears to have no casualties. The winged fames sound the clarion call of triumph and crown Newcastle with the victor's laurel wreath while the sky opens to shine down heaven's approval on him. The Garter motto, *honi soit qui mal pense*, 'shame on him who thinks badly', is borne up by cherubs, and his black pageboy, a sign of his status, carries his helmet, which signifies him as a conqueror of nations. Newcastle carries all the arms appropriate to his role, and his horse is performing a beautiful pesade, indicating the rider's skill. Recalling his days of victory and ignoring the painful irony encompassed in such images of a man who left his country after a disastrous defeat, Plate 1 presents Newcastle in his glory: a leader of men, acknowledged and approved of by heaven. The invitation has been issued for the reader to enter his demesne.

Plate 2 reinforces this image with Newcastle as a living statue upon a pedestal, which bears a verse eulogising both Newcastle and the spirit of horse, 'made by this Lord so true and so equable' that 'all Horses are subject to his law' and 'obey him as they would their King'.[250] Newcastle's status as a king to all horses, whose noble nature is refined by his skill, leaves the reader/guest in no doubt that they are to be in the company of brilliance. To reinforce the point, the couplet at the base of the pedestal reads, 'If he mounted a fiery Devil, that Devil would in all airs go truly'. Again presented as the general honoured by heaven, Newcastle is in armour and girt with a sword, but does not have the holstered pistol he wore in the first plate, suggesting that after conflict comes ceremony, with the spoils of war scattered about the plinth, symbolic of the razing of his enemies. The landscape behind him is, as are those that follow, more Flemish than English in appearance, including the silhouettes of birds, a feature of Flemish landscapes at the time. This may simply reflect the imagination of the artist, whose personal frame of reference would not be English, or be part of the fantasy locating Newcastle in the context of his Continental audience. Trevor Foulds illustrates that Diepenbeecke's involvement introduces 'a Flemish filter' to the design for Nottingham Castle and this is true also of the horsemanship plates. The production of the drawings for the plates is subject to some discussion, but letters are extant referring to visits made to Newcastle's estates by an unnamed artist, possibly Diepenbeecke.[251]

Following through the conceit of a guide to the notional visitor, here then is the statue that greets the newcomer at the entrance or gateway to Newcastle's home. These images predate and perhaps set a precedent for the life-size equestrian statue, now sadly ruined, which Newcastle commissioned to stand

---

250   See Appendix for full translations of the verses in the plates.
251   Foulds, ibid., p.86; Girouard, 'Early Drawings of Bolsover Castle' in *Architectural History*, 1957, p.512.

Plate 2

over the first-floor entrance of Nottingham Castle, and in which he is dressed very similarly to Plate 1 of the 1658 manual. Adrian Woodhouse points out that it is the earliest 'non-royal major equestrian statue' in Britain[252] so Plate 2 lays the foundation stone for the later statue in associating Newcastle with a tradition that was, in 1658, still distinctly royal.

It also contains a powerful message for its original readership. A statue both represents the person and also transforms them into a figure of power, its three dimensional solidity carrying a

---

252 'Reconstructing the Horseman of Nottingham Castle: the Equestrian Statue of the First Duke of Newcastle, c. 1679', *Transactions of the Thoroton Society of Nottinghamshire*, 104 (2000), pp.73-74.

Plate 3

stronger semiotic message than a portrait. That it would often be positioned in the open air broadens the viewing perspective and makes it also a tribute reserved only for those whose name and rank demand such public recognition. To present himself as a statue contains, therefore, a complicated psychology, whereby not only are Newcastle's expertise and *gloire* fixed in print but also by implication, fitting to be immortalised in stone.

Plates 3 and 4 suggest both in their style, content and position in the overall series of the engravings, a short masque or entertainment, such as Newcastle commissioned Ben Jonson to

Plate 4

write to welcome Charles I and Queen Henrietta Maria on their two visits to his estates. *The King's Entertainment at Welbeck* (1633), and *Love's Welcome at Bolsover* (1634), marked highly significant events so recollecting them through the plates adds an important retrospective of his career. A noble guest at Newcastle's table would find such entertainment most apt and generous, indicating the host's wealth, theatrical tastes and honour to his guests and also emphasizing that his skills have the authority of classical lineage.

Newcastle, who took part in court masques, appears in this entertainment as Lord of Horses, worshipped by nineteen muscular stallions all kneeling in acknowledgement of his skill, which is proclaimed in the verse. In the midst of this highly theatrical image, there is a small detail of simple realism, which reinforces the claims of Newcastle's expertise. The horse to the right of centre has its tail bound up ready to perform a capriole, the epitome of the art of the riding house, so as to avoid tearing the hair as it kicks out behind at the zenith of its great leap and which 'makes him appear to go higher too' (1667: p.115). Including this horse reinforces to the reader/guest that Newcastle can achieve the highest level of training and illustrates an attention to accurate detail that is consistent throughout the plates. Alongside the artistic concerns in their presentation, they are the manifestation of a precise knowledge of horses, and every plate supports that point.

Newcastle rides in a small chariot very reminiscent of those used in festivals, horse ballets and masques, dressed in classical costume, with the addition of the long horsemaster's switch, and showing a bare leg and arm. While this is keeping with his costume, it also displays a strong and muscular physique, providing convenient support for Newcastle's comments in the texts on how strong and fit this art makes the rider (1667: pp.131-140). He was in his sixties by the time this manual appeared, but this image and those throughout serve to immortalise him at the peak of his health and strength, with years of experience behind him and a confident future ahead as indicated by the wonderful estate on view.

The centaurs drawing his chariot carry spoils of war and are in keeping with the overall elevation of Newcastle above horses and men, through their classical links with both wisdom and boorishness. This suggests reference to Machiavelli's point that 'a prince must know how to use wisely the natures of the beast and the man'. This was 'taught to princes allegorically by the ancient writers, who described how Achilles and many other ancient princes were given to Chiron the Centaur to be raised and taught under his discipline. This can only mean that, having a half-beast and half-man as a teacher, a prince must know how to employ the nature of the one and the other'.[253] Rather than being educated by a centaur, Newcastle harnesses them, thus elevating himself still further. It reminds his readers once more that the first Governor of Charles II has an implicit and profound knowledge of beasts and men. The combination of elements in this plate make this scene reminiscent of a Roman Triumph, an image well-established in the conventions of the masque and horse-ballet as appropriate for the celebrations of the nobility.

This entertainment ends with a triumphal display in Plate 4, as Newcastle achieves heavenly ascension, performing a capriole on a winged horse. The accompanying verse explains that 'He flies so high that he touches the sky with his head/ And by his marvels he delights the gods to ecstasy.' This image recalls Ben Jonson's appreciation of Newcastle's riding abilities in 'An Epigram to William, Earl

---

253   *The Prince*, ed. by Peter Bondanella, trans. Peter Bondanella and Mark Musa (Oxford/New York: Oxford University Press, 1984), p.58.

of Newcastle'. Jonson declares that 'You showed like Perseus upon Pegasus', although in the classical tradition Pegasus is tamed by Bellepheron. However this misattribution is not unusual at the time and may be seen also in, for example Theodor van Thulden's Perseus and Andromeda'.[254]

In the context of Plate 3, Newcastle upon Pegasus is dressed not in classical costume, but in contemporary clothes. It seems, therefore, that he is aligning himself less with the classical heroes than the association of Pegasus with poets and artists, due to his creation of the Helliconian spring for the Muses on Mount Olympus. For this apotheosis, Newcastle chooses not the role of an ancient hero, but to play the part of himself, suggesting that he will be invited to join the assembled gods on his own merit. He is watched over by Jupiter, Juno, Mercury, Diana, Apollo, Hercules and other deities, with the cornucopia representing peace and abundance, and images of war and the arts. All areas of Newcastle's expertise are represented, and the eleven horses witness his aspiration to heavenly status. The number eleven is generally taken iconographically to represent the twelve disciples, minus Judas Iscariot, an uneasy reference in this context. There is a great deal of mixed iconography here and it is unlikely that Newcastle is associating himself with Christ. However, the subtext of these images would be well-known to readers steeped in classical and Christian imagery and it is hard to interpret them without accepting that such recognition could be made. If the winged horse is taken to make up the number to twelve, the New Testament iconography remains and this image is open to a variety of interpretations.[255]

In his poems to Margaret Cavendish during their courtship, Newcastle links the sacred and profane in a manner Douglas Grant describes as 'distressing' and it may that his tendency to solipsism blinds him to the potential offence of such links.[256] The more prosaic practicalities of artistic composition might mean that eleven horses balance the plate visually in the eye of the artist, but when the images are so rich in potential meaning, this is not an especially satisfying conclusion. Clearly Newcastle is aiming to impress, not to offend, and in this virtual world he has created through the plates, his ascension is a climactic moment in the entertainment of his guests. Newcastle's winged steed is performing a capriole, but does not have a dressed tail, perhaps having transcended such earthly concerns in this exalted moment of transilience between heaven and earth.

The entertainment is rounded off with acknowledgment of the king and Newcastle's political affiliation as his devoted supporter. To portray Charles II as King of Great Britain, as the legend proclaims, deliberately ignores the state of the English monarchy in 1658, befitting both Newcastle's personal affiliations and the acknowledgement of Charles as lawful king by the Continental nobility. The Commonwealth appears as a hydra pursued by Mars, under the command of Charles II in the role of Jupiter. Mercury with his caduceus appears to offer this attack upon the evil monster for Charles'

---

254   *Major Works*, pp. 383; 700.
255   I am grateful to Professor Paul Spenser-Longhurst for his assistance in interpretation of the classical iconography in the plates.
256   *The Phanseys of the Duke of Newcastle*, p.xxiii.

Plate 5

consideration. Cherubs and angels offer Charles the symbols of monarchy over England, Scotland, Ireland and Wales, while Cupid acts as page, carrying his helm. He is equipped for battle and London lies below in the distance, although the trees and flocks of birds are consistent with the Flemish style overall. The most striking feature of this plate, however, as mentioned in Chapter 3, is that from the neck down, even to the white sock of the horse's near-side hind hoof and the folds of the rider's cloak, this is exactly the same figure as that in Plate 1. The only difference between them is that Plate 1 has Newcastle's head and Plate 5 has that of Charles II. It is hard to see this as saying anything other than that Newcastle and the true king are as one.

Newcastle's loyalty and closeness to the king are unequivocally established, with Charles cast in the mould of his former Governor, a bold suggestion unlikely to please many of Newcastle's peers. The verse praising Charles's virtues suggests also that Charles should aspire to follow Newcastle's apotheosis so that 'your own mount be the winged Pegasus'. This reference to Charles riding Pegasus, coming hard upon the image of Newcastle doing so, suggests that he is still offering a role model to his monarch, so that Charles' subjects may 'submit to your unique power' as the horses do to Newcastle's own particular skills. His address to Charles, which follows these opening plates, refers to the influence Newcastle had over his boyhood and the natural genius he nurtured as the future king's governor when he recognised 'quelle abondance de fruits vertueux' were present in the child's nature. Respectful affection supports visual imagery in aligning the author of this text with his lawful king not only as loyal subject but as active mentor.

However, there is a great and poignant irony in these plates. Newcastle, far from being seen at this time as a victorious general was, to his own side, the man who lost the battle of Marston Moor and left the country in disarray, if not disgrace. The days of glorious entertainments in his own estates were over and the pattern already established with Charles whereby Margaret Cavendish would later observe 'his gracious master did not love him so well as he [Newcastle] loved him' (*Life*: p.245) . However, to his credit, he never wavered in his devotion and the plates, taking this notional guest around his estates, state clearly from the outset that he is the king's man.

These first five plates are followed by the thirteen-page dedication to Charles 'Au Roy de Grande Bretagne' and an address to Newcastle's sons, Charles and Henry Cavendish. The host is not only the king's man, but a family man also, continuing an aristocratic dynasty who will recognise the worth of horsemanship in supporting the ideals and honours of their lineage, 'parce qu'il n'y a rien plus proper a un Gentil-homme que d'etre bon Homme de cheval' (1658: 'A Mes Tres-Chers Fils').

The entertainment over and loyalties established, the virtual guest is then invited to view Newcastle's stud horses, against the backdrop of the estate at Welbeck Abbey. These plates support the commentary on breeds of horses in the manuals (1658: pp.14-16;1667: pp.49-76) but also, in displaying Newcastle's own horses on his estates, recall a mentor of Newcastle's own, Sir Henry Wotton, who believed that a nobleman's home 'is a kind of private princedom'.[257] The plates become a studbook also, displaying the stallions Newcastle chooses to introduce Spanish blood to English stock, while illustrating his text on choosing fine stallions. Thus these plates, as those that precede them, can be read on a number of different levels. While the fantasy has now given way to realism in the presentation of Newcastle's estates and horses, the presentation of his status and expertise remains, rooted in the practicalities of breeding good stock and managing fine property. He aligns himself with the elite who

---

257   *The Elements of Architecture: collected by Henry Wotton, Knight, from the best authors and examples* (London, 1624), p.82.

Plate 6

can recognize and afford fine horses from several countries, demonstrating that he is among those aristocrats whose power and aesthetic sensibilities cross cultural boundaries.

Plate 6 is a Barb named 'Paragon'. This breed, although long known in Europe, was originally of North African descent. Newcastle believes that 'there never came out of Barbery, The best Horses that Country affords', because merchants and 'horse-coursers' 'Buy those Horses that are Cheapest for their Advantage' (1667: p.57) and he discusses at some length the difficulty and high cost of obtaining a Barb. This makes it the more desirable and the more prestigious a horse to have in his stud. The Barb is handled in Plate 6 by the same black page who waited upon Newcastle in Plate 1. As well as the Barb,

Plate 7

this young man handles the Turkish horse in Plate 8, for he, like the horses, has exotic associations, reinforcing that Newcastle can reach beyond European Christendom to encompass and acquire. By this time this tradition of displaying power and magnificence through the ownership of fine horses was well-established and the inclusion of non-European breeds and their handler implies Newcastle's buying power and ability to take the foreign exotic and locate it within his own context. To have a black servant was still unusual in Europe in 1658, and so adds an additional dimension of elitism.

The impressive yet homely appearance of the house reinforces the welcome for the notional guest. Smoke from the chimney shows that Welbeck is active, staffed and hospitable, with the fine façade well-displayed as a backdrop to the horse, which is positioned so that its body does not spoil the view of the house. The overall impression is one of refinement and grandeur, while the legend in a cartouche ensures no reader can mistake whose house it is.

Plate 7 shows 'Le Superbe', a Spanish horse, which is of a more rounded overall carriage than the Barb. Newcastle commends the Spanish horse as 'the noblest horse in the World' and 'Fittest for a King', due to their combination of 'great spirit […] Best Action' and 'Lovingest and Gentlest' nature (1667: p.50). These attributes are recognisable today, further illustrating the accuracy of the text and also the prepotency of the breed, one of the reasons for its popularity in the riding house. The best of the Spanish bloodlines he considers to be from 'Andalousia' especially that of the king of Spain at Cordova' (1667: p.21). The smoking chimneys and standard flying on the house behind indicate again that the family is in residence, even though at this time Newcastle was in exile and his houses either abandoned, fallen into disrepair or being managed by a few remaining staff and family members.

The plates may have served also to remind the author that his heart still had its home, and to assure those who viewed them that he intended to regain his estates, at that time 'confused, entangled and almost ruined'. Newcastle's great love for his homeland is best illustrated by Margaret Cavendish's anecdote that on his eventual return to England when 'he was able to discern the smoak of London, which he had not seen in a long time, he merrily was pleased to desire one that was near him, to jogg him out of his dream, for surely, said he, I have been sixteen years asleep, and am not thoroughly awake yet' (*Life*: pp.90, 87).

Plates 8 and 9 build on the idea of the guided tour in the plates, as the design and dimensions of the stables and riding house are detailed above the buildings. Again, the manuals provide an opportunity for Newcastle to share his expertise on the most practical level, while impressing his reader/guest. Newcastle's stables were so impressive that Jonson declared 'I began to wish myself a horse',[258] and were architecturally significant in the development of the riding house and stable in Britain.[259] These plates aim at disseminating Newcastle's innovative designs to his Continental audience and become another aspect of the colonisation he attempts through the manuals. Plate 8 simply describes the stately dimensions of the riding house, but Plate 9 adds much more detail. With a granary, stone vaulted stables, pillars, feeders and paved floor 'a l'Italienne' and most impressively, the running water and ventilation system for up to eighty horses, these stables could not fail to impress any reader interested in the good management of expensive horses or imaginative practicality in architecture.

The horse in Plate 8 is a 'Turke', led again by the black page. In both manuals, Newcastle claims little knowledge of Turkish horses as 'I have seen very Few of them' because 'the Grand Signor is very Strict, in not Suffering any of his Horses to Go out of his Territory' (1667: pp.69,

---

258   Already cited.
259   Designs for Newcastle's riding houses and stables are extant and discussed in detail by Giles Worsley, Lucy Worsley and Tom Addyman and Adrian Woodhouse, already cited.

Plate 8

71). However, one appears to be part of his own stud. As it is unlike Newcastle to consider himself inexpert on any subject on which he has even some small experience, it seems likely that not all the horses illustrated existed outside the notional estate contained within the manual. Although the horse in the plate is named, Newcastle does not include any Turkish names in his list of suggestions of 'Excellent Names' and considers that those he had seen 'appeared not so Fit for the manage, as for to Run a Course', due to their action (1667: pp.353, 70). This horse, like the Barb, is not as rounded in outline as the Spanish stallion, illustrating the different attributes of the various breeds

Plate 9

that could be used to enhance English bloodlines.

Although Newcastle says that Neapolitan horses, a Spanish cross-breed, are 'ill-shaped' (1667: p.21), the horse shown in Plate 9, is particularly attractive and well-proportioned. He has the rounded musculature of the Spanish, with the long top-line (poll to withers) of the Barb and a splendid mane, falling to his shoulder. His sloping muzzle is characteristic of certain Spanish types and the deep-set eye suggests intelligence. The Neapolitan courser had been a popular choice as a war-horse across Europe in the sixteenth century due to its strength and courage, but Newcastle's criticism is that too much cross-breeding had caused the breed to become 'Bastarded, and Spoyled'.

Plate 10

This point is supported by the Marquis of Caracena's assurance to Newcastle that even though war had an impact on the breed, 'they began now to Repair it, and that he Hoped within Fourteen Years it may be Established as formerly it hath been' (1667: pp.68-69).

This horse bears the brand which displays Newcastle's lineage as part of an ongoing agenda of elevating his status as explained by Adrian Woodhouse:

Newcastle quartered the Ogle and even older Northumbrian Bertram arms with
Cavendish; blithely used the Bertram baronial title although he was not entitled to do
so; had the Ogle barony bumped up to an earldom with his dukedom in 1665 and used
the Ogle sun-in-glory badge ubiquitously.

This enabled him to claim a long noble lineage through his mother, even though his father's
family had only started to climb social ladder in the sixteenth century. As Woodhouse points out, the
association with 'traditions of chivalry […] inextricably linked with horses and knightly service on
horseback' through this noble descent served his image of himself, as presented in all aspects of his
life, including the horsemanship manuals.[260]

The young man in Plate 9 is the second of the four attendants, angels and gods aside, who
appear in the plates alongside Newcastle and Captain Mazin. This is unlike the Pluvinel manuals
which are crowded with students and admirers of the author, including the young king. Newcastle
in the context of his estates is not a riding master but a horsemaster, a subtle difference and even
when he taught the young Charles II, he did so not as the master of an Academy, but as his personal
governor. Plate 9 also gives an impressive view of the riding house and stables at Welbeck, along
with full gloss of the interior, as discussed above.

The final stallion, in Plate 10 is 'Rubecan un Rousin', displayed in a Flemish landscape.
'Rousin' is a very old French term for a war horse and as this animal is a shorter more heavily
boned horse, while still displaying the high-stepping muscular quality favoured by Newcastle. This
suggests a cross-breed capable of weight-bearing but with the capacity also to be agile, necessary if
he were to be used on the battlefield.

The reader/guest having viewed the stallions, is taken in plates 11 and 12, to view Newcastle's
stock at large. As well as a fine stallion, whose active gait illustrates his disposition, there are mares
and well-fleshed foals, whose large numbers and rounded shape suggest abundance and fertility. The
leafy trees and flowers and grazing for the horses also give the impression that under Newcastle's
hand, the land is well managed and fertile. Art and realism support and inform one another in all these
images, as the accepted symbolism is portrayed through notional observation of actuality. The stallion
in plate 11 is branded again, and one of the mares has her tail tied up, suggesting she has only recently
foaled, as the tail would be tied out of the way to prevent it becoming soiled during the birth. This adds
another small element of good management and realism to the idyllic images of this equine paradise.
The foals are rather shaggy, which is entirely consistent both with the downy first coat of all foals, and
with the tendency of the Spanish horse to be born looking unrefined but develop into graceful animals
as they mature. Another feature combining symbolism and realism is the veins showing on the horses,

---

260   Woodhouse, p.76; fn. 8.

Plate 11

which in artistic terms can represent vitality and health, but would also be an accurate representation of a finely-bred, fine coated horse of this type. The man and dog in this and the following plate are recommended to watch over the horses 'Day and Night; not only to tell you when they are Served, but that no other horse comes to the Mares, or other Mares put to the Horse watch them day and night' (1667: p.92). In the highly competitive and expensive world of horse breeding, the less than efficient landowner or unscrupulous breeder might threaten the purity of the bloodlines or take advantage of fine stock.

Plate 12

Plate 12, the final one in this initial tour of land and property, shows thirty-six young weanlings at play in open pasture. Again there is a great sense of growth and vitality, with summer foliage, in keeping with Newcastle's advice to time foaling for May. Some of the youngsters play-fight, which is common behaviour among young horses as they work out their place in the herd. Others however, are executing highly complicated caprioles and curvets, implying both natural aptitude and perhaps also that because he has trained the natural abilities of their fathers, they are born imbued with the skills they will refine in their adulthood. It also illustrates the practice of breeding for desired attributes, common at the time and ever since. This combination of realism and idealism may be seen also in

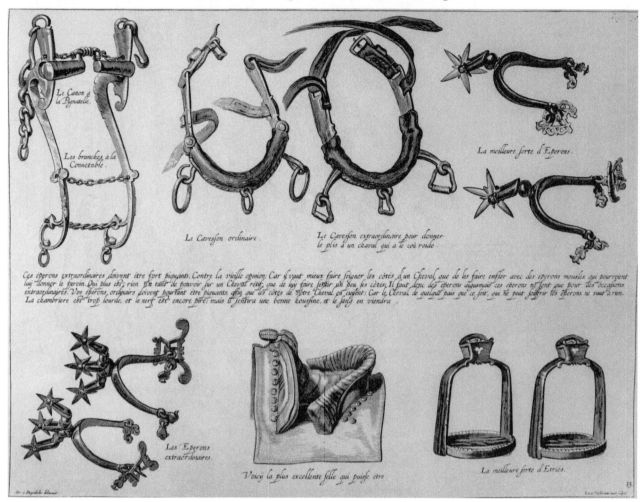

Plate 13

some of the life-size portraits of horses at Welbeck Abbey, where the stallions are running free and yet performing airs above the ground. A similar message seems likely: the movements are based on nature and that Newcastle's training impresses itself upon nature and is assimilated by nature.

The notional guest has now been welcomed, introduced and entertained by the host then shown his stud horses and innovative stable and riding house design, while given a running textual commentary. A tour of the pastures has shown the natural management skills of the master and the time for riding approaches. Newcastle will show his skill as a trainer and then ride himself for the pleasure of his guest.

Plate 14

Plate 13 begins the explanation of training methods by a display of tack and equipment, including Newcastle's own design of cavesson, explained by the legend. From the point of view of a guest who is a rider and keeper of horses, this is a very logical progression from the horses, their management and gear and then the riding: training followed by display. This order introduces first the philosophy of the host and then the demonstration of his skill in both training and performance. His tack would be of prime interest to other riders. Once the horse has the bit in its mouth or the saddle on its back, any hidden tortures, such as a raw edge on the bit, or rigid spurs would be easily hidden. As Newcastle comments in such detail on bitting (1658: pp.263-269; 1667:pp.343-350), clearly he would

Plate 15

wish his guest to understand the mechanics of the items he chooses for his own horses.

Plate 14 shows Newcastle himself, demonstrating the true seat for a horseman, as described in both manuals (1658: p.35; 1667: p.203). This also shows the military general, seen previously surrounded by the spoils of war, now at leisure demonstrating the skill and beauty of his art, which is clearly suitable for 'Persons of the greatest quality' (1667: sig. c). The illustration of his method to the guest begins with a vision of perfection: the master in the saddle.

Plates 15- 29 are a training session for a fairly advanced horse, a very suitable entertainment for a house-guest with an interest in the art. The technical accuracy of the plates as discussed in detail

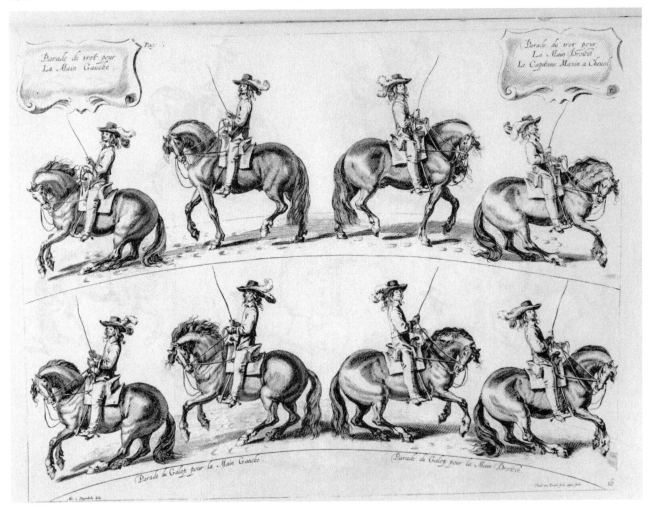

Plate 16

in Chapter 4, ensures that they illustrate the method expounded in the text. However, in the conceit of the plates as a re-creation of the personal space Newcastle demands due to his lineage and status, they reinforce his position and create a stage upon which he can perform.

In plates 15-19, Captain Mazin warms-up the horse for its training session and undertakes the initial exercises, with Newcastle directing the training from the ground, reinforcing his role as expert. The outlines of circles and hoof marks on the ground, like choreographic floor-patterns, show the pattern the horse will make on the ground when moving correctly. The horse in these plates is wearing

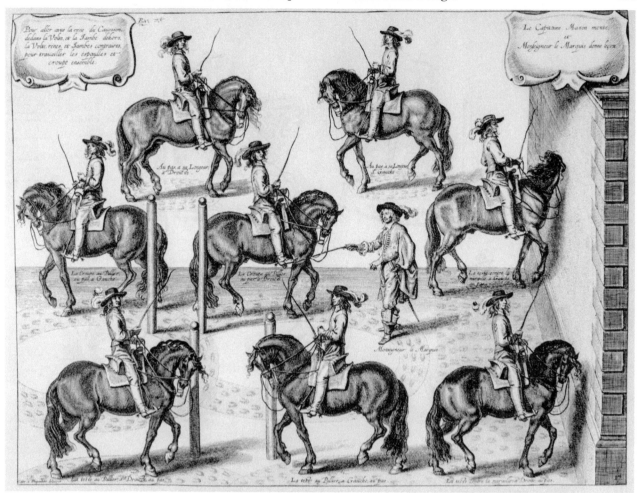

Plate 17

Newcastle's cavesson, with the rein through the noseband ring. Newcastle's method involves careful progressive training but it is also innovative and encompasses science and philosophy as well as art. In the plates, these messages are reinforced by the calm confidence and authoritative stance of the master, typified by his own method as a man of grace, reason and personal presence.

The school in which the lesson takes place is suggested by the pillar (plates 15, 17-28), while sections of a dressed stone wall (plates 17, 18, 22) recall the beautiful riding house in plate 9 without detracting from the training with full details the interior. Also, as Welbeck and Bolsover have riding houses, both may be represented through this device.

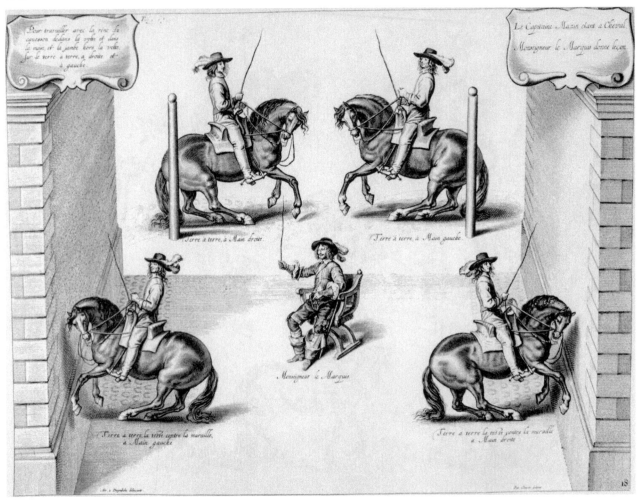

Plate 18

In plates 15- 29, the exercises are shown on both hands, that is, in both directions, a key feature of training for balanced muscle development. For the basic exercises, needing only the rider and the master teaching the lesson, Newcastle stands in the center. The horse works different steps of the same circle around him, illustrating the use of his innovative cavesson, the positioning of the horse for the correct effect and the way the pillar is used. Aside from the practicality of this, so that whole exercises may be illustrated, it also gives a sense of dynamism to the image so that Newcastle appears to be the center of a scene of great activity and learning. This is emphasized by the changes in the scene as the training progresses.

Plate 19

In plate 17, Newcastle wears a cloak bearing the Star of the Garter and carries a sword while directing the lesson with the switch. In plate 18, he has removed the cloak and sits in a throne-like chair, while by plate 19, he stands in front of the chair attended by 'Mr. Proctor', who carries his cloak. John Proctor was Newcastle's personal servant for fifty years and the engraving makes him appear to be a young man, though he had already served Newcastle for around twenty years by 1658. Like his master, he is immortalised him in his prime. His plain dress illustrates that he not among the gentlemen-servants and his posture makes it is clear that he is not involved in the equestrian activities, but simply there to attend to his master's needs. His presence testifies to Newcastle's status and prepares for plates

Plate 20

20-29 when Newcastle either rides or takes an active part in the training for the advanced airs above the ground.

When Newcastle is directing the exercises, he either watches actively or points the whip to refine Captain Mazin's execution, reinforcing that he is in charge as the expert in the situation. In plates 20 and 21, when Newcastle rides, Mazin stands in the center, watching respectfully. His posture is one of waiting and observation, his switch held in his right hand and tucked back through his left elbow. There is no possibility of the reader thinking he has an active teaching role when his master is

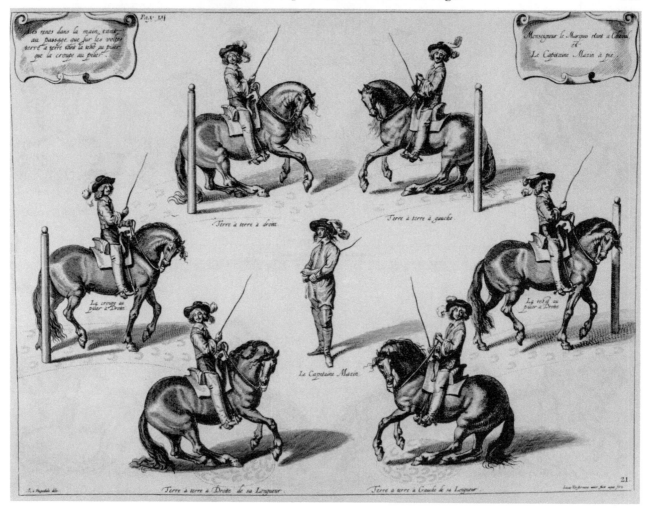

Plate 21

riding.

Newcastle takes over as training has moved into its advanced stages and while Mazin would be fully capable of completing the procedure, with visitors present it would be appropriate for Newcastle to demonstrate his own expertise at this point, rather than any other. The horse now works off the shanked bit, not the cavesson, demonstrating that these are advanced exercises and in plate 21 he moves from two hands on the reins, to the finished one-handed style of perfection.

From the conceit of the virtual tour, while to hear the host speak about his horses would be very

Plate 22

worthwhile, to see him ride would be an experience indeed. This may be compared with the anecdote Newcastle tells of being persuaded to ride even though he had been ill, when the Marquis of Caracena said, 'It would be a great Satisfaction to him, to see me on Horseback, though the Horse should but Walk' (1667: p. sig. b2). His willingness to put his views into practice illustrates his genuine skill.

In plate 22, he rides the horse one-handed in the shanked bit at the *galop* to a turn over the haunches, demonstrating first the training attitude of a flexed neck and then the finished performance with the perfect 'apuy', that is self-carriage and balance, of the horse. All these images support the

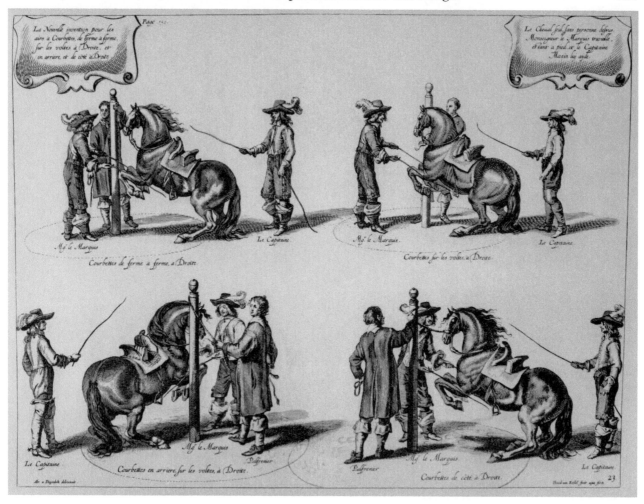

Plate 23

practical use of the text with their accuracy, but repeatedly emphasise the strong confident position of the author in his riding house.

In plates 23 – 29, the display moves into the area of real excitement for the reader/guest as Newcastle demonstrates the execution of the airs above the ground, for which all else is but preparation. All the exercises shown in the fourteen training plates are chosen for their difficulty. No-one without skill and authority could begin to train a horse to perform these challenging movements so the message of the plates as a whole in the 1658 manual is that Newcastle is the current master on the Continent as

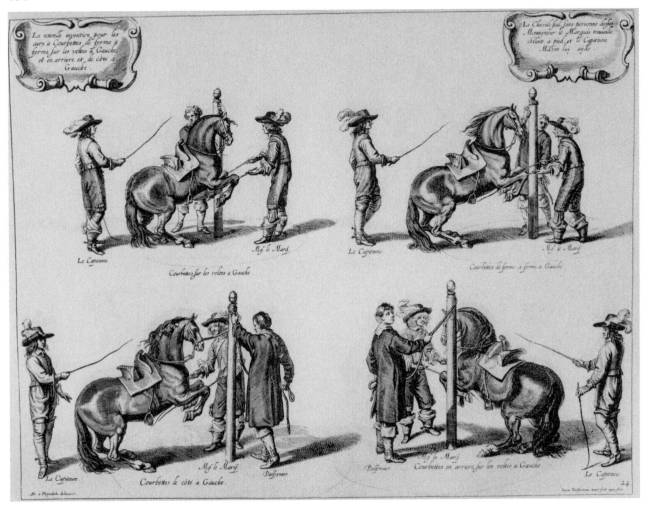

Plate 24

well as in England.

Plates 29 – 35 move outside to a display of the finished work by Newcastle himself. Having shown Welbeck Abbey in the stud plates and a general riding house interior in the training plates, the final display provides a suitable vehicle for showing the beauties of Bolsover Castle in the background. This progression from practical to theatricality fits in with the uses made of Newcastle's properties as while Welbeck was for everyday use, Bolsover Castle was for entertaining and pleasure.[261]

---

261   Lucy Worsley, 'Habitation', p.140.

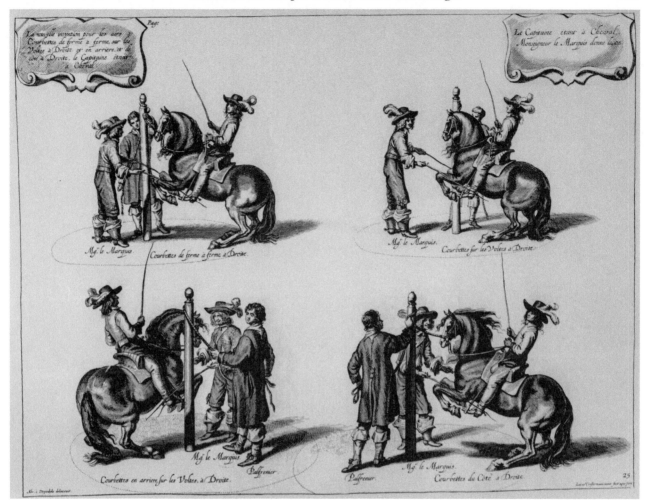

Plate 25

The relationship between the display areas and the castle are not accurate but Bolsover itself is recognisable within the context of artistic licence. These plates offer Newcastle, the exile, the opportunity to show his true location and social position, in relation to the beautiful castle built with his input. This series of plates offers not only seven examples of Newcastle and his horse executing highly advanced moves, but also seven perspectives of Bolsover Castle, illustrating its impressive position, aspects of the 'Little Castle' containing the reception and living accommodation, and the impressive gallery and riding house. While the legends on each plate are in the third person, describing 'Monsieur

Plate 26

le Marquis' and his properties, in plate 30 there is a slight slip in the note below the depiction of 'Ma Maison de Bolsover', and this use of the possessive first person indicates perhaps more clearly what these plates represent to the author of the text they accompany.

Plates 36 and 37 seem out of context as they return to the riding house, but the text also returns to matters Newcastle says he has forgotten to include earlier (1658: pp.a-19). In the conversational style of the text and the conceit of the tour, a return to the riding house to answer questions arising from the display offers greater continuity.

Plate 27

In plates 38, 40 and 41 the display is over and the guests accompany Newcastle out hunting. However, as he is not a great lover of the hunt, he displays his horse in airs while the chase is going on in the background, illustrating that, as noted by Edward Berry, 'Descriptions of hunting in parks suggest that, unlike par force hunting, this sport was not considered an end in itself [.......] but an adjunct to courtly pageantry.'[262] The legend establishes that plate 38 illustrates 'Le Parc de Welbeck', which is evidently an estate of some size, while the attractive long avenue between the trees giving a

262   *Shakespeare and the Hunt: A Cultural and Social Study* (Cambridge: Cambridge University Press, 2001), p.18.

Plate 28

fine vista. As with the horses, nature is perfected by the artistry of the landowner. There is considerable activity, with Newcastle presiding at the front of the scene on his curvetting horse. One other horse in the scene is clearly a riding house horse, as its tail is tied up for airs above the ground. This indicates the versatility Newcastle is always keen to emphasise (1667: p.6). Among the trees are hunters pursuing deer on horseback and on foot with dogs and long spears. Marksmen hunt with bow and arrow and firearms and the fecundity of the land is suggested by the many birds, including waterfowl, who supplement the five separate herds of deer as hunting quarry. The trees would not be out of place in a Flemish landscape and the rugged background is not especially evocative of England, though could

Plate 29

perhaps suggest the countryside of 'la Province de Nottingham'. More importantly, the scene is easily recognisable as a flourishing environment to the Continental reader enjoying the tour.

Plate 39 appears at first to be another slight diversion from the hunting plates it lies between, as it is a page of bits. However, it illustrates the point Newcastle is making in the text about the versatility of his method outside the riding house (1658: pp.263-268) and the correct bits for all activities. It serves in this respect almost as a 'close-up' of what is happening in the scene, so that the detail of tack that would be apparent to the interested guest in an actual visit to Newcastle's estates, is not denied to the reader.

Plate 30

Plate 40 removes the party to 'Le Chateau d'Ogle', Newcastle's Northumbrian estate, a similar scene of fertility and ordered nature. This is a more agricultural environment, with cattle and ploughed fields between the hunters and the moated house. Ducks again present themselves for the benefit of the wildfowlers who hunt with spaniels, suitably soft-mouthed dogs, rather than hounds, and a hawk, on foot and horseback. A female rider is among this group, but Newcastle again is alone in the foreground, executing a pesade. He and the other male riders carry riding-switches though the lady does not, indicating not only the male prerogative of the riding house, but also that the riders in this plate are observing rather than joining the hunt.

Plate 31

Plate 41 is another very active hunt scene in front of 'Le Chateau de Bothel dans la province de Northumberland'. Newcastle performs a ballotade in front of a wilder environment than either the neat deer park or the farmland seen so far but within the pale fence surrounding his mansion, nature is more ordered. While the hunters pursue the deer with hounds through the trees, inside the fence, a couple walk hand-in-hand on the drive leading to the house and ducks are settled on the moat, where a boat is moored and a man rows towards them. The smoking chimneys remind the guest that all these properties are thriving and active with occupants. Within the confines of the house and immediate lands, the peaceful mood contrasts with the hunt, but Newcastle, on the outside, still illustrates refinement and

Plate 32

control on his manège horse. Even in the wilderness, his hand is literally and figuratively on the reins.

Plate 42 ends the visit with a fantasy in which Newcastle, Margaret Cavendish, and all his sons, daughters and their spouses are gathered together to watch Charles and Henry Cavendish ride. In a similar way to plate 4, this echoes a religious iconography, perhaps unconsciously. Newcastle and Margaret Cavendish hold the positions of Christ and the Virgin in 'Coronation of the Virgin' art, with their family members as the court surrounding them. This is a dynastic gathering and also echoes the

Plate 33

Holbein Tudor dynastic portrait, which was destroyed in 1698.[263]

    Charles Cavendish's horse is on the left, which is correct in the left-to-right importance which in art recognises the natural movement of the human eye, as he is the elder of the two, while the spaniel-type dog running away is of the sort favoured by the Stuart kings. A peacock, symbol of constancy, is perched on a balustrade, and the smoking chimneys of a house can be glimpsed over the roof of the colonnaded seating area. The scene is one of aristocratic familial accord, as the observers chat and

---

263   Again, I am indebted to Professor Paul Spencer-Longhurst for his insights into this plate.

Plate 34

gesture towards the expertise displayed in the riding. The reader is also reminded of Newcastle as part of a dynasty, passing not only his blood, but skills which reinforce all that it is to be a gentleman to the next generation.

There is poignancy in the idealisation of his family and aristocratic environment Newcastle presents to round off this virtual tour of his estates. The people in this plate were never altogether in life and at the time the manual was published were scattered by his exile. The idyllic charm of this scene creates not only a virtual but parallel reality. Before the civil war, Newcastle's first wife was still alive, and after he left England, his estates were sequestered. In 1658, his favourite house, Bolsover,

Plate 35

was a 'castle ruin'd by war'[264] and he had no way of knowing if he would ever see his home or children again, yet in his faith and optimism, he presents an idyll of restoration and reunion.

A great subtlety underlies this guided tour for the guest who can only visit the estate of the great grandee and horsemaster through art. The virtual tour is able to visit properties that an actual visitor would need several days to view, and the Continental reader can be easily offered an effective guide-book, prefiguring those that became available in the eighteenth century for great houses. In the

---

264 *Poems, and Fancies*, p.89.

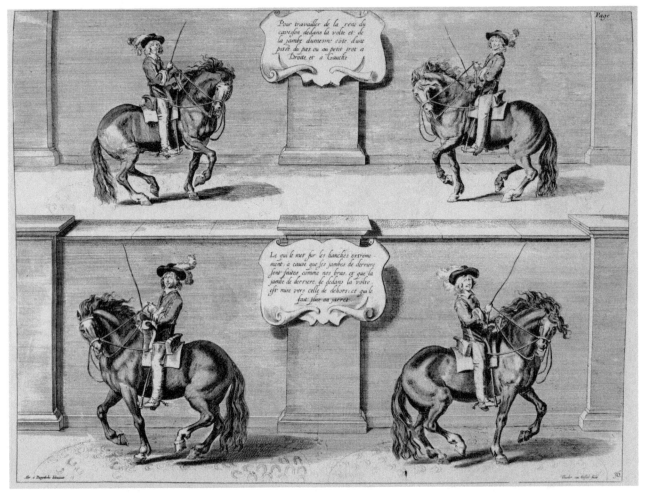

Plate 36

peaceful world of the plates, war and exile do not exist, all is fertile and flourishing and a man's grace and nobility may be demonstrated with due grandeur.

In the context of art and court culture, Newcastle uses imagery familiar to his own kind to underline his message. The subtext of the plates would have spoken to the contemporary reader of his 1658 manual to assert his lineage and status. With detailed technical accuracy he illustrates his expertise with his horses, and through the attention to small detail, such as his relationships with Captain Mazin and John Proctor, he positions himself in the social scale. He always has a servant in attendance and does not work in an Academy, surrounded by students and courtiers, but rides and

Plate 37

trains in his own inherited estates, drawing his peers to admire him through the manual itself.

The 1667 manual with its accounts of those peers and their lavish praise of his work in the small colony he established in 'my own private Riding-House at Antwerp', to some extent brings to fruition the intent of the first, but it lacks the beauty of the plates themselves. This could be interpreted as a loss of faith in the importance of statements of personal status had not Newcastle at that time been undertaking the complete renovation of Nottingham Castle. Acquired following his return from exile, his plans were for the utmost grandeur in all aspects of its presentation, including the life-size statue of himself on horseback discussed above. The absence of the plates in the 1667 manual is

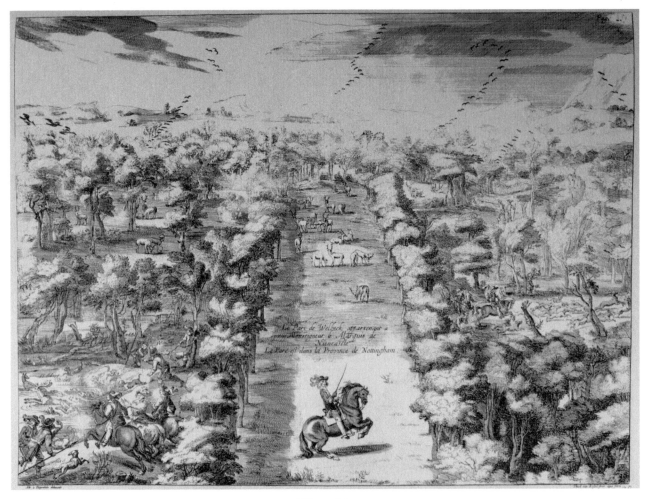

Plate 38

most likely simply to do with unavailability: they may have been temporarily lost or misplaced in the upheaval of the relocation of Newcastle's household from Antwerp to England. The creation of new plates, of indifferent quality, for the translation of the 1667 manual into French in 1674 supports that possibility.[265]

An alternative possibility is that financial considerations meant that including the plates was not possible. The horsemanship manuscript that can be firmly given a post-restoration date, states clearly the intent that 'Heer mingled In the mos proper places I woulde have figures putt' (PwV 22,

---

265   Toole-Stott, p.87; see Chapter 1, p. 5, for an example of one of the new plates from a German/French edition of 1700.

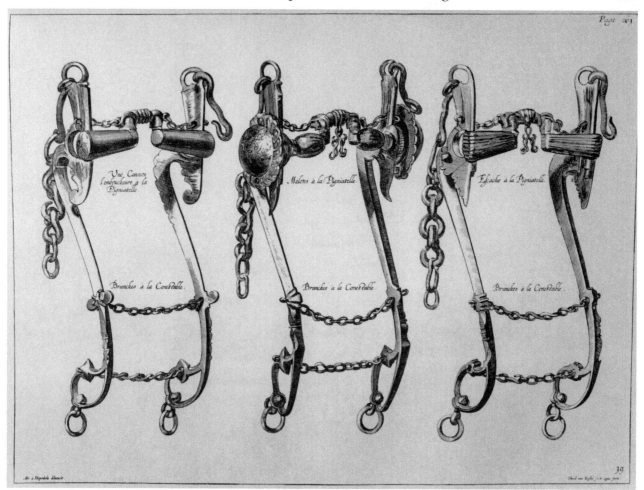

Plate 39

fol.7). Therefore, the absence of any plates was a change in his plans. The reclamation process after the return home caused continual financial worries, both in the need to pay off debts and to meet his determinedly liberal spending on rebuilding his estates. But the precipitous path between financial ruin and aristocratic liberality was one Newcastle trod all his life so that, with the plates to hand and the desire to use them, it seems likely that he would have found the financial means do so somehow.

A final consideration is that the plates depict Newcastle and his estates in their pre-war splendour, including an image of his son Charles, immortalised forever through Diepenbeecke's detailed illustrations. But that illusion could not be maintained in the face of his return to England.

Plate 40

By 1667, Newcastle was an old man at seventy-four, his estates were still being rebuilt after the deprivations of the Civil War and Charles had died of a stroke in 1659. While his plans for the future of his estates were very grand, the 1658 plates show a world that had irrevocably changed. It may be that some combination of all three possibilities led to the absence of the engravings from his second manual and it not possible to draw an emphatic conclusion. But their absence is notable and gives a sparse quality to the second manual that is uncharacteristic of the author.

Plate 41

As with much of the subtext to the manuals, loss adds desperation to Newcastle's attempt to hold on to those places and activities in which he has such faith. In the life of the manuals, the plates are a key to the motivation behind the 1658 text and perhaps the lack of them is the key to that of 1667. As Malcolm Smuts says, 'paintings and rituals can be analysed as non-verbal systems of communication analogous to language'[266] so the inclusion and later absence of the plates in the manuals may be seen

---

266 *Court Culture and the Origins of a Royalist Tradition in Early Stuart England* (Philadelphia: University of Pennsylvania Press, 1987), p.6.

Plate 42

as eloquent. The insights they provide into Newcastle's activities and beliefs are invaluable alongside their role as very beautiful records of an idyll that had gone forever by the time they came into being.

Chapter 7

Conclusion

A man, the vicissitudes of whose life were like the changes of an April sky.
Edward Jenkins, *The Cavalier and his Lady*

Newcastle's horsemanship manuals are not readily classifiable. They are books about training horses and key texts in the history of man and an animal that has helped shape human development. This alone makes them worthy of close attention. Yet they also offer an insight into the influence of court culture upon the individual and the way in which political and personal motivation may be approached though a life's passion. In this respect they are as much biographies as Margaret Cavendish's *Life*, though written in a language not all can read.

As both anachronism and innovation, the manuals appear in many respects to be a means of working through a grieving process for a lost way of life, while attempting to offer a model for the future. Anne Barton comments that, 'Political and socioeconomic dislocations force people to filter, select, and reconstruct a past' which despite its vagaries at the time becomes a way of 'affirming the essential continuity of the self'. She adds that such nostalgia 'is bound up, too, with what psychologists call "the life review": the impulse, in late middle age, to evaluate and re-possess the world of one's youth'.[267] Newcastle's nostalgia for the good old days of his boyhood is particularly evident in his 'little book' of advice to Charles II, but the horsemanship manuals follow the pattern Barton suggests in a way which is both for the public domain and 'also intensely private'.[268] Therefore, despite their specialist content, the manuals as a whole are evidence of Newcastle's coping strategy both during his exile and at the Restoration. They illustrate the balance between traditionalist and forward thinker as he roots himself in the security of established skills and beliefs, but then reshapes and develops models for the future.

This leads inevitably to the question of the impact of the work, both on the art of horsemanship and for Newcastle himself. His concerns for the art of riding are evident through both manuals and, after the Restoration, Charles II's loss of interest can only have harmed the popularity of the art. By the

---

267   Anne Barton, 'Harking back to Elizabeth: Ben Jonson and Caroline Nostalgia', *ELH*, 48.4 (1981), p.724.
268   Ibid.

time the second book appeared and the new normal was being established, Newcastle was almost more socially adrift than during his exile. Having anticipated an active role in the Restoration court, he:

> went to his gracious Sovereign, and begged leave that he might retire to the country, to reduce and settle, if possible, his confused, entangled and almost ruined estate. "Sir," said he to his Majesty, "I am not ignorant, that many believe I am discontented; and 'tis probable they'll say, I retire through discontent: but I take God to witness, that I am in no kind or ways displeased; for I am so joyed at your Majesty's happy restoration, that I cannot be sad or troubled for any concern of my own particular; but whatsoever your Majesty is pleased to command me, were it to sacrifice my life, I shall most obediently perform it; for I have no other will, but your Majesty's pleasure" (*Life*: p.131).

Even allowing for Margaret Cavendish's romanticising of her husband's life, this touching withdrawal speech rings true in essence from the evidence of the 'little book', and the dedications to Charles in the two horsemanship manuals. Absence from the court reduced Newcastle's opportunity to actively raise the profile of the art but his second manual set out to counter that problem. Also, his continued practice at Welbeck continued to fulfil the model he laid out in both manuals. Reports that his horses 'exercise their gifts in his magnificent Riding-House' and were 'more extraordinary than are to be seen in Europe' suggest an ongoing and developing post-Restoration reputation. The more homely account of daily life at Welbeck relates that 'the horses were a Riding and we present as usually' [269] even after Newcastle himself had ceased to ride, due to his wife's concern that 'after he had overheated himself, he would be apt to take cold' (*Life*: pp.208-209). He also actively continued aiming his work at the Continent with further editions and translations of his manuals as discussed in previous chapters.

Whether any of this fulfilled Newcastle's emotional need for a secure locus is impossible to say but the small collection of unpublished epigrams in the Portland Collection suggests an ongoing frustration. [270] While some of the songs, verses and letters in this collection are dated, others are not, but evidence of revision suggests, as seen in the horsemanship manuals, ongoing editing over a period of time.

There is a sadness in these fragments as records of a man whose life went out of fashion. The epigram 'On Runninge Horses' that considers racing a 'Vayne' waste of 'ritches' causing injury and death is regretful that a pastime 'Worthless of Honor' should now be so popular, which suggests a

---

269   Quoted in Whitaker, p.342; Pw1 315, fol.5; observed rehearsal serves a practical purpose in preparing for performance and is still current at the Spanish Riding School of Vienna.

270   PwV25.

post-Restoration date. The bitterness that realises 'Eatch seemes a loyall Harte, with Cristall Breste; Butt Heese thought wisest that can ['doth' deleted] jugle Beste' seems weary with fruitless trying and the poem 'Of Courte Hopes' realises 'Courte hopes do['th' deleted] make men ['me' deleted] waytye neer yet att Large'.[271]

The revisions in Newcastle's hand that change this from a personal to a general observation are revealing in removing his own experiences from the focus of the complaint. Yet these unhappy verses show by contrast the hope and the fear evident in the horsemanship manuals, when Newcastle attempted through his writing to keep his profile high and relevant, both for his faith in himself it seems, as well as for the security of his future.

However, there is evidence in near-contemporary sources that Newcastle's manuals had impact and perhaps served to prevent a complete decline of the art in this country, while making an impression upon the Continent. Whether he was aware of that is difficult to say, as these published references to his manuals did not appear until after his death.[272] Perhaps the greatest contemporary compliment, and the strongest evidence of Newcastle's importance in his own time, is the tribute to his work in the writing of Jacques de Solleysel.

The friendship between Newcastle and Solleysel seems to have lacked any of the rivalry that might be expected between two masters aiming to establish themselves in the same art. Solleysel's offer to translate Newcastle's second manual into good French, following the poor edition of 1671, was in itself a generous gesture, importing further material by the English author into French riding houses.[273] However, in Solleysel's own manual, which is on the choice and care of horses rather than training, he includes a long consideration of Newcastle's work, which is not the hyperbolic praise common at the time, but an objective appreciation and critical appraisal of work he considers to be of great importance.[274]

Solleysel was a horsemaster to Louis XIV in the Royal Academy of Riding at Paris and his own manuals were highly influential in France and translated into English in 1696, by Sir William Hope.[275] Solleysel writes modestly that even though he has taught riding and been complimented on his skill,

---

271 PwV 25, fols. 19, 38, 144.

272 While effusive letters of praise for the horsemanship manuals may be found in *A Collection of Letters and Poems [...]to the late Duke and Duchess of Newcastle*, already cited, these are not helpful in gauging a genuine response, due to their nature as courtesy responses to gifts of his book made by Newcastle.

273 London: Thomas Milbourn, 1671; Traduction nouvelle [...] par Monsieur de Solleysel (Paris: Gervaise Clousier, 1677).

274 Jacques de Solleysel, *La Parfait Mareschal*; Solleysel's manual went through various editions and revisions between 1664-1782 (see Toole-Stott, pp.190-110). Hope's title page says that he used 'the latest Paris edition' for his translation, which seems likely to have been that issued by Gervaise Clousier in 1694.

275 Already cited. All subsequent references to Solleysel's work are to this translation, which also includes Hope's own analysis. References to Hope are therefore indicated by his name, but still refer to this publication.

he does not presume to write his own training manual. Instead, he recommends that, 'if any person relish the little I have said, and that his curiosity excite him to know more, Let him read the works of Monsieur de la Broue and those of the great Duke of Newcastle'.[276]

This recommendation of an English author, while omitting any mention of Pluvinel is intriguing, especially as Solleysel adds that old methods of horsemanship are 'much improved of late, as you will see by what I faithfully relate, from the Writings of the Duke of Newcastle upon this matter'. His high opinion of Newcastle does not preclude differing with him occasionally or adding his own ideas as well and this text is a most fascinating and unusual one in this approach, and therefore, of much greater value in considering Newcastle's impact. There can be little greater assurance of Newcastle's contribution on the Continent than for a high status French rider to recommend his work and include it in his own manual. Solleysell carefully ensures that his comments are distinguished by a figure in the margin, so he should not be thought to be writing 'a Treatise taken Verbatim from another author, without so much as either mentioning the Author's name or the Title of the Book from whence he Coppied it'.[277]

Sadly this tribute did not appear until after Newcastle's death, as it would surely have been a great pleasure to him. However, it testifies to his influence among his contemporaries and when Sir William Hope translated Solleysel into English some twenty years later, he added his own testimony, referring to 'the Prince of horseman, the Unparalleled and Famous Duke of Newcastle (whose Memory for his extraordinary skills in this Art will be for ever an Honour to his Nation)'[278]. His text follows immediately from his translation of Solleysel but has its own title page, which proclaims Newcastle to be among 'the Best and most Modern Authors' on horsemanship. Hope's 'most Compendious and Excellent Treatise of Riding' is a gathering of information from 'the very best of writers upon this Subject', such as 'La Brow, Pluvinel and the Great Duke of Newcastle; But chiefly out of this last', along with his own comments.

Unlike Solleysel, Hope assimilates the work of his heroes without reservation, making no attempt to distinguish which author's writing he is using. Most of his material is an illustration of the point made by Solleysel about wholesale unreferenced use, which is ironic, as it is Hope who translates this comment. Even his title page claims that by his treatise 'all kinds of Horses may be wrought according to Nature and Perfected by the Subtility of Art', a direct use of the legend from Newcastle's title page. This assimilation continues on the first page of text, so that his opening paragraph is easily recognisable to any reader familiar with Newcastle's manual:

---

276   Solleysel, p.79.

277   Ibid.

278   Hope, sig.**2-***v.

The Art of Riding is so Noble and Gentile an Exercise, that it would require a
whole Book merely to deduce and express the Excellency; For as to Pleasure and
State, what Prince or Monarch looks more Great or more Enthron'd than upon a
beautiful Horse, with rich Furniture, and waving Plumes, making his Entry through
great Cities, to amaze the People with Pleasure and Delight.[279]

This plagiarism is clearly as much by way of tribute as Solleysel's carefully referenced text and both are highly unusual and especially interesting in the close proximity of Hope's translation. Gerard Langbaine pays tribute to Newcastle's influence in his 1685 text *The Hunte: A Discourse of Horsemanship* and later in 1691, in his *Account of the English Dramatick Poets*. In 1685, Langbaine, while writing about the hunting horse, nevertheless notes that 'his readiness to obey the hand and heels, equals him to the Mannag'd Horse'. Newcastle is referred to as an authority, both in his assertion of the riding house as a demanding sport, and across other areas of breeding and preparation of the horse. Langbaine repeatedly adds 'as the Duke of Newcastle says' when requiring affirmation of his own ideas. Langbaine is somewhere between Solleysel and Hope as he does reference his sources but in a fairly casual way, so that their words are mingled with his own. He refers also to Markham and de Grey but Newcastle is, in his opinion, the real expert.[280]

In his later text, after praising Newcastle as 'our English Mecaenas' [*sic*] for his writing in general, he focuses on the horsemanship manuals. Freely borrowing from the 1667 manual to illustrate Newcastle's importance on the Continent, he declares that the first book was 'the most Magnificent, and withal the Best Book of Horsemanship, that was ever extant'. The author's skill 'in that Noble Art of Dressing Horses in the Manage, is well known not only to our Countrymen but to all Nations of Europe'. Most interesting in Langbaine's rhetorical and enthusiastic praise is his reference to Solleysel 'one of the best Writers that I have met with amongst the French' and his tribute to Newcastle when he 'borrowed the Art of Breeding from the Duke's Book, as he owns in his *Avis au Lecteur*; and stiles him *Un des plus accomplish Cavaliers de nôtres temps'*. With some pride he adds:

But having nam'd this Foreigner's borrowing from his Grace, I should justly
deserve to be branded with Ingratitude, should I not own, That 'tis to the Work of
this Great man, that I am indebted for several Notions borrow'd from his Grace, in
a little essay of Horsemanship, printed [....] 1685. Nay, further, I think it no small
glory that I am the onely Author that I know of who has quoted him in English.

---

279 Hope, sig. **2-***v.
280 Langbaine, *The Hunte* (Oxford: Nicholas Cox, 1685), sig. A2; p.4; pp.9, 52; *An Account of the English Dramatic Poets* (London: 1691; rpt. Augustan Reprint Society, University of California, 1971).

18th century engraving by Elias J. Ridinger, showing use of Newcastle's cavesson design.

This is a useful historical detail, assuming that Langbaine is correct, so that Solleysel appears to be the first author to quote Newcastle, with Langbaine ten years later and Sir William Hope ten years later still. Langbaine also adds what seems likely to be the first bibliographical references to his texts:

> He has written two Books of Horsemanship; the first in French, called *La Methode nouvelle de Dresser les Chevaux, avec Figures,* Fol. *Ant.* 1658. The other in *English,* stiled *A New Method and Extraordinary Invention to dress horses [....],* Fol. *Lond.* 1667.

Langbaine is aware that he is fulsome in his praise and adds, 'I beg my Reader's Pardon, if I have dwelt upon this Subject, to the tryal of his Patience; but I have [....] such Respect for the Memory of the best of Horseman, that I cannot refrain from trespassing yet further', and so ends with Jonson's epigram to Newcastle upon horseback.[281] These rather charming and effusive few pages offer useful evidence for the reception of Newcastle's books and at least some continuing interest in the art, despite the popularity of the race-track. The anonymous poem *The Horsemanship of England,* while 'Most particularly relating to the Breeding and Training of the Running-Horse', nevertheless opens its dedication to the ill-fated Duke of Monmouth by declaring that 'To observe you guiding the manag'd Horse, and how becoming your seat is there, would out-do all Complement to express'.[282] While the dedication goes on to assure Monmouth of his skill on the race course also, the mention of the 'manag'd Horse' suggests that not all of the royal circle had abandoned the art, so that, as in Langbaine's text, it remains a point of reference for other styles of riding.

While the rush of new manuals between the mid-sixteenth and seventeenth centuries had slowed, texts were still being printed and Newcastle had evidently joined Grisone and Pluvinel as a seminal author. Also translations and editions of Newcastle's manuals continued after his death across the Continent into the middle of the next century, from Louis Imbotti de Beaumont's derivative text, borrowing almost word for word from Newcastle, in 1682, to Claude Bourgelat's simplified version, *Le Nouveau Newcastle* in 1744. The next seminal horsemanship author, Francois de la Guérinière, considered that Newcastle's work was unique with his book being one of only two early manuals he considers useful, the second being that of Salamon de la Broue. Like Solleysel, he quotes Newcastle directly, deferring to his ideas as 'it would be foolhardy not to follow such opinion'.[283]

---

281   Langbaine, *English Dramatick Poets*, pp.386, 388, 389.
282   London: Thomas Parkhurst, 1682, sig. A, in *Early English Books Online* < http://gateway.proquest.com/openurl?ctx_ver=Z39.88-2003&res_id=xri:eebo&rft_val_fmt=&rft_id=xri:eebo:image:154211>[accessed 31 August 2004]
283   La Guérinière, p.87.

These responses to Newcastle's manuals demonstrate not only that his work was innovative to his immediate readers but also of sound and lasting influence to later generations. He remains the only English author to make a serious and lasting contribution to the development of an art that has survived to the present day. From the perspective of value to modern scholarship, this locates him as unique in many ways.

As a noble author, Newcastle's high status and patronage of arts and sciences placed him in the public eye as that most desirable of Renaissance figures, the glass of fashion and mould of form. His struggles with bad luck and unfulfilled ambition are not apparent through beautiful and impressive texts. Therefore, his confident voice and opinionated stance impress upon his reader that the uniqueness of his contribution is linked to noble birth, reinforcing his royalist philosophies. However, from the perspective of Douglas Bush's point that 'Renaissance heroes, like classical heroes, are eminent in worldly position as well as character' so that 'moral success or failure is so much more impressive and far-reaching in its effects',[284] it may be that Newcastle's stormy history added to the impact of his heroic self-presentation for those readers that knew of his past.

He is also unique in that his horsemanship manuals are only part of a large canon of work, in a great many genres and styles. Through the horsemanship manuals, Newcastle created a private court through which he could locate himself in the public domain, so that writing offered a literal 're-creation' of himself. In this respect, proximity with the mercurial mind of Margaret Cavendish and their evident influence upon one another as writers becomes significant. It is impossible to say if Newcastle's creation of riding house worlds influenced Margaret Cavendish, or whether her ability to create fantasy worlds for herself influenced him. Certainly he was training horses in riding houses before she was born. However, they were in Antwerp together in the early years of their marriage and when she returned to London in the 1650s to petition for funds from his sequestered estates, and created a notional space for herself through her writing, he was defining his own space in Rubens' studio. Cavendish writes in *Sociable Letters* (1664) of how she enjoyed the recollections of performances she saw in Antwerp within her own mind, where 'to please me, my Fancy set up a Stage in my Brain'.[285] As Sophie Tomlinson says, 'Cavendish's writing is acutely conscious of 'Fancy's' power to substitute the scene of the mind for the theatre of the world'.[286] John Berger considers that a man's 'social presence' is 'dependent upon the promise of power which he embodies'. That power may be 'moral, physical, temperamental, economic, social, sexual', but 'its object is always exterior to the man'.[287] Close links in the writing practice of this husband and wife partnership demonstrate that the meeting between her satisfaction with her imagination and his restless need for such social presence may have enabled them

---

284   'The Isolation of the Renaissance Hero' in *Reason and the Imagination*, already cited, p.60.
285   *Sociable Letters* (London: William Wilson, 1664), p.408.
286   Clare Brant & Diane Purkiss, eds., *Women, Texts & Histories: 1575-1760* (London: Routledge, 1992), p.135.
287   *Ways of Seeing* (London: BBC/Penguin Books, 1977), p.45.

both to manifest 'fancy' into reality in ways that assisted the psychological survival of their exile.

Along with all the multi-layered purposes of the horsemanship texts, Newcastle's attempt to locate himself as still belonging to England and his family estates, yet claiming a synonymous influence on European horsemanship, is written into the subtext. In the first manual, by locating himself visually through the plates amid his own estates, by implication he also restores Charles to his throne. In the plates, the ravages of the Civil War are either unacknowledged or repaired so that all's right with the English countryside and its government once more. The fecundity of the landscape, amid which gentlemanly pursuits can be followed, offers evidence that life is rich and secure, which it can only be with the rightful monarch on the throne. Thus the writing of the first manual becomes not only nostalgic, but prophetic. His writing style serves to persuade, assert and educate and its great value is in the strong sense that he can be 'heard', so the contrast between his style and that of other authors becomes another aspect of his individuality. The tone of voice in his texts is not the polite refined deference of Pluvinel to his monarch. Newcastle's sweeping assured style is the voice of a confident man, at ease in the company of the highest nobility, with a mission to rally his Continental peers in times of unease.

However, his defensiveness and arrogance reveal his own unease and Insecurity. This is especially true in the second manual, where his fury erupts against Blundeville and those who are more interested in 'wearing Fine Cloaths and Feathers' (1667: p.9) than aspiring to true nobility in the riding house. Therefore, his emphasis on practice rather than theory offers a strong sense that the manuals do not simply fulfil an idea of himself as the focus of European horsemanship, but set out a blueprint for how that will be achieved.

His reference to 'my own private Riding-House at Antwerp' (1667: sig. B^v) becomes a form of colonisation that served him especially well during his exile, creating a notional court suitable for the 'tres-puissant Prince' his title-pages assert him to be. By locating himself in the context of earlier writers, Newcastle claimed the solidity and security of a sense of place that was important to him throughout his life.

A personal place, a 'room of his own' in whatever situation he found himself to establish a *ménage* that went far beyond the simple needs of the *manège*, and that he could be recognised as occupying, was quintessential to him. Therefore comparisons with the work of other authors and the ways in which he related his two manuals to earlier texts illustrate that he used the context both of his English lineage and Continental exile to make each manual work as a retrospective that contextualised him. While his horsemanship manuals may seem small stuff after war and political upheaval, the first text rooted Newcastle in a world that seemed lost and reminded his readers of the importance of nobility and appearance for the aristocracy. The second established his exile as a time of great influence and impact upon his Continental peers.

Stephen Greenblatt says that Renaissance figures 'understand that in our culture to abandon self-fashioning is to abandon the craving for freedom, and to let go of one's stubborn hold upon selfhood, even selfhood conceived as fiction, is to die'.[288] Newcastle typifies this awareness in his self-conscious and deeply held belief that he must make a place for himself, regardless of the circumstances. The manuals create a personal location, fixed in print, which the winds of change could not influence. In this too, he is unique. No other significant horsemanship author in the early modern period writes during a time of enforced exile or in circumstances where his personal emotional survival is so evidently linked to his method of horse-training.

Yet this never compromises their practical application as not only beautiful and philosophical reminders of an elite way of life, but as genuine 'hands-on' guides to living that life through skill, hard work and dedication. Through the reiteration of values such as noble display and the loving fear for the superior, writing the riding house enables him to write himself, so that in using the method he reinforces his life. The great sense of indignation against those who say 'that all things in the Mannage is nothing but Tricks, and Dancing, and Gamballs, and of no use' (1667: p.5), reveals perhaps a secret fear that the value of beauty for its own sake is lost or become worthless. His long list of noblemen who support his views sounds anxious and while he states 'I leave every one to his own Wayes, and his own Delights, desiring they will do the like by Me', the very act of writing and publishing reveals a need to persuade. Thus, when he declares 'But if it Chances they will not be Gracious, and Just to me [.....] I shall Sleep never the Worse'(1667: p.14), it is hard to believe him. It seems likely that Newcastle frequently lost sleep over the future of horsemanship and though he assures his readers that 'the King takes it for no Disgrace to be an Excellent Horseman', knew full well that the days of the king's enthusiasm for the art were over (1667: p.7).

As the service of the horse does not degrade but ennobles it, so his service to the monarchy ennobled him, and if little service was required then he accepted that. There was a freedom in this, through the perspective offered by Hobbes, that again casts light upon Newcastle's method as well as his own life. Quentin Skinner's analysis of Hobbes' theory of freedom under law perfectly describes Newcastle's expectation of his horses as their natural leader and also of himself in his own natural relationship to his monarch:

> We can now see the sense in which you remain free according to Hobbes when you act in obedience to law. When the law coerces you into obeying by activating your fears about the consequences of disobedience, it does not do so by inducing you to act against your will, thereby causing you to act less freely. It always does so by inducing you to deliberate in such a way that you give up your will to disobey, and thereafter act freely in the light of the will you have acquired.[289]

---

288   Greenblatt, p.257.

289   Quentin Skinner, *Liberty before Liberalism* (Cambridge University Press: 1998), p.8.

As a man who was acutely aware of the role of host, patron and aristocrat, the manuals become the idealised performance of his life. No earlier or subsequent horsemanship author attempts such an enterprise and in the successful combination of art, technique and propaganda, Newcastle's work is significant in ways that travel far beyond the presentation of a courtly art.

Therefore, in this study I have shown that a comprehensive approach to Newcastle's manuals reveals horsemanship as a paradigm for life as theatre that he fully exploited and celebrated, both philosophically and practically. As a man who achieved a lifestyle notable in its grandeur yet never quite reaching the heights of court influence he desired, the theatricality of the riding house suited his temperament and offered a means of influencing his peers. The overall achievement of the manuals is that they create harmony in a time of chaos; they provide their author with a platform from which he can rally the like-minded, instruct the eager mind and forge ahead in the development of an influential art. He builds upon the precedent of the horsemanship manual as guide to an elite art to achieve his aims and then speaks clearly and with passion. His sweeping enthusiasm for all that he believes in creates a place where it can thrive beyond the time of its creation so that the manuals become a triumph both of exile and of restoration.

Yet they remain poignant also, full of the fear of loss and the awareness that one man's faith may be insufficient to repair the ravages of time and fashion. However, rather than giving their author pause, this doubt inspires him rather to attempt to save the art of the riding house, as well as reminding those who had forgotten his true worth that he still had much to offer.

Newcastle's last great building project was at Nottingham Castle, which he managed to buy only two years before his death at the age of eighty-three. Although he did not survive to see the project completed, his plans were ambitious and show no lessening over time of his belief in noble display. Today, at Nottingham Castle, the remains of the statue of Newcastle upon horseback, like Oxymandias, offer mute evidence of the way in which time resists human attempts at immortality though works. However, they still recall a character of great charisma and resilience, and in opening the horsemanship manuals that character is released, as vigorous, arrogant and confident now as when he set pen to paper to seek a less visible but more lasting means of immortality.

Any rider today who works a horse from a lunging cavesson would recognise the illustration in Plate 13, because, despite changes in modern usage, they are employing equipment Newcastle designed. Anyone who rides a horse in a 'shoulder-in' uses an exercise that has hardly changed since he created it. In considering his texts in their early modern context, we see at once his relationship to the horsemasters of his own time, while by opening any comprehensive modern manual we can easily locate his legacy. Even developments in horse handling in the last fifteen years, based on the horse's comfort in leadership, seem less innovative having looked at Newcastle's manuals.[290]

---

290   Monty Roberts, Pat Parelli and Mark Rashid are just three of a considerable body of American trainers who have

My aim has been to identify the value of Newcastle's manuals as a whole, to both the early modern scholar and the rider. For the historian, they are evidence of the importance that a contribution to horsemanship meant in the early modern period not simply as a leisure activity but also as a manifestation of Newcastle's personal philosophy. To the rider, they offer sound common-sense advice about approach and handling horses. Even where they are outdated by modern understanding and attitudes, they reveal the extent to which our own ideas are received and rooted in the culture of a much earlier time.

The manuals themselves, however, offer the most direct contact with the vital spirit of a humane man whose wit and knowledge can be found untouched by time or opinion, and whose essential enjoyment of his art perhaps offers the ultimate interpretation:

> I beseech my Readers, to take in good part, That I have set down, as clearly as I
> could, without the Help of any other Logick, but what Nature hath taught me, all
> the Observations about Horses and Horsemanship; which I have made, by a long,
> and chargeable, though I must needs say, very pleasant, and satisfactory,
> Experience (1667: sig. B^v).

---

made their mark on British and European riders today much as the Italian trainers did in Newcastle's youth. Newcastle would consider many of their methods his own.

Appendix

Prefatory material and verses with translations:
La Methode Nouvelle et Invention Extraordinairre, 1658

Au Roy de la Grande-Bretagne (1658 : sig.^{1}- d^{1v}),

Elle,

Plus grande-honneur je n'ay jamais eu, & je n'en puis souhaiter de plus sur-eminent, que celuy d'avoir été le premier Gouverneur de Votre Majesté, lors qu'Elle toit Prince de Galles, & âgée de huit ans seulement. Je remarquay alors par les tendrons d'un naturel Royal, quelle abondance de fruits vertueux Elle nouse apporter oit en son age plus meur. Je considéray Sa douceur naturelle, pour être autant au dessus du commun, comme l'avantage de Sa naissance l'élevé pardessus le reste des homes, comme si Dieu & la nature l'eussent destine a présider sur le bon naturel mesme, qui est la base & le fondement de toute bonté.

Mais le temps où nous sommes me fait croire, que la nature a départi tant de douceur, & de bonté à Votre Majesté, qu'elle n'en a point laisse à la plus grand-part de Vos sujets. De sorte que Votre Majesté pourroit recevoir du désavantage des libéralités de la Nature envers Elle, si elle ne luy avoit donne un jugement tres-serain & tres-net, pour rectifier leurs défauts par Sa justice. Et comme Elle est le Député de Dieuenterre & sonvray Oint, Elle peut imiter la Divinité, qui châtie sans être fâchée ; ainsy Elle preservera Sa douceur, & montrera a Ses sujets que Sa miséricorde surpasse Sa justice.

Je vis aussy aux jeunes ans de Votre Majesté les trois parties d'une boneame (& il ni en a que trois) l'espirit, le jugement, & la mémoire, ou bien les facultés, par lequelles nous comparons les choses ensemble, nous en souvenons. Vous les avies alors pour Votre age au plus haut degré, & avec L'admiration de tout le monde. Je m'asseure que Votre Majesté, a cause de ces troubles mal-heureux, est apresent parvenue a la Maitrisede Sa charge Royale, qui est deconnoitre l'espirit, & le naturel des hommes, qui sont, pour la plus part tromeurs, d'autant qu'il y en a plus des meschans, que des bons ; & comme dit l'Escriture Sainte PLUSIEURS SONT APPELLES ET PEU ELUS.

Il ne faut pas, SIRE, que j'oublie, que j'ay eu l'honneur de Vous mettre le premier a cheval dans le Manège, ou Votre Majesté a tellement proufite, qu'a l'age de neuf a dix ans ; Elle n'avoit pas seulement la plus belle, & la plus ferme assiette que j'aye jamais veue, mais aussy la plus grande addresse, & jugement : outre qu'Elle avoit des aides les plus délicates pour faire aller un cheval parfaitement, fust a la Soldade, Passades, Terre a terre, ou par Haut. Votre Majesté monta deux chevaux dispos DESPERATO, & BALOT, quoy que tres-rebours, avec tant de bonne-grace, d'aise & de justesse, que les meilleurs Cavaliers quietoient auprès d'Elle, & la regardeoient avec admiration, en etoient tous étonnes.

Quelques-uns, qui etoient la, & qui avoient appris aux Académies étrangères, eussent été, sinon tout a fait, au moins presques jettes par terre par les mesmes chevaux. Le Roy Votre Père, de glorieuse Mémoire, disoit, qu'il n'avoit jamais veu aucun de Votre age qui Vous approchât de bien loin a monter a cheval (Sa Majesté etoittre-capable d'en juger) il disoit qu'il cherchoit quelque faute, mais qu'il n'en pouvoit treuver. Par tous ces titres, SIRE, ce liure de la Cavaleries est Votre : & je n'aurois pas présume de le dédier a Votre Majesté, si je n'avois sceu, qu'il apporte au monde des nouvelle dans le vray Art de dresser les chevaux, lesquelles jusques icy n'ont point été connues. Puis donc que Votre Majesté est Maître en cet Art, aimez les chevaux : car un Prince n'est jamais accompagne de tant de majesté, mesmement sur son throne, comme il est sur un beau cheval. C'est la créature, entre toutes les autres, a qui l'homme a le plus d'obligation, tant pour l'usage, que pour le plaisir, & tant pour son honneur, que pour sa vie ; comment donc peut-on faire trop grande estime d'un bon cheval ?

Combien de Roys & grands Princes y a-t-il, qui ontevite le reproche d'être pris prisonniers, & ont sauve leur vie & leur honneur tout ensemble par la bonté & excellence de leurs chevaux ? dequoy plusieures histoires nous font foy. Qui plus est, un Roy, étant bon Cavalier, scaura beaucoup mieux comme il faudra gouverner ses peuples, quand il faudra les récompenser, ou les châtier ; quand il faudra leur tenir la main serrée, ou quand il faudra la relâcher ; quand il faudra les aider doucement, ou en quel temps il sera convenable de les éperonner. Il ne faut jamais les monter jusques a leur faire perde l'haleine, ou bien ils deviendront rétifs, & rebelles, ou (comme l'on dit) ils prendront la bride aux dents, & s'emporteront ; mais il faut plutost les traiter doucement, & ne prendre que la moitie de leurs forces, affin qu'ils puissent être gaillards, & faire toutes choses de leur bon gré, & avec vigeur.

Il ne faut pas que d'autres les montent trop souvent, ni les harassent : mais il faut les garder pour la selle de Votre Majesté seulement, c'est a dire, en ses affaires particulières, & celles du public. Or on se doit toujours modérer dans les passions, parce que la multitude capricieuse est une beste a plusieures testes, de sorte qu'il faut qu'elle ait plusieures brides, mais non pas plusieures éperons ; car plusieures testes doivent avoir plusieures brides, mias la République, n'ayant qu'un corps, elle ne doit avoir qu'une paire d'éperons, & qui doivent être ceux de Votre Majesté, contre lesquels ils ne se rebelleront jamais, mais obéiront toujours, & les prendront pour une Aide, plutost que pour un Châtiment. Ils se rebellerot contre les éperons de ses sujets, & combie qu'ils les montent sans éperons, comme des poulains, neantmoins ils les jetteront par terre, & peut-être leur feront prendre quelque tour de Rosse, en sorte que Votre Majesté pourroit être en danger a la prochaine-fois qu'Elle monteroit dessus. Mais Votre majesté est excellent Homme de cheval, comme je desirerois qu'Elle fut, & je m'asseure, qu'Elle est telle ; ce qui la rendra glorieuse & les sujets heureux. Voicy l'augure, & le souhait, de celuy qui est, jusques au dernier soupir.

SIRE,
DE VOTRE MAJESTE

Les tres-humble, & tres-fidel serviteur, & sujet
Guillaume de Newcastle

To the King of Great Britain,

Sire,

I have never had a greater honour, and I could not wish for a greater distinction, than that of having been the first Governor to Your Majesty, when You were Prince of Wales and just eight years old. I know then from seeing the most tender years of a Royal being, the abundance of the qualities and virtues You would bring to us as you matured. I consider Your natural grace, which is so much above that of the common man, as coming from the advantage of Your birth and elevating You above the rest of men, as if God and nature had destined You to preside over natural qualities themselves, this being the base and foundation of all bounty.

But the times in which we find ourselves make me believe that nature has bestowed upon Your Majesty much gentleness and bounty that is not granted to the vast majority of Your subjects. To the extent that Your Majesty could have been granted the gifts of nature to a fault, had she not also bestowed upon You supreme serenity and clarity in judgement to overcome the faults of these [gifts] by Your justice. As Your Majesty is the deputy of God on earth and the Anointed Sovereign, Your Majesty may imitate the Divine, which chastises without anger; thus Your Majesty will preserve your gentleness and will show Your subjects that Your mercy surpasses Your justice.

I also saw, during Your Majesty's young years, the three parts of a good soul (and there are only three) spirit, judgement and memory, or indeed the faculties, by which we compare all things together, and remember them. You showed these to the highest degree for your age and with the admiration of the whole world. I am assured that Your Majesty faced with these unfortunate troubles, has at present succeeded in mastering Your royal burden, which is to recognise the nature and spirit of men, who are for the most part deceivers, especially since there are more wicked people than good ones; and as the holy scripture says, *many are called and few are chosen.*

Sire, I must not forget that it was I who had the honour of first putting You on a horse in the manège where Your Majesty derived so much benefit, between the ages of nine and ten; Your Majesty not only had the most beautiful and firm seat that I have ever seen, but also the greatest skill and judgement: apart from the fact that You had the most delicate helps to make a horse go perfectly, whether this be Soldade, Passades, Terre a Terre, or Par Haut. Your Majesty mounted two alert horses, Desperato and Balot, although very difficult to handle, with such grace, ease and justice, that the best cavaliers were reassured by You and looked on with admiration, and were all completely amazed.

Some of them who were there and who had learned in foreign Academies, were if not completely, at least almost, thrown to the ground by these horses. The King, Your Father, of blessed memory, said that he had never seen anyone of Your age who came anywhere near to approaching You in riding a horse, (His Majesty being quite capable of judging that); He said that he looked for some fault but could not find any. Because of all these things, sir, this book on Horsemanship is Yours: and I would not have presumed to dedicate it to Your Majesty if I did not know that it brings to the world something new in the true art of dressing horses, which has not been known at all until now. And also since Your Majesty is a master in this art, You love horses: because a Prince is never accompanied by so much majesty, even when on his throne, as he is when mounted on a beautiful horse. This is the creature among all others to whom man owes the greatest debt, as much for use as for pleasure, and as much for his honour as for his life; how, then, is it possible to place a good horse in too great esteem?

How many Kings and great Princes are there who have avoided the shame of being taken prisoner and who have saved their life and honour, all because of the goodness and excellence of their horses? There are so many histories which give us proof of that. And what is more, a King being a good Cavalier will know so much better how he will govern his people, when he should recompense them or chastise them; when he should keep them under a tight rein or when he should give them more freedom; when he should aid them gently or when it would be appropriate to spur them on. They should never be ridden to the extent that they are made to lose their breath or that they become stubborn and rebellious, or (as it were) they take the bit between their teeth and bolt; but rather they should be treated gently and only ridden to half of their strength, so that they may be good-humoured, and do everything willingly and vigorously.

Others should not be allowed to ride them too often nor to harass them: but they should be kept for Your Majesty's saddle alone, that is to say in his private affairs and those of the public. One should always be moderate in passions because the capricious multitude is a many-headed beast, to the extent that it has several bridles but not several spurs; because many heads should have many bridles, but the Republic, having but one body, should have only one pair of spurs and those should be those of Your Majesty, against which they will never rebel, but will always obey and will regard them as a Help rather than a Chastisement. They will rebel against the spurs of Your Majesty's subjects, and to the extent that they ride them without spurs, like foals, nevertheless they will throw them to the ground and will perhaps act badly with them, to the extent that Your Majesty may be in danger when You mount again Yourself. But Your Majesty is an excellent horseman as I desired that You should be and I am assured that You are; which makes Your Majesty glorious and Your subjects happy. Here is the omen and the wish of he who is, to his dying breath,

Sir,

Your very humble and faithful servant, and subject
William Newcastle

A Mes Tres-Chers Fils

Le Seigneur Charles, Vicomte de Mansfield,

et le Seigneur Henry Cavendish (1658 : sig. d²- e),

Mes Tres-Chers Fils,

Je vous prie pour l'amour de vous mesmes d'étudier ce livre, & de le mettre en pratique ; parce qu'il n'y a rien plus propre a un Gentil-homme que d'être bon Homme de cheval : & il n'y a aucune créature de qui'l homme reçoive tant d'avantage que du cheval, soit pour l'usage, ou la plaisir. Prem ierement, l'homme ne paroist jamais tant homme comme sur un beau cheval. Peuton pour le plaisir recevoir plus de contentement qu'à voir manier un cheval parfait en toutes sortes de beaux airs ? En outre, quel exercice y a't'il plus noble, plus sain, & de qui la Cour fasse & de tournois, ou aux nopces des grands Roys & Princes toute la variété de bien manier un cheval a toute sorte d'airs ; soit a courir la bague pour le pris, ou la lance, ou la lice, & venir par après a l'épée ; il ne sauroit y avoir une pompe plus glorieuse, ni plus digne d'un homme ; ni aucun spectacle public qui délecte d'avantage le genre humain.

Soit pour servir sa Majesté a cheval, lors qu'Elle fait ses entrées dans ses grandes villes. Les beaux chevaux ornes de riches caparassons, de riches selles & housses, & de plumes ondoyantes, sont une pompe digned'etonner les spectateurs avec contentement & plaisir. Il n'y a rien de semblage par pais, ou aux recontres publiques, soit pour l'usage, soit pour l'honneour. Devez vous combatre un Duel a cheval ? votre honneur & votre vie tout ensemble dépendent d'un bon cheval & d'un bon Cavalier, parce que le meilleur cheval du monde n'étant pas bien conduit, l'homme est perdu, & le meilleur Cavalier du monde sur un méchant cheval, est aussy en péril. De sorte que vous ne deves pas seulement avoir des bons chevaux, mais aussy être bons hommes de cheval ; car l'un ou l'autre défaillent, l'homme se perd. Le plus vaillant home qui soit sur la terre n'étant pas home de cheval, & ayant un méchant cheval, doit infailliblement périr contre un bon-homme de cheval & sur un bon cheval ; parce qu'il ne sert que d'enclume a éprouver dessus l'épée de celui-ci, ou comme d'une cotte de mailles a recevoir ses estocades. Le courage d'un tel homme ne luy sert de rien en une rencontre de cette nature, a cause qu'il ne sauroit s'en servir.

De ces deux maux, un bon-homme de cheval sur un cheval médiocre vaut mieux qu'un mechant-homme de cheval sur un bon cheval ; car un bon-homme de chavel paroit raisonnablement bie sur un cheval médiocre, au lieu qu'un mechat-homme de cheval ne sauroit rien faire sur un cheval dresse, quoy que bien dresse, parce que le mondre mouvement luy commande, & l'ignorance du Cavalier luy donne tant de contre-temps & des faux-mouvemens, qu'ille rend pire qu'un qui est plus-mal dresse. C'est pourquoy tant plus un cheval est bien dresse, tant plus est-il nécessaire de le monter avec art & connoissance ; parce qu'il est sensible a tout mouvement. Quoy que je confesse qu'un bon cheval fasse beaucoup, toute fois un bon-homme de cheval, sur un bon cheval, a de l'avantage asses. Et je souhaitte que vous soyes tels, tant pour les duels a cheval, que pour la guerre. Combien avons nous d'example des Roys, Princes, & autres braves Cavaliers, qui ont sauve leur vie, & remporte l'honneur de plusieures batailles par leurs actes merveilleux, & le tout par le seul courage ; bonté & excellence de leurs chevaux ? Si donc un cheval vous apporte la santé, la préservation & l'honneur tout ensembles en temps de paix, de guerre, & de duels particuliers, ne l'aimes pas seulement, mais aiez-en des bons & toutes façons pour l'amour de vous mesmes. Et puis que le meilleur cheval du monde ne sert de rien, si on ne le scait pas bien monter, pratiques en l'Art, d'ou vous recevres le plaisir & le proufit aussy ; & d'avantage, l'honneur de Cavaliers. Ainsy Dieu, en ses miséricordes, vous veuille benir tous deux.

Je suis,

Mes chers fils

Votre affectionne Père, Guillaume de Newcastle

To My Dearly Beloved Sons,
Lord Charles, Viscount Mansfield, and Lord Henry Cavendish.
My dearly beloved sons,

  I am asking you from my love for yourselves to study this book and to put it into practice; because there is nothing more right in a gentleman than to be a good Horseman: and there is no other creature of greater benefit to man than the horse, whether for use or for pleasure. Firstly no man ever seems such a man than when he is mounted on a beautiful horse. Is there any greater source of pleasure and contentment than to see a perfect horse handled and made to perform all kinds of beautiful paces? Besides, what exercise is there which is more noble, more healthy, than that which the Court undertakes in the form of tournaments or at the weddings of great Kings and Princes, that is the good and varied handling of horses in all kinds of paces; whether running the ring for the prize, or with the lance, or in the lists, and coming later to the sword; he will not be able to achieve a more glorious spectacle, nor one which brings greater dignity to a man; nor any public spectacle which will be of greater delight to humankind.

  And indeed to serve His Majesty on horseback, when He enters into major cities. Beautiful horses adorned with rich caparisons, with rich saddles and trappings, and waving feathers, are a dignified spectacle to amaze spectators with delight and pleasure. There is nothing to rival it in peacetime or at public meetings, either from a point of view of usefulness or honour. Should you fight a Duel on horseback? Your honour and your life depend completely on a good horse and a good Cavalier, because even given the best horse in the world, if he is not well ridden the man is lost, and given the best Cavalier in the world, if he rides a bad horse, he is also in danger. And so you should not only have good horses, but should also be good horsemen; because if the one or the other is deficient, the man will be lost. The most valiant man on earth, if he is not a good horseman or if he has a poor horse, must inevitably perish when faced with a good horseman mounted on a good horse; because he only serves as an anvil to be tested by the sword of the latter, or as a coat of mail to receive his death blows. The courage of such a man will be of no use whatsoever to him in such an encounter, which means it will be of no use to him. Of these two evils, a good horseman on a poor horse will fare better than a poor horseman on a good horse; because a good horseman will appear reasonably adept on a mediocre horse, whereas a poor horseman will not be able to do a thing on a well-trained horse, however well-trained, because the slightest movement will command the horse, and the ignorance of the Cavalier will give it so many misunderstandings and false signals that it will be rendered worse than a horse which is not so well-trained. This is why the better trained a horse is, the more it requires riding with art and knowledge; because it is sensitive to all movement. And so I own that a good horse may achieve a lot, but a good horseman on a good horse has a substantial advantage. And it is my wish that you should be such, whether for duels on horseback or for war.

How many examples do we have of Kings, Princes and other brave Cavaliers, who have saved their lives and achieved honour in numerous battles by their marvellous acts, and all this by the courage, goodness and excellence of their horses alone? If, then, a horse brings you good health, preservation and honour in times of peace, war and individual duels, do not merely love it, but do so in earnest and in all possible ways out of love for yourselves. And since the best horse in the world is worth nothing if you do not know how to ride it well, practise the Art, from which you will derive both pleasure and benefit; and the honour of Cavaliers besides.

Thus God, in His mercy, will bless you both.

I am,

My dear sons,

Your affectionate Father,

William Newcastle

Aux Cavaliers (1658 : sig. e^{1v}- e^{3v}),

Je ne seray pas long-temps à vous môntrer comme ce mot Cavalliero en Italien est derivé de Cavallo, qui signifie un cheval; & Cavalliero un homme de cheval, ou Chevalier; tout de mesme que Equus en Latin signifie un cheval, d'ou est derivé le mot Eques, un homme de cheval, ou Chevalier. Mais je vous asseure, qu'il n'y a aucune creature de qui l'homme reçoive plus d'avantages que de cheval, soit pour le plaisir, ou l'usage, la seureté, l'honneur & le proufit tout ensemble. Aimes-le donc & le traites bien pour l'amour de vous mesmes, & soiés expert en l'art que professent les Gentils-hommes, qui est d'etre Cavaliers; parce qu'autrement un cheval vous est de petit usage, & ceux, qui par leur ignorance meprisent un cheval & la Cavalerie, pourront en étre plûtost tués. Je souhaiterois à telles personnes, pour leur châtiment, qu'elles fussent condamnées d'aller á pied toute leur vie. Mais les vrais Cavaliers ont plus de jugement & de generosite.

Il faut, Nobles Cavalerizzes, que je me plaigne un peu à pressent du mal-heur du cét Art, ou excellente Profession, de ce que châcun pense avoir sa provision de Cavalerie tout aussy tôt qu'il sçait mettre une jambe de châque coté de son cheval: voire mesme les mecaniques, jusques aux Cuiseniers & Tailleurs (comme aussy tous citoyens) s'imaginent de monter à cheval aussy bien qu'aucun Cavalier; combien qu'ils croient qu'aucune autre profession, quoy que vile, ne sauroit être apprise en moins de huit ou neuf ans. Et la plus-part prennent a disgrace, s'ils nesont tenus aussy bons hommes de cheval qu'aucun autre, qui certes est une injustice bien grande, & une chose tres-fausse. Car il n'y aucun Art dans le monde si difficile a apprendre, comme a être parfait homme de cheval. Ce n'est pas monter une haquenée de Cambridge à Londres, ou de S. Germain à Paris, qui fait un bon homme de cheval. Un tres-brave Gentil-homme, que etoit & soldat & écolier, disoit, qu'on prist deux garçons qui eussent l'espirit également bon, qu'on en mist l'un aux écoles, & l'autre a apprendre a monter a cheval, & que celuy-la seroit bon Philosophe, auparavant que celuy-cy fust médiocre homme de cheval; ce qui est véritable. C'est pourquoy voicy des nouvelles que je vous apporte dans l'Art parfait de dresses les chevaux. Lisez-les donc, c'est à dire, entendez-les, & les mettes en pratique, & le proufit vous en demeurera. Je ne veux pas vous ennuyer par longs discours comment les Pages doivent boutonner leur pourpoins, ou attacher leurs aiguillettes; ou quand c'est qu'ils doiver doivent dire leurs priers (ce que je laisse à leurs Directeurs spirituels) ou comment ils doivent lire la Philosophie morale, laquelle leçon je reserve à leurs Pedagogues. Je n'ay pas aussy dessein de vous troubler de châque boucle, sangle, clou, ou frange, ny comment il faut épouster une selle. Je vous present non plus la figure d'un chandelier de trios sols, ny je vous dis pas ou c'est que le Maitre Palfrenier doit monter à cheval ny combine de chapeaux, gans, ou paires de bottes il doit avoir; parce que j'écris de la façon la plus courte qu'il m'est possible (non pas aux écoliers, mais aux Maîtres) l'Art de bien dresser les chevaux, lequel n'a jamais étée connu. Ce qui m'oblige à ne faire pas un livre de plusieures repetitions de choses qui paroissent comme secrets, mais en esset ne le sont pas, puis quelles sont connues à châque Cavalerizze. Je ne veux non plus faire un livre entire pour diviser un cercle en plusieures parties; parce qu'un cercle peut etre diuise entant de parties (ce que Arithmetique, ou Geometrie pevvent faire, ou quelque methode ennuïeuse de la mesme nature) qu'un cheval ne sauroit vivre asses pour etre dresse. Je ne veux pas d'ailleurs être si court, comme quelques-uns, qui, par la routine de leurs piliers, se hâtent tant de dresser un poulain & le rendre cheval parfait, qu'ils le continuënt de las sorte poulain toute sa vie, sans le mener jamais hors du lieu où on a de coútume de la monter. Je ne veux non plus faire comme en quelque pais, où on se sert si long-temps de cavesson fait à la vieille mode, que le cheval ne peut pas aller avec la bride; ou comme quelques autres font, en d'autres pais, qui se servent si long-temps de la bride, que le cheval ne veut aller, ni avec le cavesson, ni avec le bride. Mais cette Methode enseigne l'un & l'autre parfaitement, & leur apprend a obéir a la main, & au talon, avec tant de perfection, qu'ils vont par tout aussy bien comme en leur lieu ordinaire du Manege; ce que vous verres par de vérité de mes leçons suivantes. Ainsy je demeure,

Messieurs,
Votre tres-humble et tres affectionate serviteur,
Guillame de Newcastle

To Cavaliers,

I will not take long to show you how this word Cavalliero in Italian is derived from Cavallo, which means a horse; & Cavalliero a horseman, or Chevalier [in French]; similarly, that Equus in Latin signifies a horse, from which is derived the Eques, a horseman, or Chevalier. But I assure you, there is no creature from which man receives greater advantage than the horse, either for pleasure, or usefulness, safety, honour and benefit all together. Therefore love them and treat them well, for love of yourselves, and be expert in the art practised by Gentlemen, that is [the art of] being Cavaliers; because otherwise a horse is of little use to you, and those who, by their ignorance, misunderstand horses and *Cavalerie*, may even be killed by this. I would wish to chastise such persons by condemning them to have to walk on foot all their lives. But true Cavaliers have better judgement and greater generosity.

Noble Cavalerizzes, I feel obliged to complain a little at present about the poor state of this Art, or excellent Profession, where anyone thinks that they are sufficiently versed in *Cavalerie* as soon as they can place a leg on each side of the horse: see how even the mechanics, up to Chefs and Tailors (as, indeed all citizens) imagine that they can ride a horse as well as any Cavalier; while they believe that no other profession, however lowly, may be learned in less than eight or nine years. And the majority consider it a disgrace if they are not considered horsemen as good as any other, which is indeed a great injustice, and a very bad thing. Because there is no Art in the world which is as difficult to learn as how to become a perfect horseman. There is more to being a good horseman than riding a palfrey from Cambridge to London, or from St. Germain to Paris.

An outstanding Gentleman, who was both a soldier and a scholar, said that if one took two boys with equally good spirit, and put one in school and taught the other how to ride, that the former would be a good Philosopher before the other became a mediocre horseman; which is true. This is why I am bringing you these new ideas in the perfect Art of dressing horses. Read them, that is to say, understand them, and put them into practice, and the benefit will remain with you. I do not want to bore you with long discourses on how pages should button their *pourpoints*, or attach their spurs; or when they should say their prayers (I leave this to their spiritual guides) or how they should read moral Philosophy, which lesson I leave to their Teachers. Nor do I have any designs on troubling you with every buckle, strap, stud or fringe, nor how a saddle should be polished. Nor shall I present you with a diagram of a three-tier candelabra, nor will I tell you if Master Palfrenier wishes to ride a horse, what combination of hats, gloves or pairs of boots he should have; because I am writing in as brief a manner as possible (not to students, but to Masters) about the Art of properly schooling horses, which has never been recognised. Which obliges me not to produce a book containing numerous repetitions of things which appear to be secrets, but in fact are not, since they are known to every Cavalerizze.

Nor do I want to produce an entire book on how to divide a circle into several sections; because a circle may be divided into so many parts (which Arithmetic or Geometry may do, or some other tedious method of similar nature) that a horse would not live long enough to be schooled in them. Nor do I want to be too brief, like some who, by the routine of their grinding, are in such a hurry to school a foal and make him into a perfect horse, that they continue to make of him a foal all his life, without ever taking him away from that place where he is used to being ridden. Nor do I wish to behave as in some countries, where one continues for such a long time with cavesson in the old style, that the horse is no longer able to respond to the bridle; or like some others do, in other countries, who use the bridle for such a long time that the horse refuses to go, neither with the *cavesson* nor with the bridle.

But this Method trains in the one and the other perfectly, and teaches them obedience to the hand, and the heel, with such perfection that they will go anywhere just as well as in their usual place in the Manège; you will see this to be true from my lessons which follow. And so I remain,

Sirs,

Your very humble and affectionate servant,

William Newcastle

(1658 : sig. Zzz^v)

Si à cét Art des Roys tu pense parvenir,
Pratiquiz ces leçons assin de t'en garnir;
Tout vice de cheval est icy curable,
Par la methode de ce livre admirable,
Qui le Manege tellenebt subtilise,
Que les dessein de Routine place n'a prise :
A tous Airs ; au Pas, Trot, Galop, à la Course,
La raison toûjours vous conduît, & vous pousse;
Tellement que le cheval est obeïsant
A la main, & talon, par ce livre sçavant.

M.D.V.

If you seek to attain the Art of Kings,
Practise these lessons in order to equip yourself;
All the vices of the horse are curable here,
By the methods in this admirable book,
Which refines so much the given practice of the Manège
Where the Routine practices have no place.
In all Airs, Walk, Trot, Galop, and the Race-track[291]
Reason always drives you and pushes you;
So much so that your horse is obedient
To the hand and the heel, by knowing this book.

---

291   Newcastle does not discuss the riding house as preparation for racing, so this translation is not satisfactory, but the alternatives of 'tilting' or 'hunting' are no better.

Par ces reigles, le cheval est obeïssant,
Ou bien vous étes peu sçavant, ou ignorant,
Si justement en vôtre cause vous jugés ;
Et la quinte-essence de cét Art ne negligez.
Tu ne la sçavras dés la premiere veuë,
Par la seule pratique elle te sera connuë.
Ma peine, & mon labeur te mettent en repos;
Tu n'as qu'à joüir de mes travaux & propos.
Dés le premier, tu ne dois pas étre Maître,
La nature si injuste ne peuy étre :
En cét Art jamais elle ne te flatera,
Ni le cheval si tôt ses vices delairra.
Si tu y treuve par trop de difficulté
Cherche un autre métier qui te soit plus aisé.
M. D. V.

By these rules, the horse is obedient,
But if you know little or are ignorant,
If you just judge by your own actions,
And neglect the quintessence of this art,
You won't realise it at first
By practice alone it will make you able.
My endeavour and my labour will bring you ease,
You have but to put into practice my works and proposals,
From the start don't expect to be a Master,
This cannot be because nature is so unjust,
In this art it will never flatter you,
Nor will the horse be able to hold back its vices so soon.
If you lag behind because it's too difficult
Look for another skill which will be easier for you.[292]

292　The use of both first and third person does not help in deciding the identity of the author, but is an interesting feature of the verses. The general tone and manner makes Newcastle himself a very likely candidate.

Translations of Verses in Plates 2, 3, 4 & 5,

Plate 2

After man the Horse the most noble animal,
Is made by this Lord so true and so equable,
By this Method that all the world admires
That one easily believes that he is subject to His Empire.
His beautiful seat, his secret helps;
All with studied ease, so beautifully done
Are to us a valid and powerful argument
That to his heels and Bridle he [the horse] is obedient,
And that all Horses are subject to his law;
Then that they obey him as they would their KING.

If he mounted a powerful Devil, this devil would go in true Airs.
                                        Mr. D. V.[293]

Plate 3

Newcastle, the power of your genius
Which makes you triumph over other horseman;
Who to the furious encounter for the love of glory,
In combat carries off the victory.
Inside your circles, you do nothing but conjure,
When you mount, you Philosophise;
And then you tame the fiery and the wise
And altogether they pay you homage.
                                        M. D. V.

---

293   Plates 2 & 4 have Mr. D. V., rather than the initials only.

Plate 4

He mounts with the hand the spurs, and whips
The Horse Pegasus, who flies in a Capriole;
He flies so high that he touches the sky with his Head
And by his marvels he delights the Gods to ecstasy.
The mortal Horses who down there on the ground
In Courbettes, demi-airs and terre à terre go
With humility, submission and servility,
Adore him like God and the author of their skill.

Mr. D. V.

Plate 5

May Pallas be your guide and Cupid your page,
Mars the captain who guides your courage;
May your own mount be the winged Pegasus,
And Mercury serve you always at your side.
May Fortune to your unique power submit,
She who sits over us.[294]

---

294   There are no initials on this verse, although the positioning might suggest that they were lost in setting out the plate.

Bibliography

Primary Sources:

Manuscripts

The British Library, London

Additional MS 4278

Additional MS 45865

Additional MS 70499

Harleian MS 6320

Harleian MS 6796

University of Nottingham, Department of Manuscripts and Special Collections

Portland MSS:
Pw1
PwV 21, 22.
PwV 23, 24, 25, 26

Public Record Office, London

State Papers (domestic) 29/46/145; 77/31

Works on Horsemanship

Anon, *The Horsemanship of England* (London: Thomas Parkhurst, 1682)

Astley, John, *The Art of Riding* (London: 1584)

Baret, Michael, *An Hipponomie or the Vineyard of Horsemanship* (London: 1618)

Blundeville, Thomas, *A Newe Booke containing the Arte of Ryding and breaking greate Horses* (London: Willyam Seres, 1560)

> *The fower chiefyst offices belongyng to Horsemanship* (London: Humfrey Lownes, 1609)

Caraciollo, Pasquale, *La Gloria del Cavallo* (Ferrari: 1567)

Cavendish, William, *La Methode Nouvelle et Invention extraordinaire de dresser les Chevaux* (Antwerp: Jacques van Meurs, 1658)

> *A New Method, and Extraordinary Invention, to Dress Horses* (London: Thomas Milbourn, 1667)

> *Methode nouvelle, et invention extraordinaire de dresser les chevaux* (London: 1671)

> *A General System of Horsemanship, Vol. 1* (London: J. Brindley, 1743)

> *A General System of Horsemansh* (London: J. A. Allen, 1970, rep. 2000)

> *A New Method to Dress Horses* (Virginia: Xenophon Press, 2015)

Clifford, Christopher, *The schoole of horsemanship* (London: 1585)

Corte, Claudio, *Il Cavallarizzo* (Paris: 1562)

Corte, Claudio, *The Art of Riding*, trans. by Thomas Bedingfield, (London: 1584)

De Grey, Thomas, *The Compleat Horseman and Expert Ferrier* (London: 1639)

Guérinière, François Robichon de la, *School of Horsemanship*, trans. by Tracey Boucher (London: J. A. Allen, 1994)

> *Ecole de Cavalerie Part II*, trans. by EDA Corp. (Virginia: Xenophon Press 1992, 2015)

Grisone, *Federico Gli Ordini di cavalcare* (Naples: 1550)

> *Ordini di cavalcare et modo di conoscere le nature de'cavalli* (1558)

> *L'écuirie du Sr. Federic Grison* (Paris : Ch. Pellier: 1559)

> *The Rules of Riding : An Edited Translation of the First Renaissance Treatise of Classical Horsemanship*, ed. by Elizabeth Mackenzie Tobey; trans. by Elizabeth MacKenzie Tobey and Federica Brunori Deigan (Arizona: Arizona Cente for Medieval and Renaissance Studies: 2014)

La Broue, Salamon de, *La Cavalerice François* (Paris: 1602)

Langbaine, Gerard, *The Hunte: a Discourse of Horsemanship* (Oxford: Nicholas Cox, 1685)

Markham, Gervase, *Cheape and Good Husbandry* (London: Roger Jackson, 1614; repr. Amsterdam: Theatrum Orbis Terrarum, 1969)

The Compleat Horseman, ed. by Dan Lucid (Boston: Houghton Mifflin, 1975)

Morgan, Nicholas, *The Perfection of Horse-manship, drawne from Nature; Arte and Practise* (London: Edward White, 1609)

The Horse-man's Honour or, The Beautie of Horse-Manship (London: John Marriott, 1620)

Pluvinel, Antoine de, *Le Maneige Royal* (Brunswig: Gottfridt Muller, 1626; repr. London: J.A. Allen, 1970)

The Maneige Royal, trans. by Hilda Nelson (London: J. A. Allen, 1989)

The Maneige Royal, trans. by Hilda Nelson (Virginia: Xenophon Press, 2010)

Russius, Laurentius, *Hippiatria sive marescalia* (Paris: 1532)

Saunier, Gaspard de, *A General System of Horsemanship, Vol. II* (London: John Brindley, 1743)

Solleysel, Jacques de, *Le Parfait Mareschal* (Paris, Gervaise Clousier, 1694)

Le Parfait Mareschal or Complete Farrier, trans. by William Hope, and including The Compleat Horseman: A Compendious Treatise of the Art of Riding. Collected from the best Modern Writers on the Subject. (Edinburgh: George Mosman, 1696

Xenophon, *The Art of Horsemanship*, trans. by M H. Morgan (London: J. A. Allen, 1962)

General Titles

Alciato, Andrea, *Emblematum liber* (1531)

Bacon, Francis, *Essays* (London: Henry Frowde, 1904)

Castiglione, Baldassare, *The Book of the Courtier*, ed. by Virgina Cox (London: Everyman, 1994)

Cavendish, Margaret, *Life of the Duke of Newcastle, to which is added the True relation of my Birth, Breeding and Life*, ed. by C. H. Firth (London: J. M. Dent, 1915)

Poems, and Fancies (London: J. Martin & J. Allestrye, 1653; rpt. Menston: Scolar Press 1972)

Philosophical and Physical Opinions (London, 1655)

Nature's Pictures (London: J. Martin & J. Allestrye, 1656)

Playes Written by the Thrice Noble, Illustrious and Excellent Princess, the Lady Marchioness of Newcastle (London: J. Martin, J. Allestrye & T. Dicas, 1662)

Sociable Letters (London: William Wilson, 1664)

The Blazing World and Other Writings, ed. by Kate Lilley (London: Penguin, 1992)

Cavendish, William, *Witt's triumvate or the Philosopher*, ed. by C. A. Nelson (Salzburg: Institut fur Englische Sprach, 1975)

The Humorous Lovers, ed. by James Fitzmaurice (Oxford: Seventeenth Century Press, 1997)

The Country Captain, ed. by Anthony Johnson (Oxford: Malone Society Reprints, 1999)

Cavendish: Dramatic Works, ed. by Lynn Hulse (Oxford: Malone Society Reprints, 1996)

A Declaration made by the Earl of Newcastle, (London: 1624; rpt. Leigh-on-Sea: Partizan Press, 1983)

The Phanseys of the Duke of Newcastle, ed. by Douglas Grant (London: Nonesuch Press, 1956)

A Collection of Letters and Poems, Written by several Persons of Honour and Learning [...] to the late Duke and Duchess of Newcastle (London: Langley Curtis, 1678)

Cox, Nicholas, *The Gentleman's Recreation* (London: 1686)

Dando, John and Harrie Runt, *Maroccus Extacticus or Bankes Bay Horse in a Trance* (Cuthbert Burby, 1595)

Descartes, Rene, *Meditations and Other Metaphysical Writings*, trans. by Desmond M.Clarke (London: Penguin Books, 2000)

Elyot, Thomas, *The Boke called the Governour* (London/New York: J. M. Dent/ E. P. Dutton, n. d.)

Hobbes, Thomas, *Leviathan*, ed. Kenneth Minogue (London: J. M. Dent, 1994)

Hutchinson, Lucy, *Memoirs of the Life of Colonel Hutchinson*, ed. by Harold Child (London: Kegan Paul Trench, 1904)

Hyde, Edward, *The History of the Rebellion and Civil Wars in England*, ed. by W. D. Macray, 6 Volumes (Oxford: 1888)

Jonson, Ben, *A Critical Edition of the Major Works*, ed. by Ian Donaldson (Oxford:Oxford University, 1985)

Langbaine, Gerard, *An Account of the English Dramatic Poets* (London: 1691; rpt. Los Angeles: Augustan Reprint Society/ University of California, 1971)

Machiavelli, Niccolo, *The Prince*, ed. Peter Bondanella, trans. by Peter Bondanella and Mark Musa (Oxford/New York: Oxford University Press, 1984).

Montaigne, Michel de, *The Complete Essays*, ed. by M. A. Screech (London: Penguin Books, 1991)

Peacham, Henry, *The Compleat Gentleman* (London: 1634)

Rolleston, John, *Being Commanded by his Excellency, the Lord Marquis of Newcastle, to publish the following Articles for his new Course* (Oxford, 1662[?])

Sidney, Philip, *Defence of Poesie, Astrophil and Stella and Other Writings*, ed. by Elizabeth Porges Watson (London: Everyman, 1997)

Vernon, John, *The Young Horseman or, The honest plain-dealing Cavalier*, ed. by John Tincey (Leigh-on-Sea: Partizan Press, 1993)

Warwick, Philip, *Memoires of the Reign of King Charles I* (London: 1702)

Wotton, Henry, *The Life and Letters of Sir Henry Wotton*, ed. by L. P. Smith (Oxford: Oxford University Press, 1966)

The Elements of Architecture: collected by Henry Wotton, Knight, from the best authors and examples (London: 1624)

Secondary Sources:

Albrecht, Kurt, *A Dressage Judge's Handbook* (London: J. A. Allen, 1996)

Amussen, Susan Dwyer, *An Ordered Society: Gender and Class in Early Modern England* (New York: Columbia University Press, 1988)

Anzilotti, Gloria, *An English 'Prince': Newcastle's Machiavellian Political Guide to Charles II* (Pisa: Giardini Editore e Stampatori, 1988)

Aston, Elaine and George Savona, *Theatre as Sign-System: A Semiotics of Text and Performance* (London: Routledge, 1991)

Barratt, John, *Newcastle's War: The Royalists in the North 1642-1644* (Merseyside: Caracole Press, 1997)

Becket, John, ed., *Nottinghamshire Past: Essays in honour of Adrian Henstock* (Nottingham: Merton Priory Press, 2003)

Beneden, Ben van, *Royalist Refugees: William and Margaret Cavendish in the Rubens House, 1648-1660* (Antwerp: BAI, Schoten, 2006)

Berger, John, *Ways of Seeing* (London: BBC/Penguin Books, 1972)

Berry, Edward, *Shakespeare and the Hunt: A Cultural and Social Study* (Cambridge: Cambridge University Press, 2001)

Brant, Clare and Diane Purkiss, eds., *Women, Texts and Histories 1575-1760* (London/New York: Routledge, 1992)

Camins, Laura, *Glorious Horsemen: Equestrian Art in Europe 1500-1800* (Massachusetts: Springfield Museum of Fine Arts, 1981)

Cruickshanks, Eveline, ed., *The Stuart Courts* (London: Sutton Publishing, 1998)

Darnell, Greg, *A Bit of Information* (Colorado: Western Horseman Inc., n.d.)

Davies, Alice I., *16th and 17th Century Dutch and Flemish Paintings in the Springfield Museum of Fine Arts* (Massachusetts: Springfield Museum of Fine Arts, 1993)

Dent, Anthony, *Horses in Shakespeare's England* (London: J. A. Allen, 1987) *The Horse Through Fifty Centuries of Civilisation* (London: Phaidon, 1974)

Duncan-Jones, Katherine, *Sir Philip Sidney: Courtier Poet* (London: Hamish Hamilton, 1991)

Edwards, Peter, *The Horse Trade of Tudor and Stuart England* (Cambridge: Cambridge University Press, 2004)
    et. al. *The Horse as Cultural Icon* (Leiden: Brill, 2012)

Evans, David, *The Battle of Marston Moor, 1644* (Bristol: Stuart Press, 1994)

Felton, W. Sidney, *Masters of Equitation* (London: J. A. Allen, 1962)

Freeman, Rosemary, *English Emblem Books* (New York: Octagon Books, 1978)

Froissard, Jean and Lily Froissard, eds., *The Horseman's International Book of Reference* (London: Stanley Paul, 1980)

William Cavendish Duc de Newcastle Sa Vie et Son Oeuvre (Paris: Crepin-Leblond, 1983)

Fudge, Erica, ed., *Renaissance Beasts* (Urbana/Chicago: University of Illinois Press, 2004)

Perceiving Animals: Humans and Beasts in Early Modern English Culture (New York: St. Martin's Press, 1999)

Fudge, Erica, Ruth Gilbert and Susan Wiseman, eds., *At the Borders of the Human* (London/New York: Macmillan/St Martin's Press, 1999)

Fumerton, Patricia and Simon Hunt, eds., *Renaissance Culture and the Everyday* (Philadelphia: University of Pennsylvania Press, 1999)

Guirard, Felix, ed., *The Larousse Encyclopedia of Mythology*, trans. by Richard Aldington (London: Hamlyn, 1983)

Girouard, Mark, *Robert Smythson and the Elizabethan Country House* (New Haven: Yale University Press, 1983)

Goody, Peter C., *Horse Anatomy: A Pictorial Approach to Equine Structure* (London: J. A. Allen, 1983)

Goulding, Richard W., *Letters from the originals at Welbeck Abbey* (London: John Murray, 1909)

Grant, Douglas, *Margaret the First* (London: Rupert Hart-Davies, 1957)

Greenblatt, Stephen, *Renaissance Self-Fashioning: From More to Shakespeare* (Chicago/London: University of Chicago Press, 1980)

Hale, J. R., *Renaissance War Studies* (London: Hambledon Press, 1983)

Handler, Hans, *The Spanish Riding School: Four Centuries of Classical Horsemanship*, trans. by Russell Stockman (New York: McGraw-Hill, 1972)

Heal, Felicity and Clive Holmes, *The Gentry in England and Wales, 1500-1700* (London: Macmillan, 1994)

Huth, F. H., *Works on Horses and Equitation: A Bibliographical Record of Hippology,* (London: Bernard Quaritch, 1887)

Hyland, Ann, *The Medieval Warhorse from Byzantium to the Crusades* (Stroud: Sutton Publishing, 1994)

The Warhorse 1250-1600 (Stroud: Sutton Publishing, 1998)

James, Mervyn, Society, *Politics and Culture: Studies in Early Modern England* (Cambridge: Cambridge University Press, 1988)

Jardine, Lisa and Jerry Brotton, *Global Interests: Renaissance Art between East and West* (London: Reaktion Books, 2000)

Jenkins, Edward, *The Cavalier & his Lady* (London: Macmillan, 1872)

Johns Adrian, *The Nature of the Book: Print and Knowledge in the Making* (London/Chicago: University of Chicago Press, 1998)

Liedtke, Walter A., *The Royal Horse and Rider: Painting, Sculpture and Horsemanship 1500-1800* (New York: Abaris Books/Metropolitan Museum of Art, 1989)

Lindley, David, ed., *Court Masques: Jacobean and Caroline Entertainments 1605-1640* (Oxford: Oxford University Press, 1998)

Loch, Sylvia, *The Royal Horse and Rider* (London: J. A. Allen, 1987)

McCormick, Adele von Rüst and Marlena Deborah, *Horse Sense and the Human Heart* (Florida: Health Communications Inc., 1997)

McMullan, Gordon, ed., *Renaissance Configurations: Voices, Bodies, Spaces 1580-1690* (New York: Palgrave, 2001)

Mazzeo, J. A. and others, *Reason and the Imagination: Studies in the History of Ideas 1600-1800* (New York: Columbia University Press; London: Routledge and Kegan Paul 1962

Mennessier de la Lance, Gabriel-René, *Essai de Bibliographie Hippique* (Paris: L. Dorbon, 1917-21)

Mertes, Kate, *The English Noble Household 1250-1600* (Oxford: Blackwell, 1988)

Parelli, Pat, *Natural Horse-Man-Ship* (Colorado: Western Horseman, 1993)

Perry, H. T. E., *The First Duchess of Newcastle and Her Husband as Figures in Literary History* (Boston: Ginn and Company, 1918)

Piggot, Stuart, *Wagon, Chariot and Carriage: Symbol and Status in the History of Transport* (London: Thames and Hudson 1992)

Podeschi, John B, *Books on the Horse and Horsemanship: Riding, Hunting, Breeding and Racing, 1400-1941* (London: Tate Gallery, 1981)

Podhajsky, Alois, *The Complete Training of the Horse and Rider* (London: Harrap, 1983)

Poynter, F. N. L., *A Bibliography of Gervayse Markham* (Oxford: Oxford Bibliographical Society, 1962)

Raber, Karen, & Treva J. Tucker, eds., *The Culture of the Horse : Status, Discipline, and Identity in the Early Modern World* (New York: Palgrave Macmillan, 2005)

Rees, Lucy, *The Horse's Mind* (London: Stanley Paul, 1991)

Reese, M. M, *The Royal Office of Master of the Horse* (London: Threshold Books, 1976)

Reytier, Daniel, ed., *Les Écuries royales* (Versailles: Association pour l'Académie d'Art Équestre de Versailles, 1998)

Roberts, Monty, *The Man who listens to Horses* (London: Arrow, 1997)

Seddon, P. R., *Letters of John Holles, 1587-1637* (Nottingham: Thoroton Society Record Series 31, 1975)

Skinner, Quentin, *Liberty before Liberalism* (Cambridge: Cambridge University Press: 1998)

Smith, Geoffrey, *The Cavaliers in Exile, 1640-1660* (New York: Palgrave Macmillan, 2003)

Smuts, R. Malcolm, *Court Culture and the Origins of a Royalist Tradition in Early Stuart England* (Philadelphia: University of Pennsylvania Press, 1987)

    Culture and Power in England 1585-1685, (New York: St.Martin's Press, 1999)

Stevens, Michael J., *A Classical Riding Notebook* (Buckingham: Kenilworth Press, 1994)

Stone, Lawrence, *The Crisis of the Aristocracy 1558-1641* (Oxford: Clarendon Press, 1965) *Social Change and Revolution in England 1540-1640*, (London: Longman, 1965)

Strong, Roy, *Henry: Prince of Wales and England's Lost Renaissance* (London: Thames & Hudson, 1986)

    Van Dyck: Charles I on Horseback (New York: Viking Press, 1972)

    Art and Power: Renaissance Festivals 1450-1650 (Suffolk: Boydell Press, 1984)

Strong, S. A., *A Catalogue of Letters and other Historical Documents Exhibited in the Library at Welbeck* (London: John Murray, 1903)

Stoye, John, *English Travellers Abroad 1604-1667*, rev.edn., (New Haven/London: Yale University Press, 1989)

Thirsk, Joan, *Horses in early modern England: for Service, for Pleasure, for Power*, (Reading: University of Reading 1978)

Thomas, Keith, *Man and the Natural World: Changing Attitudes in England 1500-1800* (London: Penguin Books, 1983)

Tomassini, Giovanni Battista, *The Italian Tradition of Equestrian Art: A Survey of the Treatises on Horsemanship from the Renaissance and the Centuries Following* (Virginia: Xenophon Press, 2014)

Toole-Stott, R. S., *Circus and Allied Arts: A World Bibliography 1500-1959* (Derby: Harpur & Sons, 1960)

Trease, Geoffrey, *Portrait of a Cavalier: William Cavendish, First Duke of Newcastle* (London: Macmillan, 1979)

Vale, Marcia, *The Gentleman's Recreation: Accomplishments and pastimes of the English gentleman 1580-1630* (Cambridge: D. S. Brewer, 1977)

Vlieghe, Hans, *Flemish Art and Architecture 1585-1700* (New Haven: Yale University Press, 1998)

Walker, Elaine, *Horse* (London: Reaktion Books, 2008)

    To Amaze the People with Pleasure and Delight: The horsemanship manuals of William Cavendish, Duke of Newcastle (London: Long Rider's Guild Press, 2010)

    The Horse (London: Parragon, 2014)

Watanabe-O'Kelly, Helen, *Triumphall Shews: Tournaments at German-speaking Courts in their*

European Context 1560-1730 (Berlin: Gebr. Mann, 1992)

Whitaker, Katie, *Mad Madge: Margaret Cavendish, Duchess of Newcastle, Royalist, Writer and Romantic* (London: Chatto & Windus, 2003)

Willey, Basil, *The Seventeenth-Century Background: Studies in the thought of the age in relation to Poetry and religion* (London: Routledge and Keegan Paul, 1986)

Wooton, David, ed., *Divine Right and Democracy: An Anthology of Political Writing in Stuart England* (London: Penguin Books: 1986)

Worsley, Giles, *The British Stable: An Architectural and Social History* (Yale University Press, 2004)

Worsley, Lucy, *Cavalier: A Tale of Chivalry, Passion and great Houses* (London: 2007)

Wrightson, Keith, *English Society 1580-1680* (London: Routledge, 2003)

Young, Peter, *Marston Moor, 1664: The Campaign and the Battle* (Moreton-in-Marsh: Windrush Press, 1997)

Journal Articles

Barton, Anne, 'Harking back to Elizabeth: Ben Jonson and Caroline Nostalgia', *English Literary History*, 48.4 (1981), 706-731

Baughan, Denver Ewing, 'Swift's Source of the Houyhnhnms Reconsidered', *English Literary History*, 5 (1938), 207-10

Bowden, Betsy, 'Before the Houyhnhnms: rational horses in the late seventeenth century', *Notes & Queries*, (March 1992), 38-40

Clements, J., 'The Truth of the Sword – the Lost Fencing Book of the Marquis of Newcastle, c. 1650', *The Association for Renaissance Martial Arts* <http://www.thearma.org/essays/truth_ots.html> [accessed 12 May 2015]

Foulds, Trevor, "This greate House, so Lately begun, and all of Freestone': William Cavendish's Italianate Palazzo called Nottingham Castle', *Transactions of the Thoroton Society of Nottinghamshire*, 106 (2002), 81-102

Fudge, Erica, 'How a Man Differs from a Dog', in *History Today*, 53.6, June 2003, 45-50

Gagen, Jean, 'Honor and Fame in the works of the Duchess of Newcastle', *Studies in philology*, 56 (1959), 519-538

Girouard, Mark, 'Early Drawings of Bolsover Castle', *Architectural History*, 27 (1984), 510-518

MacGregor, Arthur, 'Horsegear, Vehicles and Stable Equipment at the Stuart Court: A Documentary Archaeology', *Journal of the Royal Archaeological Institute*, 153 (1996), 148-200

'The Royal Stables: A Seventeenth- Century Perspective', *Antiquities Journal*, 76 (1996), 181-200

'Strategies for Improving English Horses in the Sixteenth and Seventeen Centuries', *ANTHROPOZOOLOGICA*, 29 (1999), 65-74

Masset, Claude, 'What length of life did our forebears have?', *Population and Societies,* 380, (2002) https://www.ined.fr/fichier/s_rubrique/18771/publi_pdf2_pop_and_soc_english_380.en.pdf [accessed 10 May 2015]

Raylor, Timothy, 'Thomas Hobbes and 'The Mathematical Demonstration of the Sword'', *Seventeenth Century*, 15.2 (2000), 175-198 ed., *Seventeenth Century - Special Issue: The Cavendish Circle*, 9.2 (1994)

Walker, Elaine, 'Longing for Ambrosia: the torment of a restless mind in Poems & Fancies', *Women's Writing*, 4.3 (1997), 341-351

Woodhouse, Adrian, 'Reconstructing the Horseman of Nottingham Castle: the Equestrian Statue of the First Duke of Newcastle, c. 1679', *Transactions of the Thoroton Society of Nottinghamshire*, 104 (2000), 73-81

Worsley, Giles, The History of 'Haute École' in England', *Court Historian*, 6.1 (2001), 29-47

Worsley, Lucy, 'I Began to Wish myself a Horse' – William Cavendish and the Furnishing of Bolsover Castle', *Collections Review*, (2001), 1-7

"An Habitation not so Magnificent as Useful': Life at Welbeck Abbey in the 17th Century', *Transactions of the Thoroton Society of Nottinghamshire*, 108 (2004), 123-143

Worsley, Lucy and Tom Addyman, 'Riding Houses and horses: William Cavendish's Architecture for the Art of Horsemanship', *Architectural History*, 45 (2002), 194-229

Unpublished conference papers and theses

Draskóy, Andrew, "Se il Cavallo è Gagliardo': connections between Horsemanship and Dance in 16th Century Italy' (conference paper, International Dance Conference: Ghent, 2000)

MacDonald, Gabrielle Ann, 'Horsemanship as a courtly art in Elizabethan England: origins, theory, and practice' (Ph. D. thesis, University of   Toronto, 1982)

Somnez, Margaret J. M., 'English Spelling in the Seventeenth Century'(Ph. D. thesis, University of Durham, 1993)

'The Gentleman on Horseback: the Duke of Newcastle's writings on Horsemanship' (paper, 1994)

Worsley, Giles, 'The Design and development of the Stable and Riding House in Great Britain from the 13th Century –1914' (Ph. D. thesis, Courtauld Institute,

University of London, 1989)

Walker, Elaine, "Torment to a Restlesse Mind': an analysis of Major Themes in 'Poems, and Fancies', by Margaret Cavendish (1653)' (M. Phil. thesis, University of Birmingham, 1996) <http://etheses.bham.ac.uk/3148/>[accessed 29 May, 2015)

"To Amaze the People with Pleasure and Delight': an analysis of the Horsemanship Manuals of William Cavendish, first Duke of Newcastle, (1593-1676) (Ph. D. thesis, University of Birmingham, 2004)
<http://ethos.bl.uk/OrderDetails.do?did=7&uin=uk.bl.ethos.422352>
<http://etheses.bham.ac.uk/5920/ >[accessed 29 May, 2015]

www.XenophonPress.com

CPSIA information can be obtained at www.ICGtesting.com
Printed in the USA
LVOW01s0545280815

451693LV00012B/86/P